^AYear _{of} Reading

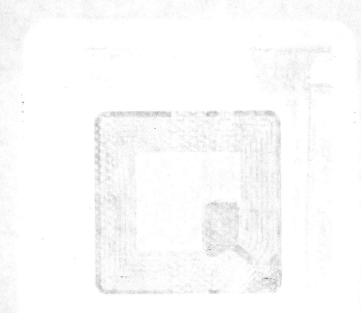

A Year of Reading

A Month-by-Month Guide
to Classics and Crowd-Pleasers
for You and Your Book Group

Elisabeth Ellington & Jane Freimiller, Ph.D.

SOURCEBOOKS, INC.®
NAPERVILLE, ILLINOIS

Published by Sourcebooks, Inc.
P.O. Box 4410, Naperville, Illinois 60567-4410
(630) 961-3900
FAX: (630) 961-2168
www.sourcebooks.com

Library of Congress Cataloging-in-Publication Data

Ellington, H. Elisabeth.
  A year of reading : a month-by-month guide to classics and
crowd-pleasers for you and your book group / by H. Elisabeth
Ellington and Jane Freimiller.
      p. cm.
   ISBN 1-57071-935-7
   1. Best books—United States. 2. Group reading—United States. I.
Freimiller, Jane. II. Title.
   Z1035.9 .E45 2002
   011'.73--dc21
                                        2002006926

Printed and bound in Canada
WC 10 9 8 7 6 5 4 3

FOR OUR MOTHERS

Contents

Acknowledgments

I'd like to thank the staffs of the Portsmouth Public Library in Portsmouth, New Hampshire, and the Dimond Library at the University of New Hampshire for assistance and suggestions. Our book group members—Elizabeth Andersen, Sarah Avery-Leaf, Cheryl Booth, Holly Brunelli, Sybille Goldberg, Vivian Harris, Erika Mantz, Paula Parisi, Cori Sharp—have been unfailingly enthusiastic and supportive of this project. I am grateful to Elizabeth Andersen for providing book suggestions, loaning books, and generally commiserating. Carmen Nge offered useful suggestions and wrote the box on postcolonial literature. Erika Mantz provided invaluable assistance by reading and commenting extensively on the manuscript, writing several boxes, and alerting us to books, places, and information that book group members would want to know about. This book greatly benefited from her careful reading and thoughtful feedback. *A Year of Reading* could not have been written without the more-than-generous assistance of my mother, Juliana Ellington. Her influence can be seen on every page. I could not wish for a better reader, editor, collaborator, coconspirator, and friend. Finally, thanks to my husband, Danny, for making me pancakes, solving all my many computer crises promptly and good-humoredly, not complaining about the paper explosion in his study, and always believing in me.

—Elisabeth Ellington

The greatest of all thanks go to my husband, Kevin Connolly, whose wisdom and enthusiasm were essential in making this book happen. Thanks also to our agent, Bob Silverstein, for his encouragement and advice. I would also like to thank Juliana Ellington for her help with the manuscript. And I would like to express my appreciation for my friends from Lowell whose encouragement over the past few years has meant more to me than they can imagine: Katherine Collins, Susan Gallagher, Jeffrey Gerson, Hilary Holladay, Alice Walters, and John Wooding.

—Jane Freimiller

Introduction

Whether you are embarking on an intellectual journey through reading on your own or eager to share literary jaunts with a book group, *A Year of Reading* provides the tools you'll need to make your journey a success.

How this book can help the individual reader

When I get a little money I buy books; and if any is left I buy food and clothes.
—Erasmus (c. 1466–1536)

People who are passionate about reading do not have to be convinced of its benefits. We know that reading opens our minds, challenges our beliefs, and expands our hearts. We turn to books when we are lonely or when other people overwhelm us. Books are there for us whether we're celebrating or in mourning. We know that a truly good book will delight us in our youth, our prime, and our old age. A person's favorite book will tell us more about him than his resumé ever can. We form bonds with people over books though we may have nothing else in common. Passionate readers easily agree with Erasmus in listing books as foremost among the necessities of life.

But even committed readers run into problems. Which among the tens of thousands of books published each year are worth reading? How can we navigate a course through all the millions of books in print? How do we make choices? And how can we get more out of our reading? How can we learn to think more deeply about the reading choices we make?

A Year of Reading is designed to help the individual reader see her way clear through the myriad choices available. It is also designed to help individual readers organize their reading more efficiently, thereby deepening and broadening their experience. And finally, it provides questions and strategies for thinking more thoroughly about what you've read.

Not every enjoyable book lends itself well to serious reflection: after we find out "whodunit" or whether the guy gets the girl, there might not be much left to say. All of the books we've chosen, though, are filled with characters and themes that should give you plenty to talk and think about. They also broaden our horizons. In narrowing our choices down to the sixty we discuss in detail here, we've focused on books that not only touch on things that matter, but do so from fresh perspectives. Finally, we've picked books that are a pleasure to read. Reading the selections for each month should never be drudgery, and we're confident that none of these will be a chore.

How this book can also help your book group

Some books are to be tasted, others to be swallowed, and some few to be chewed and digested.

—Francis Bacon (1561–1626)

We have been in the same book group together for six years. In the beginning, our discussions rarely got beyond, "I liked it," or, "I hated it." Over the years, however, we've grown as readers and as a group. We've become better at selecting books, we take more conversational chances, and we get together outside of book group for author readings or art gallery openings. Much of our improvement has come through trial and error, but much is also the result of talking to as many different people as possible about their experiences in groups. We've learned a lot about how successful groups work—whether they are brand new or have been together for years. We wanted to share our experience by providing a resource that would lay a sound foundation for beginning groups and provide established groups with fresh energy and focus. At the same time, we wanted to put the spotlight back where it belongs—on the books themselves. We believe that great books, like great meals, ought to be shared with friends. Books worthy of being "chewed and digested" are best done so with company.

How to use this book

We've organized *A Year of Reading* around the calendar year with both the individual and the book group in mind. Each chapter represents one month of reading, and each month is designated with a theme selected with the time of year in mind. For example, January encourages readers to curl up with a cup of hot chocolate while reading stories about polar expeditions, while April's selections focus on gardening and spiritual renewal. Each month, you or your group can choose one or more of the five titles you'll find listed categorically.

Crowd-pleasers are books that will appeal to almost everyone. These are titles sharing strong plots, compelling characters, and topical issues.

Classics offer an opportunity to return to old favorites, fill in educational gaps, and discover enduring literature.

Challenges are ambitious titles offering challenging subject matter or style for readers who want to stretch their limits.

Memoirs are for those interested in a more personal style of writing.

Potluck, the final category, adds an element of surprise and unpredictability to the line-up. Here you'll find essays, short stories, history and other nonfiction, as well as a few unusual novels.

Each month we provide a description of each book and information about its author enabling you to decide if it is a book that appeals to you. Next, you will find five detailed questions suitable for reflection or discussion. Whether you are reading for your own pleasure or as part of a group, we recommend visiting these questions before, during, and after reading the book. Examine the questions before you start reading in order to be aware of themes and issues you might not have otherwise noticed; review them during reading to deepen the reading experience; and revisit them after you've finished the book in order to reflect carefully on what you've read.

We offer a substantial list of further reading suggestions for each title. While these suggestions often include other books by the author, they consist primarily of books that share a similar theme or style. This section is invaluable for organizing your personal reading for the year and for book groups interested in exploring an author or theme more thoroughly. Most of our selections are available in inexpensive paperback editions. Finally, we point you toward video and Internet resources to guide you toward background information on authors, reviews, and related topics.

You will find these ideas boxed separately from the main text under these headings:

Discussion/Reflection Strategies: different ways of thinking about the text.

Extra Credit: ideas for book-related outings, activities, and adventures.

Did You Know...?: background information about books and authors.

A Year of Reading is structured but flexible; we encourage you to adapt its material to fit your style and tastes. But some strategies you might consider are:

Keeping a journal to remember what you've read and when, and what you've thought about it. Respond to *A Year of Reading*'s questions in your journal. Generate questions of your own. Write letters to characters in novels, etc.

Experiment with a theme in order to find out as much as you can about a particular author or topic. For example, read all of our recommendations on the Harlem Renaissance, see the documentaries, listen to the jazz, and read the poetry. Develop serial obsessions!

Experiment with a genre, trying poetry, nonfiction, essays, or even plays. Share your thoughts with your journal.

For readers interested in starting a book group or improving the one they're already in, information included in the appendices covers the basics, from finding other members to choosing a meeting place, as well as more complex issues such as managing group dynamics and a variety of suggestions for making meetings more engaging and enjoyable.

Our goal in writing *A Year of Reading* was to include many more ideas and suggestions than any one reader or group would have the energy or time to pursue. That way, readers can pick and choose the strategies and activities that seem most in keeping with their own spirit.

Finally, we would love to hear about your reading. What books do you wish we had included in *A Year of Reading*? What suggestions worked well for you? What advice would you give other serious readers or book groups? Email us at yearofreading@hotmail.com and tell us about your reading. We also welcome suggestions and comments about *A Year of Reading*.

A
Year of
Reading

CHAPTER 1
January
Winter's Tales

CROWD-PLEASER
Skating to Antarctica by Jenny Diski

CLASSIC
My Antonia by Willa Cather

CHALLENGE
Winter Journey by Isabel Colegate

MEMOIR
After and Before the Lightning
(Sun Tracks vol 28) by Simon J. Ortiz

POTLUCK
Arctic Dreams by Barry Lopez

The pale, cold light of the winter sunset did not beautify—it was like the light of truth itself. When the smoky clouds hung low in the west and the red sun went down behind them, leaving a pink flush on the snow roofs and the blue drifts, then the wind sprang up afresh, with a kind of bitter song, as if it said: 'This is reality, whether you like it or not. All those frivolities of summer, the light and shadow, the living mask of green that trembled over everything, they were lies, and this is what was underneath. This is the truth.'

—Willa Cather, *My Antonia*

Whether or not we agree with Willa Cather that the light of winter is the light of truth, we can agree that January is a time for reflection and resolution. The new year inspires us to take stock of our lives and make plans for the future. The weather conspires to keep us inside, giving us the opportunity for self-study. We owe it to ourselves to spend some time thinking about where we are, how we got here, and where we are going.

This month's selections are inspired by the introspection winter brings. Jenny Diski's *Skating to Antarctica* is a wrenching story of self-exploration in the context of Antarctic travel. The beauty and brutality of life in Nebraska in the nineteenth century are exemplified by the life of a pioneer woman in Willa Cather's *My Antonia*, while Barry Lopez teaches us much about the far North in *Arctic Dreams*. Both Simon J. Ortiz and Isabel Colegate reveal the richness lying behind seemingly barren and impoverished situations. In his memoir, *After and Before the Lightning*, Ortiz recalls a winter spent on a Lakota reservation in South Dakota chronicling the weather and the lives of the inhabitants. In *Winter Journey*, Colegate delicately examines the lives and loves of a brother and sister in the quiet of the English countryside.

January/Winter's Tales
Crowd-Pleaser
Skating to Antarctica: A Journey to the End of the World by Jenny Diski,1998, available in paperback from Ecco Press for $14.00

What is this book about?

Skating to Antarctica is a blend of two genres: the family memoir and the travel narrative. First-time memoirist Diski weaves a description of her Antarctic travels with an account of her horrific childhood. The connections between these two stories may not be immediately obvious; in one, Diski writes a straightforward account of traveling to Antarctica, while in the other, she writes about trying to dissuade her daughter from investigating whether Diski's mother, who disappeared from her life in 1966, is alive or dead. In the hands of a lesser writer, this would never work. But Diski is masterful and always in control of her material.

She is a curmudgeonly traveler, turning an ironic eye on her group tour to Antarctica. Diski does not do well with timetables and schedules; she finds the daily round of meals, lectures, and planned activities nightmarish. But group travel is the only way to get to Antarctica, and getting to Antarctica is the only way she knows to "write *white*." White is the color of oblivion for Diski, the color of absence, of hospital sheets, of ice. She generously describes her parents' behavior as "emotional unreliability," but readers will have no trouble understanding why a child growing up in this household of tantrums, depression, and suicide attempts, used as a pawn in her parents' endless screaming battles and as foreplay for their sexual relationship, would grow up seeking oblivion.

Diski has every right to be self-indulgent, even maudlin. But instead, she applies the humorous, detached stance she takes toward travel to herself and her parents. She turns her past into a detective story, looking up the neighbors who witnessed the abusive relationship between her parents and knew of their multiple suicide attempts, in an effort to piece together the story of her own childhood. The two narratives ultimately converge in a climactic realization about, of all things, the true color of ice. *Skating to Antarctica* is always surprising, always engaging. Readers familiar with the dysfunctional family memoirs that have flooded the market in the past decade will find Diski's transformation of the genre mesmerizing, while readers who scoff at the genre will have to reevaluate their prejudices.

What should I know about the author?

Born in London in 1947 to two mentally unstable and destructive parents, Diski had, as readers of *Skating to Antarctica* find out, a miserable childhood. In 1976, she married Roger Diski and, a year later, gave birth to their daughter, Chloe. She taught English and history from 1973 to 1983, and worked as a tutor from 1985 to 1989. She published her first novel, *Nothing Natural*, the story of a sado-masochistic relationship, in 1986. In addition to writing novels and reviews, she has also written films for British television.

Questions for reflection and discussion

1. The structure of *Skating to Antarctica* is unusual; sections titled, "At Sea," are interspersed with sections recounting Diski's childhood. But the book never feels disconnected. Why not? How does Diski tie the narratives together? What themes or metaphors appear in both stories? How does her childhood make her long for Antarctica, and how does Antarctica remind her of her parents?

2. Though Diski claims she is not interested in whether her mother is alive, she does interview old neighbors Mrs. Rosen and Mrs. Levine and visit her old apartment building. Why do you think she takes this journey into the past? What does she want to learn? Is she expecting to learn something new about her parents? About herself? What did you hope or expect Diski to discover? Were you disappointed in the outcome?

3. "But how all right could I be, genetically and psychologically, with parents like that?" Diski wonders. She considers herself a survivor; she certainly comes across as a perfectly functional adult to the reader. This is not a self-help book, nor is Diski self-indulgent. She doesn't write much about *how* she survived this experience. How do you think Diski emerged from her childhood relatively unscathed? What kind of relationship has she been able to form with her own daughter? Reviewers have praised the detachment with which Diski writes in the third person of "Jennifer," her childhood self. Why does she detach herself from her childhood experiences, and why might reviewers find this admirable? If Diski is so detached, can she also be a sympathetic character?

4. What images come to mind when you think about Antarctica? Diski's goal, she says, is to find a white landscape, but there are many other white places on earth. What draws her to Antarctica? Were you surprised by anything she saw or experienced there? Diski develops a soft spot for explorers Ernest Shackleton and Robert Scott, who both led failed expeditions to the region. Why has Antarctica exercised this kind of pull on Diski and the rest of us?

5. What triggers your own memory? Are there descriptions in *Skating to Antarctica* that remind you of your past? Why is Diski relieved to discover that her mother was as she remembered her? Diski's comments about false memories may be especially useful in thinking about this question. Do you believe all of her claims?

Other books by Jenny Diski

Diski is the author of eight novels, including *Nothing Natural* (1986), *Rainforest* (1987), *Like Mother* (1988), *Then Again* (1990), *Happily Ever After* (1991), *Monkey's Uncle* (1994), and *The Dream Mistress* (1996). Her most recent novel, *Only Human*, tells the story of the biblical Abraham and Sarah, partly narrated by God. Her short stories are collected in *The Vanishing Princess*, and her essays, mostly from the *London Review of Books*, appear under the title *Don't*.

If you like *Skating to Antarctica*, you will like...

An Unquiet Mind by Kay Redfield Jamison. Moving memoir about bipolar disorder written by a psychologist.

The Liar's Club and *Cherry* by Mary Karr. Critically acclaimed memoirs of the author's dysfunctional childhood in Texas.

Girl, Interrupted by Susannah Kaysen. Memoir about being institutionalized at the age of eighteen; also made into a film starring Winona Ryder and Angelina Jolie.

Endurance: Shackleton's Incredible Voyage by Alfred Lansing. This slender, suspenseful account of Ernest Shackleton's Antarctic expedition is a must-read classic.

Terra Incognita: Travels in Antarctica by Sara Wheeler. Wheeler spent seven months residing in Antarctic science camps; her memoir blends her own adventures with a history of previous explorations.

Video resources

Frank Hurley was the official photographer on Ernest Shackleton's 1914 expedition to the South Pole; he directed *South: Ernest Shackleton and the Endurance Expedition*, a silent film from the footage he captured in Antarctica, which has recently been restored and made available.

Internet resources

Get a taste of Diski's skills as an essayist by looking up her book reviews for the *London Review of Books* at www.lrb.co.uk. TerraQuest's website includes a Virtual Antarctica tour with photographs, expedition dispatches, and information about Antarctic history and ecology at www.terraquest.com.

January/Winter's Tales
Classic
My Antonia by Willa Cather, 1918, several paperback editions available, including one from Mariner Books for $5.95

What is this book about?

Recently orphaned, ten-year-old Jim Burden is placed on a train in Virginia and sent to his grandparents in Nebraska. He arrives in town at the same time as an Eastern European immigrant family, the Shimerdas. Jim's grandparents' farm and the poor piece of land bought sight unseen by the Shimerdas are near enough for the families to see each other often. A strong friendship develops between Jim and the fourteen-year-old Antonia Shimerda. As Jim teaches Antonia English, they both learn how to farm, do chores, and appreciate the brutal beauty of the Nebraska prairie. Although Jim and Antonia spend less time together as the years pass—he moves to town and attends school, she labors on the farm and then works as a servant in town—they remain close, and Jim's veneration of her grows steadily stronger.

My Antonia is written as Jim's memoir of his life with Antonia. Cather's treatment of the material echoes the pace and substance of memory. Some things are remembered vividly; others less so. Some characters' lives are traced in detail; others are let go. There are stories within stories—characters relate their lives or tales they have heard. The novel layers memories on top of memories, creating a text that is as much lived as it is read.

What should I know about the author?

Willa Cather was born in 1873 in Virginia. She was the eldest of seven children. In 1882, the family moved to Nebraska where they farmed for a short period before settling in the town of Red Cloud, where her father became a businessman. Cather entered the University of Nebraska determined to become a doctor, but she abandoned that plan to study literature and journalism. While still an undergraduate, Cather worked on the local newspaper as a theater critic, gaining a reputation for critical acumen and scathing reviews. After graduation, she moved to Pittsburgh to work as an assistant editor at *Home Monthly* magazine, and following several years of magazine writing, editorial work, and high school teaching, Cather accepted a position on the editorial board of *McClure's Magazine* in New York City. During her six years at *McClure's*, she tried to write fiction in addition to performing her magazine duties, but found it difficult. She resigned from the magazine and devoted herself solely to writing when she was close to forty. Twelve novels followed, along with several collections of short stories. Cather died in 1947. She and her long-time partner, Edith Lewis, are buried near their summer home in Jaffrey, New Hampshire.

Questions for reflection and discussion

1. Antonia is the central figure in the novel and in Jim Burden's memory. Do you find Antonia as compelling a person as Jim Burden does? Is she an admirable figure? What is it about her that Jim likes so much? In what ways does Antonia change over the years? How does she remain the same?

2. What sorts of help do Jim's grandparents offer the Shimerdas? What reasons do they give for offering this help? Why do they help the Shimerda family even when Mrs. Shimerda is rude to them? How does Jim's grandmother explain and excuse Mrs. Shimerda's anger? Do you think she is right? Is the grandparents' behavior attributable to their faith in God? If so, how?

3. The prairie almost outshines Antonia and Jim as the main character in the novel. How does Cather make the prairie come alive for the reader? Identify some passages that convey a sense of place. What effect does the prairie have on Antonia and Jim as they grow up? Why do you think people choose to live under such harsh conditions? What do we learn about Jim and Antonia from their feelings about the land?

4. How does Cather address the issue of social class in *My Antonia?* Why does Jim prefer the "hired girls" to members of "his own set"? What qualities does he see in them that are missing from the middle-class girls of town? Why are Jim's grandparents upset by his fondness for Antonia, Lena, and Tiny? And are the grandparents living up to their religious ideals by questioning Jim's relationships? What are Jim's criticisms of the town of Black Hawk? Why does he end up leaving Nebraska?

5. Moral courage is always an important theme in Cather's work. It is one thing to be strong physically; it is more difficult and unusual to live up to one's principles. How do we see this played out in this novel? What does the story of Sylvester Lovett demonstrate about Jim Burden's beliefs? Does Jim behave any more courageously than Sylvester did?

Did you know...?

The character Antonia Shimerda is based on a real person Willa Cather knew while growing up in Nebraska. Her name was Annie Sadilek and she lived from 1869 until 1955. She was born in Bohemia (where the Czech Republic is now), and in 1883, when she was fourteen, the Sadilek family arrived in Nebraska. Soon after their arrival, the father committed suicide. The family struggled with the farm for many years, and Annie became a hired girl in Red Cloud. She had a child, eventually married, and had many more children and a successful farm. Both the fictional Shimerdas and the real-life Sadileks lived in a "sod house" in Nebraska. To find out more about how people built houses from dirt, visit www.websteaders.com

Other books by Willa Cather

Much of Cather's fiction can be grouped by setting. Her East Coast works include *Alexander's Bridge, Sapphira and the Slave Girl,* and *Shadows on the Rock.* Two of her best novels are set in the southwestern desert: *Death Comes for the Archbishop* and *The Professor's House.* In addition to *My Antonia,* her Plains and midwestern fiction includes *O Pioneers!, One of Ours, Lucy Gayheart, A Lost Lady,* and *The Song of the Lark.* Cather also wrote short stories (including the well-known "Paul's Case"), available in many collections.

Books about Willa Cather

Sharon O'Brien's pioneering biography, *Willa Cather: The Emerging Voice,* has become the standard, but you might want to supplement it with James Woodress's *Willa Cather: A Literary Life,* or consult a British perspective on this quintessentially American author in Hermione Lee's biography, *Willa Cather.*

Did you know...?

When Willa Cather lived in Red Cloud and Lincoln, she cut her hair short, wore men's clothing, and called herself William. She had crushes on fellow female students, actresses, and opera singers. In Pittsburgh, she lived with Isabelle McClung for several years and remained devoted to her even after McClung married. Willa Cather lived with Edith Lewis for forty years. Cather never publicly addressed her sexuality (and even her surviving personal correspondence does not mention it) nor were there ever any public questions about her lifestyle even though she was well-known. Only recently have biographers begun to discuss her lesbianism. The effort to address connections between

Cather's writing and her sexuality has produced two books of academic scholarship: *Willa Cather: Queering America* by Marilee Lindemann and *Willa Cather and Others* by Jonathan Goldberg, written primarily for those familiar with literary theory.

If you like *My Antonia,* you will like...

Plainsong by Kent Haruf. A teenager who becomes pregnant is disowned by her family, only to be taken in by two elderly brothers in this novel about late twentieth-century life on the Plains.

The Country of Pointed Firs by Sarah Orne Jewett. A remote Maine town filled with memorable personalities provides the setting for this touching story of an unlikely friendship. Cather's mentor and friend, Jewett, was a well-known New England novelist and short story writer.

Angle of Repose by Wallace Earle Stegner. This Pulitzer Prize–winning novel tells of four generations of an American family. A wheelchair-bound retired historian researches his grandparents' lives, growing closer to them while becoming estranged from his living relatives.

Ethan Frome by Edith Wharton. A poor New England farmer and his hardworking wife find their lives changed forever when visited by her charming young cousin.

Nothing to Do but Stay: My Pioneer Mother by Carrie Young. A gorgeous, slim memoir about growing up on the North Dakota plains.

Extra Credit

Many authors' houses have been preserved as museums. Visit Willa Cather's childhood home in Red Cloud, Nebraska (see Internet resources for further information). The home of Sarah Orne Jewett (Cather's mentor and friend) in South Berwick, Maine, is also open to the public. Find out details about this and other New England historic homes at www.spnea.org.

Video resources

The 1934 production of A Lost Lady with Barbara Stanwyck annoyed Willa Cather so much that she refused to permit anyone to adapt her novels to film during the rest of her lifetime. The past decade has seen an excellent television adaptation of My Antonia (Joseph Sargent, 1994), as well as O Pioneers! starring Jessica Lange (Glenn Jordan, 1992) and The Song of the Lark (Karen Arthur, 2001). Treat the whole family to Sarah, Plain and Tall, starring Glenn Close as a strong-willed New Englander who moves to Kansas as a mail-order bride (directed by Glenn Jordan, 1991).

Internet resources

The University of Nebraska Willa Cather Archive is online at www. libfund.unl.edu/cather/cather.htm. The Willa Cather Pioneer Memorial and Educational Foundation in Red Cloud, Nebraska maintains a website at www.willacather.org. Two excellent sites about Cather's life and work can be found at fp.image.dk/fpemarxlind/ and icg. harvard.edu/~cather/.

January/Winter's Tales
Challenge
Winter Journey by Isabel Colegate, 2001, available in hardcover from Counterpoint Press for $23.00

What is this book about?

Edith, twice married and twice divorced, has a daughter, two grandchildren, and a relationship with a journalist named Hubert. Always energetic, Edith has been a neighborhood activist and a member of Parliament and now runs a school for foreign students wishing to learn English. She always has goals and detailed schemes for achieving them.

Her brother, Alfred, is a professional photographer who has lived all over the world and whose services are still in demand. But Alfred's success is a mystery to Edith, since his way of life is so different from hers. While she is lively, he is quiet, solitary, and guarded. His one great relationship ended in disaster, and he is content to live alone in the family home, playing chess with a local clergyman and taking pictures of the forest in winter.

When Edith visits Alfred, the siblings are impelled to consider the lives and deaths of their parents, their respective romantic relationships, and their relationship to one another. Colegate's remark that, "It's not a bad idea to get in the habit of writing down one's thoughts. It saves one having to bother anyone else with them," provides a clue to her literary concerns. The quiet beauty of *Winter Journey* is like the beauty of winter itself—difficult to see at first, but when approached with a spirit of attentive openness, it emerges to surprise and delight.

What should I know about the author?

Isabel Colegate was born in 1931, the youngest of four daughters of Sir Arthur Colegate, a member of Parliament, and Lady Colegate Worsley. Colegate left school at sixteen and chose to devote herself to writing rather than attend a university. Her first novel, *The Blackmailer*, was published in 1958. She is married with three children and lives near Bath, England.

Questions for reflection and discussion

1. How does Colegate convey to us what sort of a person Edith is? Does her professional life provide a clue to her character? What do her marriages tell us about her? How do you think Edith would describe herself? Does Edith have any "blind spots" about herself? How does the author's description of Edith provide the reader with insight that Edith does not have into herself?

2. How does Colegate write differently about Alfred than Edith? Is he a more or less finely drawn character? How does she convey what sort of person he is? What do we learn about him through his relationships with his parents and everyone else? What do we learn by having access to his thoughts? Why might Colegate use different strategies to describe two different characters? Is she suggesting that one lifestyle is better than the other?

3. To what extent do we learn about relating to the opposite sex from our brothers or sisters? Are relationships between brothers and sisters different from those between sisters or between brothers? Do Edith and Alfred treat one another as equals? How does their relationship with one another differ from the other relationships Alfred and Edith have?

4. Edith and Alfred pride themselves on having come of age during the 1960s, which enabled them to question and reject traditional ideas about class and relationships. But have they really put the ideals of the '60s into practice? Examine Edith and Alfred's interactions with Mrs. Weeks, Mrs. Jukes, Mrs. Jukes's son, Laurence Raven, and the neighbors. How are these interactions shaped by class differences? What about Edith's concern for her daughter's marriage? How does her advice to her daughter reflect her own character?

5. Reflect on the title. Who journeys in the novel? Where did they begin and where did they end up? Has anything significant happened? What do the descriptions of landscape and weather add (or take away) from the novel? Look at the quotation from Willa Cather that opens this chapter. Does Cather's observation apply to *Winter Journey*?

Other books by Isabel Colegate

Colegate's first three novels have been published in the U.S. as *Three Novels*. They are *The Blackmailer* (1958), the story of a man who believes he can blackmail his way into upper-class society, *A Man of Power* (1960), the story of an industrialist at odds with upper-class society, and *The Great Occasion* (1962), a novel about five sisters. *Statues in a Garden* (1964) was her first historical novel; set in the years preceding World War I, it covers themes she later returned to in her best-known novel, *The Shooting Party* (1980). Her *Orlando Trilogy* (*Orlando King, Orlando at the Brazen Threshold*, and *Agatha*), set in the period from 1930 to 1956, focuses on a father and his daughter and reworks the Oedipus myth. *New from the City of the Sun* (1979) is set over a similar time period and concerns a utopian community. Colegate uses the device of a biographer researching her subject in *Deceits of Time* (1988) and *The Summer of the Royal Visit* (1991). *A Glimpse of Sion's Glory* (1985) is a collection of three novellas.

If you like *Winter Journey,* you will like...

A Start in Life and *Hotel du Lac* by Anita Brookner. Brookner's quiet, melancholy novels probe the psyches of wistful heroines.

Possession and *Angels and Insects* by A.S. Byatt. Byatt's best-known works are brilliant explorations of the Victorian mindset.

The Ice Age and *The Radiant Way* by Margaret Drabble. Sister of A.S. Byatt and contemporary of Colegate, Drabble writes novels that explore class, politics, and society in England.

The Road to Lichfield by Penelope Lively. The protagonist of this novel travels the road to Lichfield to visit her father, who is dying in a nursing home; she later discovers a secret from his past that forces her to rethink her own past.

The Sacred and Profane Love Machine by Iris Murdoch. Intelligent and leisurely paced, this novel examines two British families that are falling apart.

Did you know...?

Many of the authors we recommend have been Booker Prize nominees or winners. The Booker Prize, England's most prestigious literary prize, is awarded each year to one of six shortlisted nominees for the best full-length novel written in English by a citizen of Britain or Commonwealth nations. When you can't think of what to read next, we suggest trying a Booker winner or nominee; these novels rarely disappoint. Visit the Booker's official website at www.bookerprize.co.uk.

Video resources

The Shooting Party was made into a film starring John Gielgud and James Mason (Alan Bridges, 1985). Both it and the film version of

A.S. Byatt's *Angels and Insects* (directed by Philip Haas, 1996) are excellent movies.

Internet resources

The *New York Times* review of *Winter Journey* is online at www.nytimes.com/books/01/02/18/reviews/010218.18connt.html.

January/Winter's Tales
Memoir
After and Before the Lightning (Sun Tracks vol 28) by Simon J. Ortiz, 1994, available in paperback from the University of Arizona Press for $17.95

What is this book about?

This unusual memoir of a winter spent on the Rosebud Indian Reservation in South Dakota is a mix of poems, prose poems, and journal entries. Appointed writer-in-residence at Sinte Gleska University, Ortiz, a native of New Mexico, found himself ill-equipped to deal with the hardships of a Plains winter. As in any severe climate, "the weather is always 'news,' whether it is good or bad." Writing *After and Before the Lightning* becomes an act of spiritual survival.

Through his poetry, Ortiz discovers what there is to be thankful for in winter. We tend to think of spring with its new growth, summer with its lush productivity, even fall with its vibrant colors, as the proper seasons to appreciate nature. Winter, especially a Dakota winter, is an altogether more difficult season to value, but Ortiz discovers that writing poetry about the landscape and the human activity that goes on in spite of the snow and the cold enables him to reconnect with nature in this alienating climate. The keen observation demanded by his poetry awakens Ortiz to stark beauties and variety in the winter landscape. Moreover, he learns to be thankful for the "small necessary comforts" which we so easily overlook in the warmer months. In fact, by forcing the poet to meditate, to wait, to reflect, winter ultimately creates the ideal conditions for poetry and memoir.

What should I know about the author?

Simon J. Ortiz, a member of the Acoma Pueblo tribe of New Mexico, was born in 1941 in Albuquerque. He served in the Vietnam War, which he writes about in *From Sand Creek*. He has been publishing poetry since 1971, when his first collection, *Naked in the Wind*, appeared. Ortiz has worked as an instructor at many colleges and universities. His work has been honored with many prizes and awards.

Did you know...?

About two million Americans identify themselves as belonging to one of the five hundred different tribal groups in the United States. Among them, they speak 149 native American languages.

Questions for reflection and discussion

1. Writing poetry was a way for Ortiz to survive the hardships of a South Dakota winter. He claims that poetry reconnects his life "to all Existence with a sense of wonder and awe." What does he mean? How does this happen? Why does it happen with poetry instead of through prose? How does the form of poetry help Ortiz express his meaning?

2. Poetry is Ortiz's personal survival strategy, but he writes more generally of the importance of story: "Story, though it's still of the bitter cold, helps." He compares the comforts offered by stories to the basic needs satisfied by "good bread and a warm fire." Why do we need stories? Why is storytelling such an important part of Native American traditions and literature? Does reading satisfy our need for story, or do we also need the physical act of telling a story to others? We don't always think of poems as telling stories. Are poetry and story mutually exclusive?

DISCUSSION/REFLECTION STRATEGY

Many of us find it difficult to respond to poetry, but poetry can be enormously rewarding. *After and Before the Lightning* is the perfect volume for the poetry-shy: the poems are thematically linked, and many of the journal entries discuss events or situations that Ortiz then addresses in a poem. Ask yourself these questions as you read a poem:

• What does the poem seem to be about? What is the poet saying?

• Look for images, striking phrases, word choice, and word patterns. What pictures form in your mind as you're reading? What lines stand out? Do these pictures or lines relate to the overall meaning?

• What impact do the poet's choices about form have on your experience of the poem? Consider both how the poem looks to the eye (the line breaks, the division into stanzas) and how it rings in the ear (the rhyme scheme, if any, and the meter). Would other choices have worked as well?

• How does the title relate to the poem?

Listening to poets reading their own works adds to the experience of their poetry. *Poetry Speaks: Hear Great Poets Read Their Work from Tennyson to Plath* is an invaluable resource. In addition to anthologizing major poems, from Alfred, Lord Tennyson to Sylvia Plath, it provides brief biographies and critical essays and includes three CDs of the poets reading their works. Many libraries carry recordings of authors reading their own poetry; recordings can also be downloaded online. For example, find video and audio recordings of Simon J. Ortiz reading his works at www.counterbalancepoetry.org /simonjortiz.htm.

Groups wanting to integrate poetry into their reading could begin by having one member each month share a favorite poem with the group as an "appetizer" before the discussion of that month's book. More ambitious groups could select an anthology grouped around one theme, such as nature poems or love poems, or a small collection by one poet. We like Adrienne Rich, Maxine Kumin, William Carlos Williams, and Sharon Olds.

3. The word "margin" is used repeatedly throughout these poems. Why? What or who, for Ortiz, is marginal? You might want to look at his November 24 journal entry and, "Comprehension," the poem that follows, and also at, "The Margins Where We Live," and, "Beyond the Margin." What other words, phrases, and images are repeated? Why are these important to the meaning of Ortiz's poems?

4. What makes this a work of Native American literature? Do we classify it as Native American because of its author's ethnicity, or because of its themes, or a combination? Ortiz's primary focus in *After and Before the Lightning* is winter, yet we never forget this memoir is set on an Indian reservation. How does he remind us? What do we learn about Native American life?

5. How are tragedies a proper subject for poetry? Ortiz refers to many tragedies: the *Challenger* disaster; a farmer in Iowa who kills his banker; two men who shoot their families and then kill themselves; a man who shoots himself in front of city hall; a young poet who dies. Why do you think he's interested in telling these stories? How do they relate to the other stories in this memoir?

Other books by Simon J. Ortiz

Ortiz is primarily a poet, but he also writes in other genres. *Howbah Indians* (1978), *Fightin'* (1983), and *Men on the Moon* (1999) are collections of short stories. His books for children include *The People Shall Continue* and *Blue and Red*. If you enjoyed *After and Before the Lightning*, you will want to read *From Sand Creek: Rising in This Heart Which Is Our America* and *Woven Stone*, which collects three of his earlier works. You might want to look at *Speaking for the Generations: Native Writers on Writing*, which is edited by Ortiz.

If you like *After and Before the Lightning*, you will like...

Choteau Creek: A Sioux Reminiscence by Joseph Iron Eye Dudley. Touching memoir of time spent at the author's grandparents' house on a Sioux reservation.

Bloodlines: Odyssey of a Native Daughter by Janet Campbell Hale. An autobiography in essays by Native novelist.

She Had Some Horses by Joy Harjo. A poetry collection by a well-respected Native American poet. Look for the audio version where Harjo reads her own poems.

Land Circle: Writings Collected from the Land by Linda Hasselstrom. A collection of writings by a poet, essayist, rancher, and environmentalist.

The Blood Runs Like a River through My Dreams by Nasdijj. A painful memoir of growing up on a reservation.

DISCUSSION/REFLECTION STRATEGY

You may have already made a commitment to exploring more diversity in your reading, but you won't be able to do justice to the new literatures you're discovering without also committing to a little background research and reading. Here are our suggestions for approaching a text by a Native American author:

Begin by reading a general overview of contemporary Native American literature at www.bookspot.com/features/nativeamerican.htm.

Visit Karen Strom's excellent website on Native American issues and literature at www.hanksville.org. Here you can learn about individual authors by clicking on "Storytellers." Get a sense of the kinds of stereotypes and wrong assumptions we're likely to bring to our reading of Native American authors by visiting "A Line in the Sand."

Find out what tribe your author belongs to. Tribal associations are deeply important in Native American culture; specific customs, beliefs, and lifestyles vary dramatically from tribe to tribe. Learn more about your author's tribe by consulting the Smithsonian Institute's *Handbook of North American Indians* at your local library.

Consult Andrew Wiget's excellent reference works, *Dictionary of Native American Literature* and *Handbook of Native American Literature*. Here you will learn about the history of Native literatures, oral and written traditions, themes, tropes, and important authors.

If your book group has decided to read more works by Native American authors, you should pool your knowledge. Initiate a discussion with your group about Native American history. What can you remember learning—or not learning—in school? A general picture will begin to emerge, which you can supplement with the information you've found online.

You can also read Native authors on your own, outside your reading group. Your discussions of Native American literature would be so much richer if each member of your book group had read one work by Leslie Marmon Silko, N. Scott Momaday, Paula Gunn Allen, Joy Harjo, Louise Erdrich, James Welch, or Linda Hogan.

Video resources

Native American Life (1995) and *Native American Heritage* (1997) are recent documentaries on Native Americans.

Internet resources

Simon J. Ortiz can be viewed reading from his poetry at www. counterbalancepoetry.org/simonjortiz.htm. Learn more about Ortiz's tribe, the Acoma Pueblo, at www.indianpueblo.org /ipcc/acomapage.htm. The Native Authors Project on the Internet Public Library includes a brief biography and a wealth of links to e-texts, interviews, and articles at www.ipl.org/cgi/ref/ native/browse.pl/A93.

January/Winter's Tales
Potluck
Arctic Dreams: Imagination and Desire in a Northern Land-scape by Barry Holstun Lopez, 1986, available in paper-back from Vintage Books for $15.00

What is this book about?

Based on the author's fifteen trips to the region, *Arctic Dreams* cele-brates the awesome beauty of the far North. Lopez's prose is full of lovingly observed details. Far from being simply an endless, barren field of white, his Arctic is rich in both human and natural interest. Lopez, a gifted storyteller, illuminates the culture of the Arctic's indigenous peoples, who forge lives for themselves by drawing on generations of deep patience and attention to their surroundings. He also vividly narrates the history of European Arctic exploration: the passions that led people to undertake voyages of almost unimaginable hardship, the folly that led to the ruin of many, and the heroism of those who endured to add to the fund of human knowledge.

As a naturalist, Lopez is able to provide explanations of phenomena of the region, from the dramatic optical illusions experienced by visitors to the region to the behavior of narwhals and polar bears. His final chapter on industrial development in the Arctic—the encounter between cultures—and between culture and the land—is a careful, thoughtful account of how human "imagination and desire" affect, and are being affected by, the "northern landscape."

What should I know about the author?

Barry Holstun Lopez was born in 1945 in Port Chester, New York. He grew up in southern California and New York City and attended Notre Dame University. He has lived in Oregon since 1968. Lopez's writing is frequently anthologized in nature writing and travel writing collections. In addition to writing, Barry Holstun Lopez has worked as a landscape photographer and frequently collaborates with artists in other media. He occasionally teaches and lectures at universities. He won the National Book Award in 1986 for *Arctic Dreams*.

Extra credit

Take your book discussion outdoors on a winter nature hike! Visit the American Hiking Society's www.americanhiking.org to find trails near you or consult a hiking guidebook for your state (check your local bookstore or library). Wear comfortable hiking shoes, pack a picnic lunch and plenty of water, and discuss this month's book while enjoying the great outdoors.

Questions for reflection and discussion

1. Why do strange animals appeal to us? Why do we go to zoos, watch nature documentaries, and revel in descriptions of odd beasts? Lopez addresses the characteristics and habits of musk oxen, polar bears, and narwhals. Did his descriptions come alive for you? Share your favorite parts from these chapters. What surprised you most?

What did you find most difficult to imagine? Would you like to see any of these animals in the flesh?

2. What do you think of hunting? What role, if any, does it play in your life or the life of your family? What do you think are its pros and cons? In the chapter called, "Migration: The Corridors of Breath," Lopez describes hunting as a state of mind. What does he mean by this? How do the Eskimos cultivate that state?

3. Can you explain why the sun never sets in the summer and never rises in the winter in the Arctic? Have you ever experienced greatly lengthened or shortened days of sunlight? What effect did it have on you? What sorts of optical phenomena and illusions does Lopez describe in chapter six? What accounts for them? What is the aurora borealis? Solar and lunar rings? The fata morgana? Why does Lopez say that views of the aurora borealis "make the emotion of self-pity impossible?" Do you agree with him?

4. Do you think the concept of a "mental map" is a useful one? What was your "mental map" of the Arctic before you read this book? What is it now? Do you think people who live in cities have as fully developed mental maps of their terrain as Eskimos do of the Arctic? How much do you think intuition and nonverbal cues play in your ability to navigate your terrain? Do smells, sights, sounds, and memory guide you at all?

5. What do you think about industrial development in the Arctic? Lopez describes encounters with people involved in development projects. To his credit, Lopez refuses to label people as simply good or bad because of their stands on development. Who are the people he meets and why are they in the Arctic? How do they justify their missions? About one group, Lopez says their attitude toward the Arctic is "colonial." What does he mean by this?

DISCUSSION/REFLECTION STRATEGY

Philosophers distinguish between two types of worth or value: instrumental value and intrinsic value. Something that only has instrumental value is considered worthy only to the extent that it is useful. For example, a hammer has instrumental value—I value it for its ability to help me drive nails into a wall. Something that has intrinsic value is valued for itself. Human beings are the best example of intrinsic value—we consider humans to be worthy of consideration independent of their instrumental value. Other people may be useful for us, but they are also more than that. They are valuable in their own right. Environmental philosophers ask if there is anything else that has intrinsic value. Barry Lopez suggests that the Arctic is valuable for its own sake—that it should not be treated solely as a useful resource for human use. Is he right? What do you think?

Other books by Barry Holstun Lopez

Lopez's extensive world travels provide the basis for his writing in short stories, essays, magazine articles, and book-length nonfiction. Like *Arctic Dreams*, his other works concern the interrelationship between humans and nature. Lopez's nonfiction works include *About This Life: Journeys on the Threshold of Memory*, *Of Wolves and Men*, *The Rediscovery of North America*, and *Crossing Open Ground*. His fiction includes *Lessons from the Wolverine*, *Field Notes: The Grace Note of the Canyon Wren*, *Winter Count*, *River Notes: The Dance of Herons*, and *Desert Notes: Reflections in the Eye of a Raven*. *Crow and Weasel: A Novella* is for children. *Giving Birth to Thunder, Sleeping with His Daughter: Coyote Builds North America* is a collection of stories about Coyote, the trickster figure from many Native American spiritual traditions, compiled from oral histories.

If you like *Arctic Dreams,* you will like...

Travels in Alaska by John Muir. Story of Muir's trips to Alaska in the latter half of the nineteenth century.

Coming into the Country by John McPhee. Considers Alaska in all its geographic, social, and economic complexity.

The Last Light Breaking: Living Among Alaska's Inupiat Eskimos by Nick Jans. Jans tells of modern Arctic explorers.

Two in the Far North by Margaret E. Murie. The true story of a married couple living for fifty years on the edge of the Alaskan wilderness.

Video resources

Relevant PBS Home Video titles include, *Great White Bear*, *The Alaska Experience*, and *Restoring Alaska: Ten Years in the Wake of Exxon Valdez*.

Internet resources

Find interviews with Barry Lopez at www.calypsoconsulting. com/lopez.html and www.januarymagazine.com. Paintings by the artists mentioned in chapter six can be viewed online at www.art cyclopedia.com. See the entry on "Seasons" in www.britannica.com for a further explanation of the Arctic midnight sun. If you would like to see pictures of narwhals go to www.coloradonarwhal.com. The Public Broadcasting System has good webpages on polar bears and walruses. See www.pbs.org/wnet/nature/whitebear/ and www.pbs. org/wnet/nature/toothwalkers/.

CHAPTER 2

February
In Honor of
Black History Month:
Family Legacies

CROWD-PLEASER
Kindred by Octavia E. Butler

CLASSIC
Passing by Nella Larsen

CHALLENGE
Middle Passage by Charles Johnson

MEMOIR
Pearl's Secret by Neil Henry

POTLUCK
The Farming of Bones by Edwidge Danticat

There is no agony like bearing an untold story inside of you.

—Maya Angelou

In the mid-1920s, African-American scholar Carter G. Woodson instituted Negro History Week in February, choosing this month because
it contains the birthdays of Abraham Lincoln and Frederick Douglass.
In 1976, February was declared Black History Month; since then, each
February has seen lectures, workshops, exhibitions, concerts, dramas,
and literary readings honoring the rich history of Americans of
African and Caribbean descent.

It has become commonplace to say that race has shaped the consciousness and the history of all peoples living in the Americas. The
intersections where black and white collide (and where, sometimes,
they mix) have been crucibles in which the brave have forged self-
knowledge from the unpromising material of oppression. This
month's choices look at the fresh and vital stories which, untold for
so long, are continually emerging from those intersections. In *Kindred*, Octavia Butler takes us on a time-travel journey with a modern
American woman inexplicably drawn back in time to meet her white
slave-holding ancestor. Nella Larsen's Harlem Renaissance novel, *Passing*, recounts the story of a mixed-race woman who denies her black
family and lives as a white woman. The Challenge selection, *Middle
Passage*, shows a freed slave coming to terms with his own conflicted
feelings about family and intimacy. Neil Henry relates the story of his
genealogical research into the white branch of his family in *Pearl's
Secret*, and finally, in the lyrical and haunting *The Farming of Bones*,
Edwidge Danticat explores the labyrinthine relationships between
slaves and masters, lovers and friends.

February/In Honor of Black History Month
Crowd-Pleaser
Kindred by Octavia E. Butler, 1988, available from Beacon
Press for $13.00

What is this book about?

The year is 1976. Dana Franklin, a happily married African-American
writer, has just moved to a new house in Los Angeles. She is in the
midst of unpacking when she begins to feel dizzy and nauseated; she

collapses—and awakens to find herself on the other side of the continent over 150 years in the past. A white boy is drowning in a river, and Dana must save him. When her own life is placed in danger, the dizziness returns, and she wakes to find herself back in her own time, her perplexed husband watching over her. Over the course of the novel, Dana repeats this journey many times, always for the same reason—to save Rufus Weylin, who, it turns out, is the son of a Maryland slave owner and will grow up to own slaves himself. Recognizing the name Weylin from her own family tree, Dana realizes that Rufus Weylin must stay alive at least long enough to father Hagar, who will found Dana's family line—and Dana is the only person who can save Rufus. The complicated relationship that develops between Dana and Rufus is one of the novel's great strengths.

Time does not progress uniformly in Dana's two worlds: months spent in the antebellum South amount to only a few hours in her own late twentieth-century Los Angeles. Through her eyes, we witness the making of a slave owner and the difficult lives that so many of the Weylins' slaves led. Dana herself is considered property in 1816 because she has no papers to prove she's free. Although the novel does depend on time travel to facilitate its plot, the science-fiction element takes a backseat to the psychological development of the main characters and to Dana's quest for survival.

What should I know about the author?

Octavia E. Butler was born in 1947 in California. She began writing science fiction when she was twelve. Like Dana in *Kindred*, she worked blue-collar jobs to support her writing—even after she published her first novel. In 1984 and 1985, she won three of the top science fiction prizes: the Hugo, the Nebula, and the Locus Awards. Because Butler believes that you need to know science to write science fiction, she follows scientific trends and discoveries. She was recently a recipient of a "genius grant" from the MacArthur Foundation.

Did you know...?

The Science Fiction and Fantasy Writers of America, Inc., awards the highly coveted Nebula Award for the year's best example of speculative fiction. The sci-fi community also boasts the Hugo Award sponsored by the World Science Fiction Society. If you are trying to find your way through the maze of science fiction and fantasy, try the Science Fiction and Fantasy Writers of America's website at www.sfwa.org. Don't miss their list of the top one hundred sci-fi and fantasy books!

Questions for discussion and reflection

1. Butler is especially good at creating complex characters about whom the reader feels ambivalent. Rufus and Alice are perhaps the best examples. How does Butler initially make Rufus, a racist, slave-owning child, sympathetic? At what point does he begin to change, to become more disturbing? Dana confesses late in the novel that she doesn't hate Rufus; why not? How sympathetic do you think Butler wants the reader to be toward Rufus? Does our response to him mirror Dana's? Would you do what Dana did in this predicament? Why wouldn't she want to let Rufus die to save her ancestors from the pain of slavery?

2. The major relationships in *Kindred* are all interracial. Dana Franklin is married to Kevin, a white man. She travels back in time to the antebellum South to save Rufus Weylin, a white man. And Rufus is in love with Alice, a black woman who is originally free, but ultimately becomes Rufus's slave. Why does Butler organize her narrative around these three interracial relationships? How does it help Dana for Kevin to be white?

3. The title, *Kindred*, foregrounds themes of kinship, ancestry, and connection. Early on, Dana realizes that if she's going to survive these trips to the South, she must forge a bond with Rufus and with her fellow slaves. But she discovers that building relationships under slavery is difficult. Why? Trace how Dana's bonds with between Margaret Weylin, Sarah, Rufus, Alice, Nigel, and Tom Weylin develop over the course of the novel. Betrayal crosses racial boundaries in this novel; on whom can Dana really count?

4. The opening chapters of *Kindred* throw the reader right into the action. We meet Dana in the hospital, learn that something terrible

has happened to her, that her partner has been accused of abusing her, that she can't tell the truth about how her arm was hurt. But we don't learn more about Dana—or about her partner, Kevin—until much later in the story. What speculations did you make about them? Does Butler want her readers to form conclusions about the characters early in the novel? What reasons might Butler have for beginning her story this way? By the end of the novel, what do we really know about Dana and Kevin?

5. Octavia E. Butler has said, "When I write, there are always a lot of levels. The first level is, here's an entertaining story; enjoy yourselves. And then there's whatever I put underneath." What has she put underneath in *Kindred*? What themes and symbols did you discern? Butler has also noted, "Science fiction suffers from its *reputation* for trashiness and immaturity." How does a novel like *Kindred* refute this reputation? How does what Butler puts "underneath" help elevate her work to a different level?

DISCUSSION/REFLECTION STRATEGY

You may choose to follow up Butler's novel with one of her favorite books, Frank Herbert's *Dune*. Why do you think the follow-up book is such a favorite? Do the two authors share similar concerns, themes, styles?

Other books by Octavia E. Butler

Butler's Patternmaster series, about a society of telepaths, comprises five novels: *Patternmaster* (1976), *Mind of My Mind* (1977), *Survivor* (1978), *Wild Seed* (1980), and *Clay's Ark* (1984). The Xenogenesis trilogy, focusing on aliens and genetic engineering, includes *Dawn* (1987), *Adulthood Rites* (1988), and *Imago* (1989); the series has been published in one volume under the title *Lilith's Blood*. Her most recent series includes *Parable of the Sower* (1995), which won the Nebula for Best Novel, and *Parable of the Talents* (1998). *Bloodchild and Other Stories* (1995) collects the prizewinning "Bloodchild" and "Speech Sounds," as well as two essays on the writing life.

If you like *Kindred,* you will like...

The Between by Tananarive Due. An African-American man discovers he can walk through doorways in time.

Brown Girl in the Ring by Nalo Hopkinson. Set in futuristic Canada, this novel mixes sci-fi and the supernatural with a healthy dose of voodoo magic and spirit-calling.

Remnant Population by Elizabeth Moon. A woman eludes an evacuation party on her planet and stays on alone, only to confront an alien species she never knew existed.

Stigmata by Phyllis Alesia Perry. Powerful novel about a young girl who inherits a trunk from her ancestors and becomes possessed by their reincarnated spirits.

The Sparrow by Mary Doria Russell. Fascinating novel about the discovery of extraterrestrial life in 2019; the expedition to space is led by Jesuits. *Children of God* is the sequel.

Extra credit

Dana is sent back in time to Maryland, the state that claims Harriet Tubman as a native daughter. After escaping from slavery in 1849, Harriet Tubman became a key figure in the Underground Railroad. She returned to the South again and again, ultimately assisting about three hundred slaves to freedom. Visit the Underground Railroad/Harriet Tubman Organization in Cambridge, Maryland, (phone 410-228-0401 for information). As a free woman, Tubman lived in Auburn, New York, where her home is open to the public (http://www.nyhistory.com/harriettubman/home.htm). The Tubman African American Museum in Macon, Georgia, (http://www.tubmanmuseum.com) features exhibits dedicated to Tubman's work and the culture and history of African-Americans in the nineteenth century.

Video resources

None of Butler's novels have been made into movies, but readers intrigued by time travel have a wealth of films to choose from, including the lighthearted trilogy *Back to the Future* (Robert Zemickis; I and III); *Time After Time* (Nicholas Meyer, 1979), in which H. G. Wells time-travels and hunts Jack the Ripper; *Time Bandits* (Terry Gilliam, 1981), about a boy who travels back in time accompanied by six dwarves; *Time Chasers* (David Glancola, 1995), a low-budget feature about a scientist who travels back in time to save the world from the disasters caused by a time machine he developed; or the classic *Time Machine* (George Pal, 1960), about a scientist who invents a time machine.

Internet resources

The Octavia E. Butler page at the Voices from the Gaps website provides useful information, including a brief biography, a bibliography of works by and about Butler, and a few links at voices.cla.umn.edu/authors/OctaviaButler.html. Visit a fan site at www.geocities.com/sela_towanda/index.html. Read a detailed "chat" with Butler using questions from her readers at 204.202.137.114/ABC2000/abc2000 entertainment/Chat_Butler.html.

February/In Honor of Black History Month
Classic
Passing by Nella Larsen, 1929, available in paperback from Penguin for $10.00

What is this book about?

First published in 1929 during the Harlem Renaissance, *Passing* explores the phenomenon of light-skinned blacks breaking their ties with the black community and "passing" as white. The story is told as a series of encounters between Irene Redfield and Clare Kendry, childhood friends who lost touch with each other after Clare's black father died and her white aunts took her in. The plot is set into motion when Irene and Clare run into each other at a white hotel in Chicago; Clare has made a life of passing, hiding her black heritage and marrying a white racist, while Irene is only passing for the afternoon, temporarily taking refuge in the hotel to recover after a bout of dizziness. Married to a distinguished black physician and the mother of two dark-skinned sons, Irene has embraced her African-American heritage and become a prominent member of upper middle class black society in New York. She is horrified by Clare's choices, but she too has flirted with passing.

Clare uses her renewed acquaintance with Irene to revive relationships with other black friends and to ingratiate herself into the black community—at much personal risk to herself, as Irene never ceases to remind her. Clare's difficult position fuels the novel's suspense. She chose to abandon her heritage for marriage to a man who would disown her and her child if he ever discovered the truth, but she also longs for the bonds of community she can't seem to find in the white world. Clare's betrayal of her family and her race will lead, ultimately, to her betrayal of Irene. The tension between these two women builds to a dramatic conclusion leaving readers deliberating over the choices that are possible in a society plagued by racism.

Did you know...?

The term **Harlem Renaissance** refers to the flourishing of African-American writing, art, and culture in New York in the 1920s. Important Harlem Renaissance writers include Countee Cullen, Langston Hughes, Zora Neale Hurston, Claude McKay, Jean Toomer, and Richard Wright. See Internet Resources at the end of this section for websites related to the Harlem Renaissance.

What should I know about the author?

Born in 1891, Larsen graduated from Lincoln Hospital of Nursing and worked as a nurse before moving to New York City with her husband, physicist Elmer Imes, and beginning a second career as a librarian. Soon, Larsen and her husband were moving in Harlem literary circles, and she had begun her third career—as a writer. She published two novels and became the first African-American writer to win a Guggenheim fellowship. But things turned sour for Larsen soon after. Her only other published work was a short story called "Sanctuary," for which she was accused of plagiarism. (She was later cleared of the charge.) Her marriage to Imes was falling apart. Then, her publisher rejected *Mirage*, the novel she spent her Guggenheim year writing. By 1941, divorced from Imes and unable to support herself by writing, she returned to nursing. Larsen died in 1964, not having published in more than thirty years.

Questions for reflection and discussion

1. Why is being taken for white so important to Clare? What does she hope to find in the white world that she believes will be forever out of reach in the African-American community? Light-skinned Irene could also pass; in fact, she is often mistaken for "an Italian, a Spaniard, a Mexican, or a Gypsy." There are times when Irene takes advantage of her light skin. When does she allow people to think she's white? Is she betraying her family and her race when she does? Why doesn't she choose always to pass? You might also want to consider Gertrude, who combines aspects of both Irene's and Clare's situations. Like Clare, she is married to a white man. Like both women, she can pass for white, but like Irene, she chooses to be identified as black.

2. The theme of passing turns up frequently in African-American literature. Why would African-American authors be interested in exploring this issue? Passing obviously has a literal meaning in these novels; does it also take on a metaphorical meaning? Scholar Charles Larson notes, "No passing novel can be regarded as anything other than a strong indictment of American life; people are driven to such drastic measures because of American racism and the need for economic survival." There is much talk in *Passing* about safety and security; what connections do you see between passing and security? What aspects of American life does Larsen's novel indict? You may want to read another novel about passing to compare and contrast. See works by Chesnutt, Fauset, Johnson, and Thurman in the further reading suggestions below.

3. Author Marita Golden argues that literature at its best is a prescription. What do you think she means? A prescription for behavior,

thinking, action? Do you agree with this definition of good literature? Think about your favorite novels. Are they works of prescription? In *Passing*, what might Larsen want to prescribe to her
readers?

4. *Passing* is structured as a series of encounters between Clare and
   Irene. Their personalities dominate the novel. How much sympathy do you feel for Clare? For Irene? Do your allegiances shift
   over the course of the novel? Do you think Larsen wants the
   reader to sympathize with one character more than the other?
   Why or why not? Why is Irene so angry? Why is Clare so lonely?
   Part of their problems stem from their marriages. What is wrong
   in these relationships, and why do the women want to hold on
   to their husbands?

5. Critics and readers alike have been perplexed by *Passing*'s sudden
   conclusion. What really happens at the end? Is Irene responsible
   for what happens to Clare? Why do you think Larsen concludes
   Passing in this way? What alternative endings can you imagine?
   What would have happened to Clare? To Irene?

Other books by Nella Larsen

Larsen's first novel, *Quicksand* (1928), is often reprinted with *Passing*.
Her short stories, including the controversial "Sanctuary," along with
both novels, have been collected in *An Imitation of Things Distant: The
Collected Fiction of Nella Larsen*, edited by Charles Larson.

Books about Nella Larsen

To learn more about Larsen, we recommend Thadious M. Davis's
detailed biography, *Nella Larsen, Novelist of the Harlem Renaissance: A
Woman's Life Unveiled*.

If you like *Passing*, you will like...

The House Behind the Cedars by Charles Chesnutt. Early novel about
passing.

Plum Bun by Jessie Redmon Fauset. A novel about two sisters—one who passes and one who doesn't—by a contemporary of Larsen.
The Autobiography of an Ex-Colored Man by James Weldon Johnson. The mixed-race narrator tries to find a place for himself, but is shunned by both black and white communities.

Corregidora by Gayl Jones. The light-skinned protagonist, a blues singer in the 1930s, confronts the violent legacy of slavery.

The Blacker the Berry... by Wallace Thurman. The dark-skinned heroine of this novel escapes her light-skinned family and runs away to Harlem, in the same time period as *Passing*.

Video resources

John Singleton's *Rosewood* (1997) explores race relations in a small community in Florida in 1923, about the same time period as *Passing*. It stars Jon Voight and Ving Rhames. *A Raisin in the Sun* (Daniel Petrie, 1961), based on the play by Lorraine Hansbury, shows just how little had changed for African-Americans by the 1950s, when a black family moves into an all-white neighborhood.

Internet resources

Find tips on appreciating *Passing* at www.georgetown.edu/bassr/heath/syllabuild/iguide/larsen.html. Learn more about the Harlem Renaissance at Jill Diesman's website, where you will find poetry, prose, and paintings by Harlem Renaissance writers and artists: www.nku.edu/~diesmanj/harlem.html.

Extra credit

Find out more about the cultural contexts of Nella Larsen's fiction by visiting the Studio Museum in Harlem, located in New York City, which features rotating exhibits on African-American art and heritage: www.studiomuseuminharlem.org.

February/ In Honor of Black History Month
Challenge
Middle Passage by Charles Johnson, 1990, available from
Scribner Paperback Fiction for $12.00

What is this book about?

Middle Passage relates the adventures of Rutherford Calhoun, a twenty-two-year-old freed slave living in New Orleans in 1830. The sleazy enticements of New Orleans have led Calhoun into dangerous situations. Gangsters wish to get money from him (and beat him up), and even worse, a prim New England schoolteacher wants to marry him. To escape from these calamities, Calhoun stows aboard a ship that, unfortunately, turns out to be on its way to Africa to pick up a cargo of slaves and is under the command of a bloodthirsty, cruel, maniacal captain. *Middle Passage* recounts how Calhoun escapes execution at sea, works as the cook's assistant, and becomes the confidant of the both the captain and the first mate. He befriends members of the newly enslaved African tribe and learns of their history as well as his own.

Combining the narrative structures of the classic sea story with the first-person slave narrative, *Middle Passage* is an adventure story, a comedy, a love story, a coming-of-age story, and a profound exploration of the philosophical and spiritual dimensions of identity.

What should I know about the author?

Charles Johnson writes novels, reviews of literature and film, literary essays, works of philosophy, plays, and screenplays. He is also an illustrator. Born in 1948 in Evanston, Illinois, Johnson received his B.A. from Southern Illinois University at Carbondale. He did graduate work in philosophy at SUNY–Stony Brook. In addition to philosophy, Charles Johnson is a student of Eastern spiritual traditions, especially Buddhism, and is a practitioner of the martial arts. He has received numerous awards for his work, including one from the MacArthur

Foundation in 1998. He currently holds the Pollock Professorship for Excellence in English at the University of Washington. *Middle Passage* won the National Book Award in 1990.

Did you know…?

Allegory is the literary term for a narrative that has a literal, primary meaning, but also a metaphorical, secondary meaning. That is, the narrative, while literally representing one event or character, is actually alluding to something else. George Orwell's *Animal Farm* is one good example.

Questions for reflection and discussion

1. *Middle Passage* is not an allegory from beginning to end, but it uses allegory in places throughout. For example, the ship's name is the *Republic*. What is the allegorical significance of that name? Find the passages in the book which describe the ship, how it is built, its condition, and what happens to it. What is Johnson describing through allegory?

2. In addition to allegory, Johnson also employs "anachronism," which is the insertion of dialogue or objects that post-date the time period of the novel. For example, a novel about ancient Athens containing characters wearing sneakers and discussing fast food chains would be anachronistic. Johnson breaks one of the rules of historical fiction by deliberately employing anachronisms. What do his anachronisms add to the story, or do they detract? Why do you think the author uses this device?

3. The Allmuseri are the people being transported by the *Republic* to the United States. Find the passage where Johnson describes what the people are like and review it carefully. How do they differ from their captors? Why do the Allmuseri bring high prices from slave traders? What accounts for changes in Allmuseri character and behavior? Look at the Allmuseri allegorically. What is Johnson saying about the effects of slavery?

4. Calhoun experiences many changes on his journey. How does he cope with the shipping of slaves when he no longer is one? How does he relate to the white men on board? The greatest change comes from Calhoun's encounter with the contents of the crate that is being transported from Africa at great cost and with great secrecy. What does he experience? How does this experience change him?

5. Explore the significance of the title *Middle Passage*. To what else, besides a part of the ocean voyage, does it refer? The ship, for most of the book, is between Africa and America. What, besides continents, is Calhoun between? Think about the polarities within the novel, and discuss how Calhoun traverses them, e.g., black and white, male and female, virtue and vice, father and son, African and American.

Other books by Charles Johnson

Other novels by Johnson are *Dreamer*, a fictional account of the last year of Martin Luther King's life; *Sorcerer's Apprentice*; *Oxherding Tale*; and *Faith and the Good Thing*. Johnson has also authored two books of cartoons: *Black Humor* and *Half-Past Nation Time*. His nonfiction includes *Being and Race: Black Writing Since 1970*; *Africans in America: America's Journey through Slavery*, coauthored with Patricia Smith; and *Black Men Speaking*, edited by Johnson and John McCluskey with artwork by Jacob Lawrence. Readers may also like *I Call Myself an Artist: Writings by and about Charles Johnson*, edited by Rudolph P. Byrd.

If you like *Middle Passage*, you will like...

Invisible Man by Ralph Ellison. In his acceptance speech for the National Book Award, Johnson paid homage to this novel and spoke of its influence on his own work. A nameless black narrator travels from southern oppression to northern poverty and debasement in this classic story of race in America.

Benito Cereno by Herman Melville. An epic sea adventure from the master of the genre.

Philadelphia Fire: A Novel by John Edgar Wideman. A writer is forced to think about his failed marriage, his career, and the disintegration of his community when researching the 1985 bombing tragedy in Philadelphia.

Mumbo Jumbo by Ishmael Reed. A brilliant satire of contemporary society and Western civilization employing historical figures interacting with fictional characters.

The Intuitionist by Colson Whitehead. In this novel, elevator engineers are divided according to their modes of investigation. Some inspect elevators using the evidence of their senses, others through intuition. Whitehead creates a world simultaneously strangely familiar and very different.

Video resources

A&E Home Video's *Ship of Slaves: Middle Passage* is a documentary of the slave trade. Steven Spielberg's *Amistad* (1997), though not a critical success, is a visually stunning recreation of a revolt on a slave ship. Both *Glory* (Edward Zwick, 1989) and *A Soldier's Story* (Norman Jewison, 1984) share with *Middle Passage* an exploration of African-American identity and allegiance.

Internet resources

Southern Illinois University at Carbondale maintains a site on Charles Johnson at www.siu.edu/~johnson. For more detailed information about Johnson, look for his biographical entry at www.previewport.com.

February/In Honor of Black History Month
Memoir
Pearl's Secret: A Black Man's Search for His White Family by Neil Henry, 2001, paperback from the University of California Press for $16.95

What is this book about?

Journalist Neil Henry had always known that his great-great-grandfather was a white plantation overseer who had a long-term relationship and child with a slave named Laura. This child, Pearl, grew up in St. Louis after she and her mother left Mississippi; Pearl's own daughter, Fredda, became Neil Henry's maternal grandmother. What Henry did not know was whether his white ancestor had another family. Had he married? Did he have children? Were there descendants around today? If so, did they know about Laura and Pearl?

Pearl's Secret: A Black Man's Search for His White Family is the story of Neil Henry's genealogical research. But it is also more than that. This is the story of Henry's own life: growing up in an all-white neighborhood in Seattle during the turbulent 1960s, his four years of loneliness at Princeton University, his years as a reporter at the *Washington Post*, and his time as the newspaper's foreign correspondent in Africa. We learn about his wife, Letitia, his daughter, Zoë, his father, who was one of the first black surgeons in the United States, and his mother, who was a librarian. Family love and allegiances are no less complex than race relations throughout *Pearl's Secret*. Henry's quest to fill in all the branches of his family tree lead him and the reader on a geographic and emotional journey that resonates for anyone concerned with family and race in the United States.

What should I know about the author?

Neil Henry is an associate professor in journalism at the Graduate School of Journalism at the University of California, Berkeley. He was born in Nashville, the third of four children. Henry grew up in Seattle, attended Princeton University, and upon graduation, went to work for the *Washington Post*, where he was assigned to Africa as a foreign correspondent.

Questions for reflection and discussion

1. Have you ever done any genealogical research? How many generations back does your family knowledge extend? What or who have been the main sources of what you know about your family tree?

What do you think people wish to get from this research? Neil Henry is looking for the white branch of his family tree, but why? What is he really looking for? Does he find it?

2. What were the contradictory messages about "blackness" Henry received from his family as he was growing up? How was he taught to be proud of his heritage? What did his parents tell him about his forebears? What were the hidden messages about race that he also received? Why does being told he has "good hair" make Henry uncomfortable?

3. While growing up in Seattle, Neil Henry and his siblings are exhorted by their parents to excel in everything they do. Henry says, "I knew that, as a black kid, I was in some way carrying a flag for my race and must never let it touch the ground in disgrace." Henry's parents have lived lives of strength and dignity. Their achievements and those of their children are noteworthy. What did it cost them? How did the pressure of considering themselves standard-bearers for their race express itself in their lives? What about their children? Do you think their parents put unfair pressure on them? Why or why not?

4. Neil Henry was a foreign correspondent in Africa for the *Washington Post*. Did he have any sense of being "home"? What was his experience of Africa? Why did he decide to leave?

5. What was Pearl's secret? How does Neil Henry convey to us what she was like? Do we get any sense of Pearl herself? What was the chief source of sorrow in her life? What was she looking for? Did she ever find it? Why did the Louisiana Beaumonts refer to her as "Indian"? What legacy did Pearl leave her descendants?

Did you know...?

Genealogical research is easier than ever with more records going online. For tips on how to get started (or how to continue if you have gotten stuck), visit the site maintained by the National Archives and Record Administration at www.nara.gov. You may also wish to check the Genealogy Home Page at www.genhomepage.com. Who knows who you will find!

If you like *Pearl's Secret,* you will like...

Slaves in the Family by Edward Ball. The author searches for the descendants of slaves that his slave-holding ancestors had owned during the nineteenth century.

The Sweeter the Juice: A Family Memoir in Black and White by Shirlee Haizlip. In this excellent companion for *Pearl's Secret,* the author searches for her mother's white relatives.

In the Garden of Our Dreams: Memoirs of a Marriage by Shirlee Haizlip and Harold C. Haizlip. Contemporaries of Neil Henry's parents, the Haizlips tell a similar story of "upholding the race."

Roots: The Saga of an American Family by Alex Haley. Recommended by Neil Henry, this enormous volume traces Haley's roots back to Africa.

The Hairstons: An American Family in Black and White by Henry Wiencek. A history of an immense nineteenth-century American dynasty. Before the Civil War, the Hairstons owned more than forty-five plantations in four states and over ten thousand slaves. The complexity of the genealogical web among black, white, and mixed members of the family is astounding.

Did you know...?

The relationship between A.J. Beaumont and Laura Tullis was not an unusual relationship for the time. It has long been known that sexual relationships between slave owners and slaves in America were common. The most famous slave owner-slave relationship is the one between Thomas Jefferson, author of the *Declaration of Independence* and third president of the United States, and his slave, Sally Hemings. Ending years of speculation and rumor (going back to 1802), the Thomas Jefferson Foundation of Charlottesville, Virginia, has concluded through an examination of DNA evidence and exhaustive study of the documentary record that Jefferson did father Hemings's children. To learn how this determination was made, visit the foundation's website at www.monticello.org and click on "Resources." There have been many books about this controversial relationship; we recommend the collection of essays, *Sally Hemings and Thomas Jefferson: History, Memory, and Civic Culture*, edited by Jan Ellen Lewis and Peter Onuf. Barbara Chase-Riboud's 1979 novel, *Sally Hemings*, is also worth a look.

Video resources

The 1996 film *A Family Thing* (Richard Pearce) stars Robert Duvall as a bigoted businessman shocked to discover that he has a black brother. James Earl Jones stars as the brother in this moving story of loss and redemption. Alex Haley's majestic *Roots* (Marvin J. Chomsky) was released in 1977 to critical acclaim.

Internet resources

Find out more about Neil Henry at his webpage, www.journalism .berkeley.edu/faculty/henry/. This site links to reviews of *Pearl's Secret* and interviews with Henry.

February/ In Honor of Black History Month
Potluck
The Farming of Bones by Edwidge Danticat, 1998, available
in paperback from Penguin for $14.00

What is this book about?

The Farming of Bones is a fictionalized account of an actual event—the 1937 massacre of Haitian workers in the Dominican Republic. We see events leading up to the massacre, the slaughter, and its aftermath through the eyes of Amabelle Desir, who is a servant for the wife of a Dominican military official. Through dreams and stories, we learn of Amabelle's life in the Dominican Republic: how she came with her parents from Haiti, how as a small child she witnessed their drowning in a river, how she was made a servant by a well-to-do Dominican family. We also learn how sugar cane workers live: how they cope with the poverty and the physical and emotional toll the work demands. The stories that Amabelle and her lover, Sebastien Onius, tell one another and the conversations between servants and employers and among sugar cane workers allow the reader to become aware of the oppression under which the Haitians live. The stories and conversations also create a sense of terror once the slaughter begins. Though bloodshed, brutality, and the decades-long aftermath of memory and regret are vividly depicted, this is not a gory novel. The story of Amabelle and Sebastien testifies to the power of love.

The Farming of Bones embodies what is best about postcolonial literature. Though it is a work of fiction, it is a novel speaking for real people who were not allowed to speak for themselves.

What should I know about the author?

Edwidge Danticat was born in 1969 in Haiti. Her parents left the island for New York when she was a small child, leaving her in the care of relatives. She joined her parents in New York City when she was twelve. Her first published writings appeared when she was just fourteen. Danticat received her B.A. in French Literature from Barnard College and her M.F.A. from Brown University. Her short stories have been published in over twenty periodicals. She has received awards from *Seventeen* and *Essence* magazines, as well as the James Michener Fellowship.

Questions for reflection and discussion

1. Danticat presents us with characters who have different levels of insight into the circumstances into which they are placed. Who has more awareness about personal relationships? Who understands the political situation better? Which characters have "blind spots" about parts of their lives? Is there anyone in the book who understands all that is happening? Is Danticat suggesting that personal and political awareness can be sharpened or weakened by oppression?

2. How does Danticat introduce the reader to the tensions between the Haitians and the people from the Dominican Republic? Which

behaviors of which characters clue the reader into the political situation? How did Joel die? Who killed him? How did the various characters respond to his death? Why did they respond the way they did? What do their responses suggest about life in the Dominican Republic at the time?

3. *The Farming of Bones* uses foreshadowing and allegory. Joel's death, the circumstances under which it happened, and people's responses to it can be viewed as foreshadowing of the massacre that follows. What are the similarities between the death of the individual and the massacre? Consider the birth and death of the twins as an allegory about the island of Hispaniola. What do little Rafael and little Rosalinda symbolize? One appears stronger, but is not. If the children symbolize the divided island of Hispaniola, then what is Danticat saying about the island?

4. How is the novel constructed? The first several chapters alternate between dream sequences and reality. Does this structure change significantly? How? Why does it change? What does the change suggest about the difference between dreams and reality? Does Amabelle live in dreams or in the real world? What about Father Romain? Does the distinction we ordinarily make between dreams and real life make sense here?

5. Why do the workers refer to sugar cane farming as "the farming of bones"? Why does Danticat choose this phrase for the novel's title? What is the significance of the quotation from the Book of Judges that opens the novel? How does it symbolize the story? What is the Haitians' *shibboleth*?

Other books by Edwidge Danticat

Breath, Eyes, Memory, Danticat's first book, was chosen by Oprah for her former book club. *Krik? Krak!* is a collection of short stories. Danticat has edited *The Butterfly's Way: Voices from the Haitian Dyaspora in the United States* and *Beacon Best of 2000: Great Writing by Women and Men of All Colors and Cultures*.

If you like *The Farming of Bones,* you will like...

In the Time of Butterflies by Julia Alvarez. A fictional account of the real-life Mirabel sisters, who were involved in the resistance movement opposing the Trujillo dictatorship in the Dominican Republic.

The Kingdom of this World by Alejo Carpentier. A magical realist novel about colonialism.

Texaco by Patrick Chamoiseau. The author reimagines two centuries of history in Martinique.

In the Palm of Darkness by Mayra Montero. A novel about the inner and outer journeys of a U.S. herpetologist and his Haitian guide as they search for a rare snake in the jungle.

They Forged the Signature of God by Viriato Sencin. This novel not only won the National Fiction Award of the Dominican Republic for its compelling condemnation of the Dominican Republic's oppressive upper class, but also had the distinction of having the award *withdrawn* by that same upper class, which was enraged by Sencin's critique.

Video resources

Film director and producer Jonathan Demme has been involved in the production of several documentaries on Haiti: *Haiti: Dreams of Democracy, Haiti: Killing the Dream,* and *Courage and Pain.* To find out more about these films, visit the website of the National Coalition for Haitian Rights at www.nchr.org. *Sugarcane Alley* (Euzhan Palcy, 1983) is set on Martinique in the 1930s and explores the lives of black plantation workers.

Internet resources

Windows on Haiti at www.windowsonhaiti.com contains information about the country, including an essay by Danticat and an essay on the actual massacre depicted in *The Farming of Bones.* NPR Online at www.npr.org lists several interviews with Danticat. PBS hosts an extensive educational site called *Africans in America* that addresses the history of Haiti at www.pbs.org/wgbh/aia/part1/narrative.html.

CHAPTER 3

March
In Honor of Women's History Month: New Life in the New World

CROWD-PLEASER
Jasmine by Bharati Mukherjee

CLASSIC
Bread Givers by Anzia Yezierska

CHALLENGE
The Spirit Catches You and You Fall Down by Anne Fadiman

MEMOIR
To See and See Again by Tara Bahrampour

POTLUCK
Becoming American: Personal Essays by First Generation Immigrant Women edited by Meri Nana-Ama Danquah

Sometimes I am not sure whether home is behind me or in front of me. I am not so sure this longing is really recognizable. I might just be attaching it to those things that are familiar to me. Rwanda, that place that I have called home all my life, is a place I have only visited for one month. All I know of Rwanda is its people, my family. So home might be family and nothing more. It might be the people who make me feel. The people who define and occupy and receive my emotions. The people who reciprocate, who give me the most sought after, most valuable and intangible gifts—acceptance, trust, laughter, comfort, love. In that case, Burundi is home. And so is Swaziland. And so is America.

—Nola Kambanda, "My New World Journey"
(in *Becoming American: Personal Essays by First Generation Immigrant Women*)

Women from all over the globe have left their families, communities, and homes to pursue a better life in America. And as these books also affirm, "better" is a complex, ambiguous term. For Bharati Mukherjee's Jasmine, is it better to leave India and become an illegal immigrant in America only to be raped and abused repeatedly? For Sara Smolinsky, the heroine of *Bread Givers*, is it better to leave Russia only to nearly starve on the streets of New York? This month's selections question what it means to *be* American and *become* American. The contributors to *Becoming American: Personal Essays by First Generation Immigrant Women* arrive from different countries and for different reasons, but they must all confront their own expectations of America— and also Americans' expectations of them.

As Nola Kambanda's comments suggest, these five selections reflect on the question of what and where constitutes home. Have the Hmong immigrants Anne Fadiman investigates left home behind or brought it with them? What place do you call home when you straddle cultures as dissimilar as Iran and America, as Tara Bahrampour does? Our March reads grapple with enormously difficult questions; they provide no easy answers, but much material to reflect upon and discuss.

March/In Honor of Women's History Month: New Life in the New World
Crowd-pleaser
Jasmine by Bharati Mukherjee, 1989, available in paperback from Grove Press for $12.00

What is this book about?

Jasmine is a story of the heroine's journey west: Mukherjee covers more than half the globe as she moves her character from India to

America, from New York to Iowa, and from Iowa to California. Told in Jasmine's own words, the novel is structured as an extended flashback. We begin with Jasmine, now calling herself Jane and living in Iowa, recalling a significant childhood moment in India when an astrologer foretold her "widowhood and exile." The novel traces how this prediction, much resisted by Jasmine, comes to pass, and what Jasmine does after she becomes a young widow. The early chapters set up Jane's life as it is now: pregnant with much older banker-boyfriend Bud's baby, already mother to Bud's adopted Vietnamese teenaged son Du. The novel then travels back in time to reconstruct Jasmine's childhood in the Punjab, her marriage with the forward-thinking Prakash, the tragedy ending their marriage, and her subsequent illegal immigration to America. Each incarnation brings with it a name change—from Jyoti to Jasmine to Jase to Jane—to symbolize Jasmine's new life and new self.

In *Jasmine*, Mukherjee creates a memorable heroine capable of narrating both the chaos and the stasis of her life in poetic language. Because the novel depends so much on flashbacks, we might think that the Jasmine we meet at the beginning is largely the Jasmine we will see at the end, but Mukherjee keeps this character dynamic and surprising up to the last page of the novel.

What should I know about the author?

Bharati Mukherjee was born in Calcutta in 1940. Her father was a chemist, and the family was well off. In 1961, she emigrated to the United States, where she entered graduate school at the University of Iowa, earned her masters degree in 1963 and her Ph.D. in 1969, and met her husband, Clark Blaise, also a writer. A stint as writer-in-residence at Emory University pointed the way to her "true material": "[T]hat is immigration. In other words, transformation—not preservation." She considers herself an American writer, "I am an American. I am an American writer, in the American mainstream, trying to extend it. This is a vitally important statement for me—I am not an Indian writer, not an exile, not an expatriate. I am an immigrant; my investment is in the American reality, not the Indian. I look on ghettoization—whether as a Bengali in India or as a hyphenated Indo-American in North America—as a temptation to be surmounted." In addition to writing, she has taught at the college level since 1964.

Questions for reflection and discussion

1. Jasmine goes through a number of name changes and identity changes as she remakes herself both in India and America. "We murder who we were so we can rebirth ourselves in the images of dreams," she says. What are her names, what do they mean, and why does she have a particular name at a particular moment in her story? What has to be "murdered" in these different incarnations for her to be able to move on? Is Jasmine trying to ignore her heritage? Is she doing a disservice to herself? Transformation is part of the immigrant experience, Mukherjee suggests, but is it also an inherent part of Jasmine's character before she leaves India? What do you make of the fact that men bestow most of her names on her? What does Jasmine represent to the men in her life?

2. There is a great deal of violence in this story. Jasmine grows up amidst Hindu-Sikh clashes, domestic violence, and gang warfare. But violence is not solely an Indian phenomenon. Jasmine is raped shortly after arriving in America. Bud, her live-in partner in Iowa, is handicapped after being shot by an irate farmer. Jasmine watches a violent raid on Mexican immigrants on TV. Her adopted son, Du, has seen horrors that Jasmine can't imagine. Why is violence such an integral part of the story Mukherjee wants to tell? To what extent is the life Jasmine creates for herself in America violence-free? What connections do you see between gender and violence? Between colonization and violence? Is Jasmine's longing for a life of "absolute *ordinariness*" a result of experiencing so much tragedy?

3. Jasmine moves not only in space, but also in time; much of her story is told through extended flashbacks. At the beginning of the novel, Mukherjee drops the reader into Jasmine's present, and only slowly, over the course of the novel, fills in Jasmine's background and explains where she is and why she's there. How chronological is this novel? Did the beginning confuse you? Where does the story begin? When did you begin to feel comfortable with Jasmine, to

understand her? Why do you think Mukherjee structures this novel as a series of reflections by Jasmine on her past?

4. The newly married Jasmine is eager to escape from India because she believes she can avert the disaster the astrologer predicted for her if she leaves: "If we could just get away from India, then all dates would be cancelled. We'd start with new fates, new stars." Is starting over part of the American dream? Why does Jasmine's husband, Prakash, want to go to America? Why does Jasmine decide to go without him? What is she hoping to find? What does America represent? Jasmine is not the only immigrant in *Jasmine*: there is Devinder Vadhera and his family; Du, her Vietnamese son; the Mexican immigrants on TV. What is the American experience of the Vadheras and of Du? What does it mean to become an American in *Jasmine*?

5. A number of readers and reviewers have commented on the ending. Why do you think the novel ends this way? Has Jasmine found her fate, or is she running away again? What kind of closure does this ending provide?

Other books by Bharati Mukherjee

Mukherjee has published five novels in addition to *Jasmine—The Tiger's Daughter* (1972), *Wife* (1975), *The Holder of the World* (1993), *Leave It to Me* (1997), and *Desirable Daughters* (2002). Her short stories are collected in *Darkness* (1985) and the highly recommended *The Middleman and Other Stories* (1988). With her husband, Clark Blaise, she has written a travel book, *Days and Nights in Calcutta* (1977) and *The Sorrow and the Terror: The Haunting Legacy of the Air India Tragedy* (1987). She has also published a number of essays. Read about her experiences as an immigrant in *Letters of Transit: Reflections on Exile, Identity, Language, and Loss*, edited by Andre Aciman, and about what motivates her to write in "A Four-Hundred-Year-Old Woman," in Janet Sternburg's *The Writer on Her Work, Volume II: New Essays in New Territory*.

Books about Bharati Mukherjee

Your group may want to consult two studies of Mukherjee's fiction which appeared in 1996: Fakrul Alam's *Bharati Mukherjee* and R.K. Dhawan's *The Fiction of Bharati Mukherjee: A Critical Symposium*.

If you like *Jasmine,* you will like...

The Hero's Walk by Anita Rau Badami. After the protagonist's estranged daughter dies, Sripathi becomes guardian of his Canadian-born granddaughter, who comes to India for the first time.

A New World by Amit Chaudhuri. An Indian economics professor at an American university returns home to India.

Arranged Marriage: Stories and *Sister of My Heart* by Chitra Banerjee Divakaruni. Critically acclaimed short stories set in the U.S. and India featuring protagonists who confront cultural differences.

Love, Stars, and All That by Kirin Narayan. Gita, the heroine of this novel, leaves India for Berkeley, California, where she attends college and tries to find her perfect love match, whose arrival in her life in March, 1984, was foretold by an astrologer.

Motherland by Vineeta Vijayaraghavan. Indian-born American teenager is sent back to India as punishment and must renew her ties with her native culture.

Video resources

Mississippi Masala (Mira Nair, 1991) is about an interracial relationship between an immigrant South Asian woman and an African-American man. The delightful *East Is East* (Damien O'Donnell, 1999) follows the comic tribulations of a mixed-race family in London. *Masala* (Srinivas Krishna, 1992) is a comic look at an Indian immigrant family.

Internet resources

Emory University's Postcolonial Literature website includes a page devoted to Mukherjee, with biographical information, a thematic discussion of her works, and useful links to interviews at www.emory.edu/ENGLISH/Bahri/Mukherjee.html. Read a lengthy interview with Mukherjee at social.chass.ncsu.edu/jouvert/v1i1/bharat.htm.

March/In Honor of Women's History Month: New Life in the New World
Classic
Bread Givers by Anzia Yezierska, 1925, available in paperback from Persea Books for $8.95

What is this book about?

The word "determined" is not strong enough to describe Sara Smolinsky, the heroine of *Bread Givers*. Her Russian immigrant father nicknames her "Blood-and-Iron"; obstinate in the pursuit of her goals, outspokenly critical of her traditional father, scornful of the loveless marriages her sisters settle for, Sara resolves early on to pursue the American dream through education. She will go to college, become a teacher. Never mind that she has no time for school because she has to begin working at the age of ten selling herring on the street corner. Never mind that according to Jewish tradition and law, women are not supposed to be scholars, are supposed, instead, to support their husbands. Never mind that she can put herself through night school years later only by working ten-hour days at a laundry. Sara Smolinsky is like iron; her future husband tells her, "You've got the fiber of a strong, live spruce tree that grows in strength the more it's knocked about by the wind." She is an American.

Set in a Jewish immigrant community in New York in the early twentieth century, *Bread Givers* is peopled by characters who want to be or are in the process of becoming American. Each immigrant has his or her own dream of America, of what it means to be American, and each pursues it through filth, poverty, starvation, until he or she gives up or gets ahead. At the center of this saga is Sara's struggle with her father—New World and Old World made flesh. *Bread Givers* is not a slim novel, but it is a quick read; Sara's raw first-person narrative draws the reader in from the first sentence. The language may be the most surprising and exciting thing about this book: Yezierska brilliantly employs unusual syntax to capture the speech patterns of a nonnative speaker.

What should I know about the author?

Yezierska and her family, Russian-Polish émigrés, arrived in New York about 1890. Like Sara Smolinsky, she worked ten-hour days, attending school at night. She received help from wealthy patrons of the Clara de Hirsch Home for girls, where she lived in 1899; they offered to pay her tuition to Columbia University. College was not the idyll Yezierska had hoped for, however, because her patrons were willing to fund only a practical education in cooking and household management. She did work as a cooking teacher after college, but hating the work, she decided to become an actress instead. She won a scholarship to the American Academy of Dramatic Arts in 1907, but had trouble finding work as an actress. She made headlines when her lawyer husband Jacob Gordon filed a separation suit against her because she left him the day after their wedding. Yezierska was a revolutionary: she scorned legal marriage, lived as a single mother for a time, and became a socialist. While her works enjoyed much popularity during the 1920s and early 30s, the Great Depression ultimately took its toll and Yezierska lost her audience. She published her last book in 1950 and died in 1970, almost entirely forgotten by readers and reviewers.

Questions for reflection and discussion

1. Reb Smolinsky is an infuriating character. Powerful within his own household, which is structured to cater to his desires, he treats his wife and daughters as slaves put on Earth to care for and support him. He is a learned man and a deeply religious one, who uses his learning and his beliefs to oppress his family. What role

does religion play in justifying his control? Why doesn't he work? How does the place and importance of religion differ between the Old World of Russia and the New World of America?

2. Reb Smolinsky arrived in America believing the streets were paved with gold. What do other immigrants in the novel expect from America? What does it mean to them to be American? To make it in America? How does work fit in? Education? Marriage?

3. In what ways is Sara a feminist protagonist? Sara is the youngest in a family of daughters. What does she learn about the treatment of women from the ways her sisters are treated? What hardships in women's lives does Yezierska critique? You may want to look closely at the fate of Sara's mother, who bemoans, "Woe to us women who got to live in a Torah-made world that's only for men." Does Judaism compound the problems faced by the Smolinsky women in the New World?

4. The clash between Old World and New World is a major theme in *Bread Givers*. The older generation wants to hold on to their traditional ways, while the younger generation wants to assimilate. What criticisms of America does Sara's mother make? In what ways was the Old World better? What kinds of changes does moving to America necessitate? You might want to look at work, family relationships, love and marriage, money, and food. How do you see Sara retaining old ways?

5. Contemporary readers may cheer when Sara defies her father, refuses to marry the man of his choice, and moves out on her own. Her path throughout the novel seems to carry her ever farther from her father, but we learn in the end that her running away was not an escape. How do you read her willingness to take her father in at the end of the novel? Is this a capitulation? A disappointment to you? She believes this is her duty, but duty does not motivate us today in the way it motivates Sara. What does Sara owe her father? Has he performed his duty to her? If not, should she remain bound by hers to him?

Extra credit

If you're planning a trip to New England, be sure to stop at the Strawbery Banke Museum In Portsmouth, New Hampshire, and learn about three hundred years of life in New England. Tour the Shapiro House, home to Russian-Jewish immigrants in the early 1900s, which reflects the city's multiethnic community and shows how this family, representative of many, tried to balance its strong cultural identity with new opportunities in America. Find out more at www.strawberybanke.org. If you're planning a trip to New York, visit the Ellis Island Immigration Museum. Access their website at www.ellisisland.com.

Other books by Anzia Yezierska

Yezierska's first two works, *Hungry Hearts* (1920), a collection of short stories, and *Salome of the Tenements* (1921), a novel, made the author a great deal of money when they were sold to Hollywood. A collection of stories and essays, *Children of Loneliness*, appeared in 1923. *Arrogant Beggar* came out in 1927. Her last novel, *All I Could Never Be* (1932), is an account of a friendship between a female translator and her mentor professor. Her next work, *Red Ribbon on a White Horse: My Story*, a memoir, was not be published for nearly twenty years. Alice Kessler-Harris edited a collection of essays and stories, *The Open Cage*, ten years after Yezierska's death. All of her works, except *Children of Loneliness*, are now back in print.

Books about Anzia Yezierska

Yezierska's daughter, Louise Levitas Henriksen, wrote a biography of her mother titled, *Anzia Yezierska: A Writer's Life*.

If you like *Bread Givers*, you will like...

The Promised Land by Mary Antin. First published in 1912, this autobiography has been called the classic story of the Jewish immigrant experience, as Antin writes of her family's move from Russia to Boston.

The Rise of David Levinsky by Abraham Cahan. A novel recounting the struggles of the title character in his hometown in Russia and his subsequent move to the Lower East Side in New York in the late nineteenth century.

Jews Without Money by Michael Gold. A searing novel about ghetto poverty in the Jewish community on the Lower East Side.

Giants in the Earth: A Saga of the Prairie by Ole Edvart Rolvaag. Novel about hardships in a community of Norwegian immigrants.

Call It Sleep by Henry Roth. Classic novel told from the perspective of the son of Yiddish-speaking Jewish immigrants growing up in New York.

Video resources

You may not be able to find it, but Yezierska's collection of short fiction, *Hungry Hearts*, was adapted for the screen in 1922—it's a silent black and white. Does this plot summary, written by Jim Beaver for Internet Movie Database, sound familiar? "The story of a family of immigrant Russian Jews living and struggling to survive in New York. Hanneh, the mother of the family, strives to make a better life for herself and her family, but finds that much of her effort ends up costing her more than it's worth." Other movies about the Jewish-American experience include Barry Levinson's interesting pair, *Avalon* (1990) and *Liberty Heights* (1999).

Internet resources

An excellent general site about immigration can be found at www.ellisisland.org.

March/In Honor of Women's History Month: New Life in
the New World
Challenge
*The Spirit Catches You and You Fall Down: A Hmong Child,
Her American Doctors, and the Collision of Two Cultures* by
Anne Fadiman, 1997, available in paperback from Farrar,
Straus, and Giroux for $14.00

What is this book about?

Imagine that you are a refugee, fleeing a home you love because of war
and persecution, living in a foreign country whose language and customs you cannot understand. Imagine that you must daily confront
habits, institutions, and laws that make no sense to you. Imagine that
one of your children becomes seriously ill, and you must consult with
strangers whom you do not understand or trust. These strangers per-
form strange and invasive procedures and use odd medicines that
seem to make your child worse.

Now, imagine that you are a dedicated doctor working long hours
in the pediatric unit of a hospital catering to a refugee population you
do not understand or trust. You must explain complicated procedures
and diagnoses through an interpreter, when one is available, to families who do not even tell time the way you do, much less have any
familiarity with basic medical procedures and practices. Imagine
working hard to help a seriously ill child only to have her parents dis-
regard your instructions, change her prescriptions, and even stop giving her the medication.

Anne Fadiman's *The Spirit Catches You and You Fall Down* chronicles the life and medical treatment of a Hmong child in California.
The doctors said the child had epilepsy. The parents said her soul was
lost. What happens next is a riveting, true story.

What should I know about the author?

Born in 1953 to critic and Book-of-the-Month-Club judge Clifton
Fadiman and *Time* magazine correspondent Annalee Jacoby Fadiman,

Anne Fadiman is currently editor-in-chief of the *American Scholar* and has written for numerous magazines, including the *New Yorker*, *Civilization*, and *Harper's*. She was an editor and staff writer for *Life* magazine for nine years.

Questions for reflection and discussion

1. Discuss the origins of the Hmong. Why do they migrate? How are they able to support themselves? Summarize the role played by the Hmong in the Vietnam War era. What was their involvement? Whose side were they on? Why did the Hmong leave Laos in such large numbers to become refugees in Thailand and elsewhere? Describe the Lee family's journey from Laos to the U.S. Why might Fadiman have chosen to write the Lees' story? If you look beyond the compelling story of the daughter's illness, are there themes that belong to the immigrant or refugee experience?

2. What does the term "secondary migration" mean? How did the Lee family end up in Merced, California? Merced has become a destination for many Hmong. What strains have the sudden influx of refugees placed on this town? How do the Hmong perceive welfare payments—why do they think they are getting the funds? Do people have an obligation to assimilate to the dominant culture or an obligation to retain their own cultural practices? Fadiman suggests that the traditional Hmong resistance to assimilation accounts for the tension between themselves and American culture at large, but the cohesiveness of the clans may account for the statistically low levels of divorce, domestic violence, crime, and substance abuse within the Hmong community.

3. You don't have to be a Hmong immigrant to feel intimidated and confused by doctors and hospitals. Discuss the Eight Questions put forth by Arthur Kleinman in *The Spirit Catches You and You Fall Down*. Are they useful? Might they be useful for nonimmigrant patients as well? What do you think of Kleinman's suggestion that mediation and compromise are the keys to a successful doctor-patient-family relationship?

4. Do you like how Fadiman arranges her chapters? How does the organization affect the reader's engagement with the text? Look for places where Fadiman discusses her interactions with people and her opinions of events. Does this strategy undermine the objectivity of her reporting? Do you think this is meant to be an objective account? What might her personal voice add to the book that would be missing from a more impersonal journalistic account? Can a comparison be drawn between Fadiman's personal, participatory style of journalism and what she would like to see happen in the medical profession?

5. Is there ever any reason for a doctor not to consider saving a life as his only goal? Consider the argument between psychologist Sukey Waller and physician Bill Selvidge in the chapter titled, "The Life or the Soul." How does this issue connect with contemporary concerns about euthanasia or physician-assisted suicide?

Other books by Anne Fadiman

Ex Libris: Confessions of a Common Reader is a collection of essays on reading and books originally written for the magazine *Civilization*.

If you like *The Spirit Catches You and You Fall Down*, you will like...

Mama Might Be Better Off Dead: The Failure of Health Care in Urban America by Laurie Kaye Abraham. Follows the problems an inner city black family has receiving medical care.

Her Own Medicine: A Woman's Journey from Student to Doctor by Sayantani DasGupta. An Indian-American woman narrates her experiences in medical school.

I Begin My Life All Over: The Hmong and the American Immigrant Experience by Lillian Faderman and Ghia Xiong.

Caring for Patients from Different Cultures: Case Studies from American Hospitals by Geri-Ann Galanti. Primarily a manual for health care workers, but written in a manner accessible to others.

Video resources

Documentaries on the Hmong exist, but are expensive and marketed mostly toward university libraries. For information and listings, see www.buyindies.com and www.naatanet.org. If you live near a university that offers borrowing privileges to local residents (as many do for a nominal fee), consult their video holdings. More readily available is the PBS documentary series, *Vietnam*, that addresses the role of Laos in the war.

Internet resources

Find a detailed interview with Anne Fadiman about *The Spirit Catches You and You Fall Down* at www.beatrice.com/interviews/fadiman/. You can find links to this and other interviews and reviews at www.ksu.edu/english/nelp/links/anne_fadiman.html. The Hmong are well-represented on the Web with several comprehensive sites, including www.hmongnet.org, www.hmongcenter.org, and www.hmongonline.com.

Did you know...?

As Fadiman notes in her book, the Hmong women are known for the beauty and intricacy of their embroidery. You can find out more about Hmong design in *Hmong Textile Designs* by Anthony Chan, *Southeast Asian Textile Designs* by Caren Caraway, and *Richly Woven Traditions: Costumes of the Miao of Southwest China and Beyond* by Zhang Fumin and Lin Yaohua. The websites listed above also show some examples of the embroidery.

March/In Honor of Women's History Month: New Life in the New World
Memoir
To See and See Again: A Life in Iran and America by Tara Bahrampour, 1999, available in paperback from the University of California Press for $17.95

What is this book about?

When Tara Bahrampour was a teenager in an American school during the Iranian hostage crisis, a fellow student snarled, "Go home, Iranian." Her complicated set of reactions to the incident—anger and shame, but also exhilaration and excitement—stem from her complex understanding of her identity and her love for both Iran and the United States.

Tara Bahrampour was born in the United States to an American mother and Iranian father, but spent most of her childhood in Iran. Her family left Iran during the revolution in the late 1970s and settled in the Pacific Northwest and then California. Bahrampour returned to the country of her youth in the 1990s in an effort to discover whether the Iran of her childhood still existed, if it had disappeared during the Islamic revolution, or if it had only ever been the product of her happy childhood and hence no more recoverable than childhood itself.

To See and See Again evokes an Iran that few Americans know about: a country of closely knit extended families, strong religious faith, and deep connections with the land and with the past. It was also, in the days of the Shah, a country deeply enamored of the West. Bahrampour is at her best when describing the mix of feudal and modern which characterizes Iran in her childhood and in the 1990s. This memoir of crosscultural identity never resorts to taking sides. The author's openness, honesty, and complete lack of self-pity provide both her and the reader with an exciting adventure.

What should I know about the author?

Tara Bahrampour is a journalist living in New York City. She has written for the *New York Times, Wall Street Journal, New Republic, Village Voice,* and *Travel and Leisure.*

She is a graduate of the University of California Berkeley and the Columbia School of Journalism.

DISCUSSION/REFLECTION STRATEGY

"Never doubt that a small group of thoughtful, committed citizens can change the world: Indeed, it's the only thing that ever has."

—Margaret Mead

Change the world through your book group? Yes. Whenever thoughtful, caring people explore issues with candor and respect, good things will happen. Your book group is a good place to learn more about Islam. We recommend starting with Karen Armstrong's books: *Islam: A Short History* and *A History of God: The 4,000-Year Quest of Judaism, Christianity, and Islam.*

Even if no one in your book group is an authority on Iran, you still can piece together some sense of recent political history in Iran by brainstorming for a few minutes. Group members can share what they remember of the fall of the Shah, the revolution led by the Ayatollah Khomeini, and the Iranian hostage crisis with the virulent anti-Iranian sentiment that crisis provoked in the U.S.

Questions for reflection and discussion

1. Bahrampour reveals a side of prerevolution Iran that most Americans know nothing about. What, if anything, did you find surprising? Discuss the author's life in Iran. How did the family support itself? What activities did they habitually engage in? Who were their chief sources of companionship? In writing about her childhood in Iran before the Revolution, Bahrampour stays with the child's perspective, but even within that limited view we can see some of the conditions that led to the Islamic Revolution. To what extent did her family's lives resemble those of other Iranians? How did they differ?

2. Among the themes of *To See and See Again* are alienation and connection. The author describes feeling not quite at home in either the United States or Iran. Though she moves with relative ease through each culture, she always feels like an outsider. How does this alienation manifest itself? Why does she feel like an outsider in the both the U.S. and in Iran? Conversely, what provides comfort, security, and connectedness for her?

3. What is a *chador*? Who are the *komiteh*? Explore the restrictions placed on women's behavior in Iran. How does Bahrampour get into trouble when she returns to Iran as an adult? The women we meet in *To See and See Again* have different levels of accepting the conditions of their lives and different ways of coping. What are

they? Why do some of Bahrampour's younger relatives return to Iran after living in the United States? What are their attitudes toward marriage and sexuality? Why has the author returned to Iran? What does she find in Iranian women's lives that compensates (at least to some extent) for the restrictions?

4. Toward the end of her book, Tara Bahrampour surmises that the tumultuous history of Iran has produced a people who live quiet, submissive lives punctuated by bursts of cathartic releases of passion. What are some examples of the submissiveness she mentions? What are some examples of the passionate outbursts?

5. The phrase "to see and see again" is the English translation of what Farsi term? To what activity does it refer? Why do you think Bahrampour has chosen this phrase as the title of her memoir?

If you like *To See and See Again*, you will like...

Neither East nor West: One Woman's Journey through the Islamic Republic of Iran by Christiane Bird. Bird traveled to Iran in 1998.

Daughter of Persia: A Woman's Journey from Her Father's Harem Through the Islamic Revolution by Sattareh Farman Farmaian. An amazing story of growing up in a harem, moving to America for higher education, and returning to Iran to start a school of social work.

A World Between: Poems, Short Stories, and Essays by Iranian-Americans edited by Persis M. Karim, Mohammad Mehdi Khorrami, and Mehdi M. Khorrami. Impressive collection about the Iranian-American experience.

Persian Mirrors: The Elusive Face of Iran by Elaine Sciolino. The author, a reporter for the *New York Times*, spent over twenty years living in and reporting on Iran. This book synthesizes her experiences there and her understanding of the Iranian people.

Honeymoon in Purdah: An Iranian Journey by Alison Wearing. Excellent travel narrative of a journey to Iran in which the author traveled with a male friend who posed as her husband.

DISCUSS/REFLECTION STRATEGY

Gelareh Asayesh's memoir, *Saffron Sky: A Life Between Iran and America*, tells a similar story, but is different from *To See and See Again*. Together, they make an excellent choice for a **paired reading**. How are their experiences of Iran and American similar and different? How do they write about these experiences? How can such similar stories become such different books?

Video resources

In *To See and See Again*, Tara Bahrampour refers to the 1991 film, *Not without My Daughter* (Brian Gilbert) as "a one-sided view of Iran, a skittish foreigner's view." In *Saffron Sky*, Gelareh Asayesh makes a similar complaint. It may be worthwhile to view the film critically. How does the movie represent (or misrepresent) Iranian life? What cultural stereotypes does it enforce?

Internet resources

Both www.salon.com and www.savvytraveler.com offer interviews with Tara Bahrampour. www.ankaboot.com offers an index of Iranian websites. www.iranian.com is a comprehensive site about and for Iranian-Americans. This site does require registration before viewing. Find out more about Iranian film at www.iranianmovies.com.

Did you know...?

Iranian cinema has become a strong component of the international film scene in the past ten years. Award-winning Iranian-born director Mohsen Makhmalbaf has directed *Gabbeh* (1996), an allegorical film of a nomadic tribe and *The Day I Became a Woman* (2000). Director Maryam Shahriar's *Daughters of the Sun* and Jafar Panahi's *The Circle* are powerful films about women in Iran. You won't find these movies at the local megaplex, but look for them in museum or university film series.

March/In Honor of Women's History Month: New Life in
the New World
Potluck
*Becoming American. Personal Essays by First Generation
Immigrant Women* edited by Meri Nana-Ama Danquah,
2000, available in paperback from Hyperion Press for
$13.95

What is this book about?

Editor Danquah, who was born in Ghana, collects twenty-three per-
sonal essays on "becoming American" for this volume. She explains
in her introduction that the questions raised by this anthology—
"What is an American? Have I, in fact, become an American? Would
I not be the person that I am now had I stayed in the country where
I was born?" and, most pressingly, *"What does it mean to become
American?"*—are questions she has been asking for years. The contributions to *Becoming American: Personal Essays by First Generation
Immigrant Women* suggest some answers, but also raise many more
questions. The contributors' native countries range across the globe:
Japan, Korea, Ireland, Puerto Rico, South Africa, Burundi/Rwanda,
Egypt, Russia, India, and China, among others. Despite the variety
of backgrounds, certain themes emerge across the collection. In part
because most of the contributors are writers by profession, many of
these essays foreground issues of language; most of these writers
conduct their professional lives in what is their second, third,
fourth, even fifth language. "Becoming American," Danquah asserts,
"is about language." Contributors are also haunted by geography, by
the feeling of belonging to no place, but also to every place. Finally,
family emerges as a central theme. The best essays in this volume are
moving meditations on loss, identity, home, and connection; in
reflecting on their own experiences in America, these authors urge
readers to reflect on their experiences as Americans as well, and to
question what America and being American means to them.

What should I know about the author?

Meri Nana-Ama Danquah was born in Ghana and raised in Washington, D.C. She moved to Los Angeles when she was twenty and became a single parent at age twenty-three. She writes and lectures frequently on identity, place, and depression. Her own essay on becoming American, called "Life as an Alien," was published in *Half and Half: Writers on Growing Up Biracial and Bicultural*, edited by Claudine Chiawei O'Hearn.

Questions for reflection and discussion

1. Nearly every essay in this collection raises the question of what it means to be American. What do the contributors expect from America before they arrive based on television shows and books? How different is the experience of America from these essayists' expectations? The volume's title presupposes that we can determine what "Americanness" is. How is "American" defined by these essayists? You may want to look more closely at Lilianet Bruntrip's, Gabrielle Donnelly's, Helie Lee's, and Mitsuye Yamada's essays to answer this question. How does the immigrant experience of America compare to what your group thinks it means to be American?

2. The variety of experiences and backgrounds among the contributors is striking. Some of these women arrive as children with their families; others immigrate as adults. Some are forced into exile by politics or economics, while others choose to come to America for an education, for work, even for a lark. Nina Barragan wonders "if most 'New Americans' think their circumstances are unique," but believes hers really were. Why? What was different about her family and home life? What themes or experiences turn up frequently throughout this collection? Based on these essays, can we make generalizations about what an immigrant's life in America is like? What strikes you as typical? As atypical?

3. Many essays foreground themes of assimilation, acculturation, and transformation. Some contributors, like Kyoko Mori, are so

assimilated that they think of themselves as Americans, while for others, like Ginu Kamani, "becoming American" means thinking more fully about their native culture and gaining a new perspective on it—in Kamani's words, "being born again as a self-aware Indian." How much of becoming American is a giving up or repudiation of a native culture? How do contributors find a balance between new world and old?

4. Edwidge Danticat, Lynn Freed, and Lucy Grealy write about the in-between state of exile, of belonging nowhere and anywhere. Because she is "poly-geographical," Danticat considers herself a nomad rather than an immigrant. Linked to Freed's strikingly phrased "ambivalence of place" is the sense of longing that Lucy Grealy clarifies: "There is always something to want, a place we would all rather be than where we are." Other writers, however, like Gabrielle Donnelly and Kyoko Mori, have a strong sense of belonging to America. What do you think accounts for the difference in these writers' feelings of belonging? What are the advantages to being a nomad rather than an immigrant? What might be the advantages to a *writer* of a permanent sense of exile or longing?

5. For many of these women, becoming American has also meant becoming a writer. How does becoming American influence the work of Judith Ortiz Cofer, Lynn Freed, Helie Lee, Kyoki Mori, and Mitsuye Yamada? Is it in the experiences they have to write about, the way they write about these experiences, the language they write about the experiences in, or all three? Some of these writers speak an impressive number of languages. Do you think the unique language situation of the immigrant helps or hinders them in becoming a writer? In thinking about language, you may want to look at the essays by Ginu Kamani, Kyoko Mori, Nelly Rosario, and Annette Gallagher Weisman.

Other books by Meri Nana-Ama Danquah

Danquah is the author of a well-received memoir, *Willow Weep for Me: A Black Woman's Journey through Depression.*

If you like *Becoming American: Personal Essays by First Generation Immigrant Women,* you will like...

Coming of Age in America: A Multicultural Anthology edited by Mary Frosch and Gary Soto. A collection exploring universal themes in multicultural experiences.

What Are You?: Voices of Mixed-Race Young People edited by Pearl Fuyo Gaskins. Essays, interviews, and poems by mixed-race young people in the U.S.

American Mosaic: The Immigrant Experience in the Words of Those Who Lived It edited by Joan Morrison and Charlotte Zabusky. The editors collect narratives from a cross section of American immigrants.

Half and Half: Writers on Growing Up Biracial and Bicultural edited by Claudine Chiawei O'Hearn. A collection of personal essays that will appeal to readers of *Becoming American: Personal Essays by First Generation Immigrant Women.*

As We Are Now: Mixblood Essays on Race and Identity edited by William S. Penn. A stimulating grouping of essays by mixed-race writers.

DISCUSSION/REFLECTION STRATEGY

At the time of *Becoming American: Personal Essays by First Generation Immigrant Women*'s publication in 2000, seventeen of the twenty-three contributors, plus editor Danquah, had published novels, memoirs, or poetry collections. Several more were working on novels or memoirs. For a **paired reading**, we suggest each member of your group explore the writing of one contributor to this volume. Read a novel or poetry collection and review it for your group. The more widely known authors include Edwidge Danticat, Lynn Freed, Lucy Grealy, and Kyoko Mori. Explore their works, or use this opportunity to discover someone new.

Video resources

Feature films about immigrants cover a variety of genres from comedy to melodrama to farce. Try anything by director Wayne Wang including *Dim Sum* (1985), *Eat a Bowl of Tea* (1989), and *Joy Luck Club* (1993). *The Wedding Banquet* (Ang Lee, 1993) is a comedy about a gay Taiwanese man living in America; his traditional parents (who do not know he's gay) are eager to find him a wife, so he agrees to a fake marriage with a fellow Taiwanese woman in need of a green card. There is certainly more to the Italian-American story than *The Godfather* and *The Sopranos*. One of our favorite films is *Big Night* (Stanley Tucci and Campbell Scott, 1998) and don't miss *Moonstruck* (Norman Jewison, 1987). Director Gregory Nava explores the Latino-American experience in *El Norte* (1983) and *Mi Familia* (1995). Other Latino-American films include: *La Ciudad* (David Riker, 1998), *La Bamba* (Luis Valdez, 1987), and *The Perez Family* (Mira Nair, 1995), which stars Angelica Huston and Marisa Tomei as Cuban refugees.

Internet resources

Read an excerpt from Danquah's essay about growing up Ghanaian-American at www.washingtonpost.com/wp-srv/national/longterm/middleground/danquah.htm.

CHAPTER FOUR

April
Spiritual Gardening

CROWD-PLEASER
Mean Spirit by Linda Hogan

CLASSIC
The Good Earth by Pearl S. Buck

CHALLENGE
Refuge by Terry Tempest Williams

MEMOIR
Dakota by Kathleen Norris

POTLUCK
My Garden (Book): by Jamaica Kincaid

Tell me the landscape in which you live, and I will tell you who you are.
—Jorge Ortega y Gasset

In April we go back to our gardens, clear away the detritus of winter, and start sowing seeds. Warmer temperatures send us outside more and for longer periods of time, and we get back in touch with the land that nurtures and sustains us. In doing so we may, as Ortega y Gasset suggests, become who we really are.

This month's selections take for granted that land and self are connected, but each explores that connection in a different way. Linda Hogan's novel, *Mean Spirit*, dramatizes the clashing of Native American and white cultures over oil-rich land on an Osage Indian reservation. In *The Good Earth*, one of the bestselling books of the twentieth century, Pearl Buck vividly portrays the physical perils of farming and the even greater spiritual perils of prosperity. In *Refuge*, Terry Tempest Williams juxtaposes the stories of the Great Salt Lake's flooding and her mother's death from cancer. Kathleen Norris meditates on the connections between spirituality and landscape in *Dakota: A Spiritual Geography*, and Jamaica Kincaid uses gardening not only as a way of connecting with the natural world, but also as a metaphor for understanding politics and race.

April/Spiritual Gardening
Crowd-Pleaser
Mean Spirit by Linda Hogan, 1990, available in paperback
from Ivy Books for $5.99

What is this book about?

Set in the 1920s on an Osage Indian reservation in Oklahoma after the discovery of oil has turned government attention to the reservation, *Mean Spirit* is part thriller, part dirge. The murder of Grace Blanket by corrupt government officials precipitates the plot. Agents are quick to move in and declare local Indian landowners incompetent in order to provide them with white guardians who have the authority to lease their land to oil companies. It is not only land that is being stolen, however; there is theft of children and artifacts. Hogan creates a large cast of characters, but much of the action, and much of our sympathy, rests with the Graycloud family, whose matriarch, Belle, takes in Grace Blanket's daughter after Grace's murder. Belle's affinity for the land manifests itself in her gardens, her cornfields, and her bees. But affinity for the land is a common attribute among Hogan's Osage Indians, in contrast to the whites who want to exploit and destroy the land and the people who survive on it. *Mean Spirit* is fact-based fiction depicting the clash between two peoples and two ways of life and revealing the egregious offenses that white Americans committed against Native Americans in the name of oil production.

What should I know about the author?

Linda Hogan, a mixed-blood Chickasaw, is a poet, playwright, essayist, and novelist. She was born in Colorado in 1947 and has taught creative writing at various universities since 1977, but considers Oklahoma her true home. She published her first collection of poetry, *Calling Myself Home*, in 1978; her poetry, like her novels, often explores environmental issues. Her most recent book is a memoir, *Woman Who Watches Over the World*. *Mean Spirit* was a finalist for the Pulitzer Prize for Fiction and the National Book Award.

Did you know…?

The National Book Foundation "works to promote the reading and appreciation of great American literature across the country." They sponsor literacy programs, writing camps, and most notably, the National Book Award, given yearly to those works of fiction and non-fiction representing the best of American writing. Find out more about the award and past winners from www.literature-awards.com.

Questions for reflection and discussion

1. In an interview with *O: The Oprah Magazine*, Linda Hogan explained, "If you're a white man, you have only one way of looking at the world. If you're a white woman, you have two ways, two filters you have to look through simultaneously. If you are a minority woman, you view the world through three filters. It's hard work, but the result is that you become more and more intelligent the longer you have to juggle." Stace Red Hawk, the government agent

from Washington, is the only sympathetic character who straddles the two worlds of Native American and white. How many filters does he view the world through? What do we know about Stace's past and his motives for investigating the Osages' complaints? How do whites and Native Americans see the world differently because of their different filters? Although the villains are white people in *Mean Spirit,* Hogan does create sympathetic white male characters—in Will Forrest, for example. What do you think about Forrest's fate in the novel?

2. The land is an important character in *Mean Spirit,* one that suffers and changes. The action of the novel stems from what happens to the land. How does Hogan create a sympathetic and dramatic figure in the landscape? What happens to the land in this novel? In an essay she contributed to Janet Sternburg's *The Writer on Her Work, Volume II: New Essays in New Territory,* Hogan writes of listening to the earth, hearing its voice. Why is the earth so important to the plot of *Mean Spirit?* What do the Native Americans hear when they listen to the land?

3. Hogan's work often features women as the caretakers of the environment. How does this play out in *Mean Spirit?* Think especially of the character of Belle, who remarks, "The earth is my marketplace." How is the earth her marketplace? The phrase, "marketplace," is commercial, but Belle's attitude toward the land doesn't necessarily seem commercial. Does Hogan reserve the role of caretaking for women, or does she depict her male characters as stewards of the earth as well?

4. Hogan asserts, "When we get to tell our stories a healing takes place. As in the ceremonies of indigenous people, something is created that aligns the human with self and universe and world." Is this why she wanted to tell the story behind *Mean Spirit?* How does telling a story promote healing, and what kind of healing is Hogan looking for? In the novel, Michael Horse is writing a history of current events on the Osage reservation. Why does he write? Is he trying to chronicle events or to effect change, or both?

5. Several reviewers have commented on how tragic and sad *Mean Spirit* is. Why is this book painful to read? Aristotle argued that tragedy is good for us because it is cathartic: it raises painful emotions, which it then dissipates. The implication to Aristotle's theory is that we aren't troubled further by these emotions since we've worked through them. Is that the case with *Mean Spirit*?

Other books by Linda Hogan

Hogan has published six volumes of poetry, including *Calling Myself Home* (1978), *Daughters, I Love You* (1981), *Eclipse* (1983), *Seeing Through the Sun* (1985), *Savings* (1988), and *The Book of Medicines* (1993). She followed *Mean Spirit* with two novels also examining Native American issues and environmentalism: *Solar Storms* (1995) and *Power* (1998). Her short stories are collected in *That Horse* (1985) and *The Big Woman* (1987). *Dwellings: A Spiritual History of the Living World* (1995) is a collection of meditations on nature. She coedited a collection of essays on women's bonds with animals, *Intimate Nature: The Bond Between Women and Animals*. Her most recent works are an edited companion volume about women and the natural world, *The Sweet Breathing of Plants: Women Writing on the Green World*, and a memoir, *Woman Who Watches Over the World: A Native Memoir*. Read an autobiographical essay about why she writes in *The Writer on Her Work, Volume II: New Essays in New Territory*, edited by Janet Sternburg.

If you like *Mean Spirit*, you will like...

A Yellow Raft in Blue Water by Michael Dorris. Family saga following three generations of Indian women.

Love Medicine, *Tracks*, and *The Beet Queen* by Louise Erdrich. Erdrich's three novels about Native American life win high praise from readers.

Wind from an Enemy Sky by D'Arcy McNickle. A novel about cultural clashes between Native Americans and non-Native Americans.

The Grass Dancer by Susan Power. Impressive debut novel centering on a Sioux community.

Gardens in the Dunes by Leslie Marmon Silko. Historical novel dealing with many of the same themes as *Mean Spirit*.

Video resources

Michael Apted's *Thunderheart* (1992), starring Val Kilmer, is also about a murder that takes place on an Indian reservation. Like Stace Red Hawk, Kilmer's character, a half-blood FBI agent, returns to the reservation to investigate.

Internet resources

Lisa Mitten's well-maintained and absorbing site features hundreds of links to information about Native American history and culture: www.nativeculture.com/lisamitten/indians.html. Linda Hogan discusses her novel, *Power*, and Native American spirituality at www .amazon.com/exec/obidos/tg/feature/-/5195/. Find a short write-up of her remarks as a guest speaker at a UC–Davis course at www.dcn.davis.ca.us/go/gizmo/hogan.html. Listen to Linda Hogan read from her work at www.unm.edu/~ dunaway/hogan1.wav.

Extra credit

Learn more about Native American history with a visit to the Smithsonian Institute's National Museum of the American Indian at www.nmai.si.edu. Other collections of Native American art and artifacts include the Eiteljorg Museum of American Indian and Western Art in Indianapolis and the Native American Heritage Museum in Highland, Kansas. To find a museum of Native American history or art near you, visit www.hanksville.org/NAresources/indices/NAmuseums.html

---

April/Spiritual Gardening
Classic
The Good Earth by Pearl S. Buck, 1932, several paperback
editions available, including one from Washington
Square Press for $6.99

What is this book about?

The Good Earth begins on the wedding day of Wang Lung, a poor Chinese farmer, and O-Lan, a slave purchased from an aristocratic family. Wang Lung, who has been living alone with his father since the death of his mother several years earlier, is ready for a wife. She should be a slave so that she will be accustomed to hard work and an ugly woman so that she will have escaped the interest and advances of the men of the wealthy household. The novel follows the lives of this couple from the perspective of Wang Lung for the decades following their wedding. Children are born, and children die. Money is made, and money is lost. Nature rewards their hard work some years; other years there are famine, drought, flood, and locusts. Although the family gradually becomes prosperous landowners, different dangers threaten their peace and contentment. Not only must the couple deal with avaricious relatives and contentious sons and daughters-in-law, but O-Lan must also endure the insult from Wang Lung as he gives in to his own dissatisfaction and lust and turns from his old wife to take a concubine. At the close of the novel, as Old Wang faces his own death, the reader glimpses the novel's greatest tragedy in the future disposition of all that Wang and O-Lan toiled so long and hard to create.

What should I know about the author?

Pearl S. Buck lived from 1892 to 1973. She was born in West Virginia, but moved with her missionary parents to China at three months of age. She spent most of the next forty years in China, returning to the United States for her parents' sabbaticals and for her own college education. Buck was completely bilingual, as comfortable reading and speaking Chinese as English. Forty years living as a minority in a time in China's history when foreigners were routinely described as "white devils" sensitized Buck to the plights of marginalized peoples in all societies. She was an early advocate of civil rights and women's rights in the U.S. She was one of the few public figures to condemn the internment of Japanese-Americans during World War II. *The Good Earth* won the Pulitzer Prize in 1932, and Buck won the Nobel Prize for Literature in 1938. She wrote novels, short stories, poems, biographies, autobiographies, journalistic pieces, translations of Chinese literature, and children's stories. Almost all of her novels became bestsellers, making Buck one of the most widely read novelists of the twentieth century.

Did you know...?

The Nobel Prize was named for Alfred Nobel (1833–1896), who, in addition to inventing dynamite and holding over 350 patents, was a connoisseur of the arts. Nobel gave away his entire fortune to fund the prizes that still bear his name. The Nobel Prize for Literature is not awarded on the basis of one book, but is meant to honor an author's entire body of work. Winners receive a medal, prize money, and a diploma designed especially for them. To find out more about the Nobel and other literary prizes, including the wonderful Bulwer Lytton prize for the *worst* prose, visit www.literature-awards.com.

Questions for reflection and discussion

1. Many people find that *The Good Earth* provides images and emotional reactions that stay with them for years. What scenes did you find most moving? What emotions did these scenes evoke in you, and why did you find them moving? How does Buck make the experiences of her characters resonate with readers whose lives differ so much from those of her characters?

2. The evolution of Wang Lung's character suggests that prosperity can be fatal to one's moral health. Is this true? Is Wang Lung a likable and/or sympathetic character? What are his strengths and weaknesses? What connections does the novel make between farming and decent behavior? When Wang Lung needs to work to survive,

his priorities are clear and he has no problem figuring out what needs to be done. Once he has extra money and no longer works the land himself, he becomes confused and discontented. Discuss this change in Wang Lung. Is Buck describing a universal connection between discontent and wealth?

3. Though she does not say much, O-Lan is one of the most powerful figures in the book. That may seem a strange statement given the obvious and horrifying oppression she lives under, but discuss the ways she manages to assert herself in her home. What does she do and say that belies her outward demeanor of silent submission? Do you agree that she is a strong woman? Or is she a victim? Is it possible to be both?

4. *The Good Earth* was one of the bestselling books of the 1930s. Other bestsellers from this decade include John Steinbeck's *Grapes of Wrath* and Margaret Mitchell's *Gone with the Wind*. Each of these books has as one of its main themes the attachment of people to the land and the lengths they will go to maintain connection to their property. How might these themes have contributed to the popularity of these books? Do you think these themes are of perennial interest? What was going on in the 1930s in the United States that might explain readers' responses to these novels?

5. Keep in mind that Buck was the daughter of Western missionaries and the wife of a Western engineer. What is Buck saying about the presence of Westerners in China? Look carefully at those scenes in which Wang Lung is a rickshaw driver encountering Westerners. What does he think of them? How do they treat him? Think about the fate of the pamphlet given to Wang Lung by one of the Westerners. Is this a criticism of Christian missionaries? If so, what is Buck saying about their practices?

Other books by Pearl S. Buck

Pearl Buck wrote over seventy books, including novels, short stories, plays, biographies, autobiography, children's literature, and poetry. Here are just a few novels worth reading. *Sons* and *A House Divided* are parts two and three of the trilogy that begins with *The Good Earth. Dragon Seed* chronicles the life of a village family in China before and during World War II. *Kinfolk* is the coming-of-age story of four American-born Chinese siblings returning to China in the early 1900s. *Pavilion of Women* portrays an older woman exhorting her husband to take a concubine so she can live independently.

Books about Pearl S. Buck

Peter Conn's excellent *Pearl S. Buck: A Cultural Biography* recreates the social and cultural conditions of Buck's lifetime, demonstrating how powerful her literary and philanthropic work was. There are several critical studies of Buck, including Xiongya Gao's *Pearl S. Buck's Chinese Women Characters*, which offers a Chinese perspective on Buck's work.

If you like *The Good Earth*, you will like...

Wild Swans: Three Daughters of China by Jung Chang. Chronicles three generations of Chinese women.

Bound Feet and Western Dress by Pang-Mei Natasha Chang. Dual memoir of a great-aunt and her niece.

Life and Death in Shanghai by Nien Cheng. Memoir of a woman caught up in the events of China's Cultural Revolution.

Blades of Grass: The Stories of Lao She by Lao She. A collection of short stories by a Chinese contemporary and acquaintance of Pearl Buck. Lao She's stories of city life during the first half of the twentieth century nicely complement Buck's stories of the country.

Women of the Silk by Gail Tsukiyama. Novel about courageous young women silk-workers who defy management by leading a strike.

Video resources

The film, *The Good Earth* (Sidney Franklin, 1937) garnered an Academy Award for Luise Rainer as O-Lan. Katherine Hepburn's performance in

Dragon Seed (Jack Conway and Harold S. Bucquet, 1944) was not as well received. Even Hepburn fans consider casting Kate as a poor Chinese villager to be Hollywood at its strangest. Donn Rogosin and Craig Davidson made *East Wind – West Wind: Pearl Buck, The Woman Who Embraced The World*, a documentary about Pearl Buck, in 1993. Marty Martin's one-woman stage show about Pearl Buck, *The Dragon and the Pearl*, is not on video, but may come to a theater near you.

Internet resources

Peter Conn maintains a website on Pearl S. Buck at www.English. upenn.edu/Projects/Buck that includes many photographs and information about her philanthropies in addition to her life and writing.

April/Spiritual Gardening
Challenge
Refuge: An Unnatural History of Family and Place by Terry Tempest Williams,1991, available in paperback from Vintage Books for $13.00

What is this book about?

This memoir explores the notions of change and refuge in two distinct, but complementary stories: the story of the rising and overflowing of the Great Salt Lake and the illness and death of the author's mother from cancer. In 1983, the Great Salt Lake began rising to unprecedented levels, wreaking havoc at the Bear River Migratory Bird Refuge and the nearby human communities as well. At the same time, the author's mother was diagnosed with cancer. This was her second bout with cancer—the first having been in the early 1970s when her children were small. Familiarity with the pain of the disease and its treatments made Diane Tempest determined to experience the illness and her likely death in a way that was consistent with how she lived— close to her family, close to her community, and close to God. We see all the beauty and the pain of the family's coping through her daughter's eyes, and we suffer and celebrate with them. At the same time and with the same sensitivity to detail, Terry Tempest Williams chronicles the overflow of the Great Salt Lake, the death of birds, the dislocation of flocks from ancestral habitats, and the human efforts to fix what has gone wrong. At the heart of the book lie Williams's attempts to find refuge in change, to accept death, and to let go.

What should I know about the author?

Terry Tempest Williams was born in 1955. She lives in Salt Lake City with her husband. Williams has served as naturalist-in-residence at the Utah Museum of Natural History and as the Shirley Sutton Thomas Visiting Professor of English at the University of Utah. In 1997, she was awarded a Lannan Literary Fellowship and a Guggenheim Fellowship.

Questions for reflection and discussion

1. *Refuge* tells two stories: one the rise of the Great Salt Lake, the other the illness and death of the author's mother. Williams tells the stories by alternating between them. Take a few moments to consider the stories separately. What was happening to the Great Salt Lake? How did the wildlife cope with the changes? What were the consequences of its rising for people and wildlife? What steps did people take to deal with the overflow? Williams mentions a few times that one course of action is never taken seriously. What is that course of action, and what does Williams say about it?

2. Are Diane's reactions to her illness and her approaching death consistent with how she has lived her life? How is her commitment to the Mormon religion revealed through how she lives and dies? What about the other women who die during the course of the book? Does Williams present them as living by the same precepts as her mother? Do the women form a supportive community?

3. Why has Williams chosen to tell these two stories together? Why alternate the story of the Great Salt Lake with the story of her mother's dying? How does the path or trajectory of the story of the lake mirror or complement the story of the death? Does this joining

of the two create an effective narrative whole? Or did you feel you were simply reading two stories in one book? Williams has said in an interview that the question guiding her writing of *Refuge* was, "How do we find refuge in change?" Does knowing this affect your view of and response to the narrative?

4. When questioned about the subtitle, *An Unnatural History of Family and Place*, Williams said she considered the death of the wildlife habitats and the cancer of her mother to be natural phenomena. The unnatural elements in these situations were the human responses to the phenomena (attempts to "fix" the lake, the painful medical treatments for cancer). What makes the attempts to ameliorate the painful conditions of flood and cancer "unnatural"? Would it be better not to try? Why or why not? Does the final revelation at the book's end about what may have caused her mother's illness make that cancer "unnatural"?

5. Discuss Williams's claim that the obedience taught to Mormon Church members since childhood can have sad consequences. Is Williams being fair? Is Mormonism accurately represented in the book? Religious training can imbue us with a deep sense of right and wrong. Is this always a good thing? How can it cause trouble in our lives?

Other books by Terry Tempest Williams

Williams writes frequently about landscape and the environment. In *Leap*, she brings her experiences as biologist and practicing Mormon to bear on the famous painting by Hieronymus Bosch titled, *The Garden of Earthly Delights*. *Pieces of White Shell: A Journey to Navajoland* recounts her experiences learning about Navajo culture. *An Unspoken Hunger: Stories from the Field* is a collection of essays on nature and spirit. Both *Desert Quartet* by Terry Tempest Williams and Mary Frank and *Coyote's Canyon* by Terry Tempest Williams and John Telford combine Williams's essays with pictures—Mary Frank's illustrations and John Telford's photographs. Her most recent book is *Red: Passion and Patience in the Desert*, a collection of writings about the beauties of the southwestern desert and the need to preserve it. Williams has edited several anthologies, including *New Genesis: A Mormon Reader on Land and Community* with Gibbs M. Smith and William B. Smart, and *Testimony: Writers of the West Speak on Behalf of Utah Wilderness* with Stephen Trimble. She has also published books for children.

If you like *Refuge*, you will like...

Desert Solitaire by Edward Abbey. A classic, yet idiosyncratic, piece of nature writing.

Horizontal Yellow: Nature and History in the Near Southwest by Dan L. Flores. Explores human and natural history in the American Southwest.

The Solace of Open Spaces and *A Match to the Heart: One Woman's Story of Being Struck by Lightning* by Gretel Ehrlich. Like Williams, Ehrlich writes about the need to redraw the boundary between nature and culture. *The Solace of Open Spaces* is about her life as a Wyoming rancher, while *A Match to the Heart* recounts her recovery after being struck by lightning.

All My Rivers Are Gone: A Journey of Discovery through Glen Canyon by Katie Lee. Williams wrote the foreword to this meditation on what was lost when Glen Canyon was flooded to provide hydroelectric power.

The Cancer Journals by Audre Lorde. A diary of the poet's illness.

Extra credit

After reading Williams, you may be inspired to do what you can to protect the environment. The Sierra Club, founded in 1892, is an organization that advocates conservation and protection of the wilderness and important natural resources. Find out more about Sierra Club activities in your community at www.sierraclub.org.

Video resources

The West (directed by Stephen Ives and produced by Ken Burns, 1996) is a miniseries covering western expansion from the perspectives of Native Americans and European settlers. The documentary, *Rachel's Daughters: Searching for the Causes of Breast Cancer* (Allie Light and Irving Saraf, 1997) follows seven women, breast cancer patients and survivors, who talk to experts about the possible causes of breast cancer including environmental toxins and radiation. Recent Hollywood treatments of toxic landscapes and government or corporation cover-ups include *A Civil Action* (Steve Zaillian, 1998) and *Erin Brockovich* (Steven Soderbergh, 2000).

Internet resources

For a transcript of a 1995 interview with Terry Tempest Williams, see www.scottlondon.com/insight/scripts/ttw.html. Williams specifically addresses Mormonism and the environment in another interview at web.nmsu.edu/~tomlynch/swlit.ttwinterview.html.

April/Spiritual Gardening
Memoir
Dakota: A Spiritual Geography by Kathleen Norris, 1993, available in paperback from Mariner Books for $13.00

What is this book about?

Dakota is a series of interrelated essays about landscape and spirituality. Kathleen Norris lives in a small town in South Dakota, far from any major metropolis, far from airports, and even far from other small towns. She and her husband, the poet David Dwyer, have made this town their home since the mid-1970s. They have learned to live with extreme manifestations of nature: blistering heat, huge hailstones, drought, devastating rainfall, blizzards, cold weather, and the vastness and the apparent "emptiness" of the landscape. *Dakota* is also an extended meditation on the similarities and differences between living in an isolated region and living in a monastery. Though Norris was born and reared as a Methodist, she is drawn to live and study with Roman Catholic monastic communities. She sees connections between living on the Plains and living in a monastery, with respect to honoring nature's rhythms, learning to wait, learning to sit in silence. This book functions as a memoir, a meditation on land, and an exploration of spirituality.

What should I know about the author?

Born in 1943, Kathleen Norris spent her childhood in Hawaii and attended Bennington College in Vermont. After her parents died in 1969, she inherited the family farm in South Dakota and moved there with her husband. An award-winning poet and author, she has received grants from the Bush and Guggenheim foundations. She has twice been in residence at the Institute for Ecumenical and Cultural Research at St. John's Abbey in Collegeville, Minnesota. The residence formed the basis for her book *The Cloister Walk*. For the past ten years, Norris has been an oblate (a layperson observing monastic rule without taking vows) at the Assumption Abbey in North Dakota.

DISCUSSION/REFLECTION STRATEGY

There are some books simply begging to be read aloud. You may be surprised at the insights you can have from listening that you did not get from reading. Choose some passages to read, get in touch with your inner thespian, and take turns holding forth. If your group enjoys this, you might consider adding poetry and plays to your reading schedule.

Questions for reflection and discussion

1. Why does Norris refer to the region as "Dakota" rather than North or South Dakota? What are the geographical differences between the eastern and western portions of Dakota, and why does Norris consider the east/west divide more significant than the north/south divide? What are some characteristics of the landscape? Why does Norris find this landscape so powerful?

2. Norris says, "Dakota is a painful reminder of human limits, just as cities and shopping malls are attempts to deny them." What does this mean? What are "human limits," how does Dakota remind us of them, and why is this painful? More importantly, why does Norris think it is important to experience this pain? In your opinion, are shopping malls and cities successful in their attempts to deny human limits?

3. What does Norris like about solitude? What similarities does she note between living on the Plains and living in a monastery? What does Plains living give Norris as a writer that living in New York City did not? What does she think are the virtues of silence, of waiting, of deprivation? What is her definition of asceticism? Do you think Norris's fondness for monasticism is a way of avoiding issues in her own life? What role does solitude play in your life? Do you want more of it?

4. The solitude of the Plains can be life-enriching, but Norris is candid about the insularity and small-mindedness that also thrive in Dakota. How do these qualities reveal themselves? What does Norris think causes this? Do you think her criticisms are fair? Do you think certain character traits thrive in certain settings? What traits or stereotypes characterize your own area?

5. Discuss Norris's account of monastic life. What do the monks *do*? Why does Norris consider their lives worthy of emulation? Why do people go to visit monasteries? What are they hoping to find? Are their hopes realistic? Norris relates, "A story said to originate in a Russian Orthodox monastery has an older monk telling a younger one: 'I have finally learned to accept people as they are. Whatever they are in the world, a prostitute, a prime minister, it is all the same to me. But sometimes I see a stranger coming up the road and I say, 'Oh, Jesus Christ, is it you again?'" What is her point? How does this vignette serve her readers in their attempts to understand Norris's own choices and philosophy?

Extra credit

Once a year, it might be nice for everyone in your book group to invite their partners or adult children along for the meeting. It's a great way to widen your circle and help draw book group members closer. Prepare extra food, and choose a reading with broad appeal. Try a work of fiction set in your town or a history of your town or region. Or try something written by a local author. Your librarian can certainly help you find works with local significance.

Other books by Kathleen Norris

You may find in your library or old bookstores romance novels written by a Kathleen Norris during the first forty years of the twentieth century. She and the author of *Dakota* are not the same person. *The Virgin of Bennington* is Norris's memoir of coming-of-age in the 1960s. *The Quotidian Mysteries: Laundry, Liturgy, and 'Women's Work'* reflects on the sacredness of everyday, ordinary tasks. *Amazing Grace: A Vocabulary of Faith* examines and revitalizes the language usually associated with Christianity, such as sin and judgment. *The Cloister Walk* is about living in a monastery. *Meditations on Mary* is a beautifully illustrated book with essays on the Virgin Mary.

If you like *Dakota*, you will like...

One Degree West: Reflections of a Plainsdaughter by Julene Bair. Essays about going home as an adult.

The Prairie in Her Eyes: The Breaking and Making of a Dakota Rancher by Ann Daum. A memoir of growing up on a Dakota ranch and returning as an adult.

Seeking God: The Way of St. Benedict by Esther DeWaal. An introduction to the Rule of St. Benedict, with an introduction by Norris.

An Unknown Woman: A Journey to Self-Discovery by Alice Koller. Acclaimed memoir about the solitary life. See her further reflections on solitude, *The Stations of Solitude.*

Traveling Mercies: Some Thoughts on Faith by Anne Lamott. Essays about Christian life.

Video resources
The Farmer's Wife (David Sutherland, 1998) is a riveting documentary about a young married couple in Nebraska. David Sutherland spent three years with the couple, and the resulting film is six hours long. Kathleen Norris wrote an interpretative essay on the film. See below for details.

Internet resources
Norris's guest appearance on National Public Radio's "Talk of the Nation" can be found in the archive section of www.npr.org. Her essay on *The Farmer's Wife* can be found at www.pbs. org/wgbh/pages/ frontline/shows/farmerswife/essays/norris.html.

DISCUSSION/REFLECTION STRATEGY
If you finish discussing the book early one evening, why not try these questions? What was your favorite book as a child? What book turned you into a "reader"? Who is your favorite author? If you wrote a book, to what genre would it belong? What is your least favorite book? Which famous books or authors do you think are overrated? And of course, if you were stuck on a desert island, what five books would you take with you?

April/Spiritual Gardening
Potluck
My Garden (Book): by Jamaica Kincaid, 1999, available in paperback from Farrar, Straus, and Giroux for $14.00

What is this book about?

Readers familiar with Kincaid's work will not be surprised to find her distinctive, opinionated voice much in evidence in this collection of gardening essays, but prejudice, as gardening essayist Allen Lacy writes, serves the gardener well: "Show me a person without prejudice of any kind on any subject and I'll show you someone who may be admirably virtuous but is surely no gardener. Prejudice against people is reprehensible, but a healthy set of prejudices is a gardener's best friend. Gardening is complicated, and prejudice simplifies it enormously." In these prejudiced essays, Kincaid covers gardening territory from Antigua to Vermont to China and reflects on the ways gardening triggers memory and maps consciousness. The essays range in tone and topic from the charming and brief, "An Order to a Fruit Nursery Through the Mail," which reproduces Kincaid's order for far too many fruit trees, to "To Name Is to Possess," a profound meditation on the connections between colonialism and gardening. Readers who garden will find their passion for nature ably captured by Kincaid and will also enjoy debating the merits of her idiosyncratic gardening style. But *My Garden (Book):* is not a conventional gardening book. Kincaid uses the metaphor of the garden to tackle colonialism and race, two topics that fuel much of her work. *My Garden (Book):* thus provides much to ponder for the nongardener as well.

What should I know about the author?

In an interview in the *Missouri Review,* Jamaica Kincaid said, "I write about myself for the most part, and about things that have happened to me." Kincaid (née Elaine Potter Richardson) was born in 1949 in Antigua, which was then a British colony. She moved to the United States in 1965 to work as an au pair, an experience she drew on for her second novel, *Lucy.* Kincaid changed her name when she began her writing career; she published in the *Village Voice* and *Ingenue* magazines before she began writing "Talk of the Town" pieces for the *New Yorker.* She became a staff writer at the *New Yorker* in 1976 and, in 1979, married her editor's son, Allen Shawn, a composer. Kincaid lives, writes, teaches, and gardens in Bennington, Vermont.

Did you know...?

Beginning in the sixteenth century and continuing until the late twentieth century, European countries conquered lands and people in Asia, Africa, and the Americas. Land was plundered, indigenous ways of life altered or destroyed. Colonial governments determined how people should be educated, what they should wear, what languages they should speak, etc. Most European powers lost their colonial holdings in the aftermath of World War II. Since then, the novels, stories, poetry, and plays of the formerly colonized have had a powerful impact on literature. **Postcolonialism** refers to the study of literature coming from people who can finally tell their own stories. You will find a good overview at Emory University's excellent website: www.emory.edu/ENGLISH/Bahri/Intro.html.

Questions for reflection and discussion

1. Kincaid becomes a gardener as an adult after she gets married and becomes a mother. Digging until she has blisters and sowing seeds into inhospitable soil could be seen as a metaphor for life, for motherhood, for marriage. What links does she make throughout the book between gardening and life? What meanings does gardening have for her? How does she view gardening differently depending on the season, her mood, her location?

2. Kincaid speaks out against "proper gardens" with their conventional flowers and structured beds. What kind of garden does she prefer? Trace her gardening prejudices throughout *My Garden (Book):*. How do her own gardens and gardening preferences mirror her cultural past? If you have a garden of your own or even if you simply enjoy the beauty of others' gardens, what links do you see between what you love, what your eye perceives as beautiful, and your past?

3. Kincaid writes, "How agitated I am in the garden, and how happy I am to be so agitated. How vexed I often am when I am in the garden, and how happy I am to be so vexed. What to do?" This same push-pull, or positive-negative dynamic, can be found throughout her book. What does this suggest about Kincaid's worldview, as well as

about her personality? In what ways are all of us locked in a constant effort to balance life's negatives with its positives, to create pleasure and contentment out of the worries and difficulties of our lives?

4. In "In History," Kincaid wonders "what to call the thing that happened to me and all who looked like me?" Race, race relations, the history of slavery, and the legacy of colonialism permeate these essays. What is it about gardening that causes Kincaid to reflect on these subjects? Do you find her connections between colonial history and botany surprising? Many of the essays in *My Garden (Book):* contrast the history and use of the land in Antigua with the history and use of land in America or Britain. How does location— geographical and historical—influence what kinds of narratives can be told? How does Kincaid's narrative change depending on where she locates herself?

5. Kincaid's stylistic innovations begin in the title of the book, with the peculiar parenthesis and colon. Why do you think she uses nonstandard punctuation, repetition, long sentences? Which sentences particularly struck you? What effect do you think she was aiming for, and does she succeed? Kincaid's style may be disturbing because it's not what readers expect in a gardening book. What are our expectations for this genre of writing? Which aspects of her writing satisfy those expectations?

Extra credit

Plan an outing to a local garden. *Gardenwalks: 101 of the Best Gardens from Maine to Virginia and Gardens throughout the Country* by Marina Harrison and Lucy D. Rosenfeld will help you locate the nearest public garden. Or look online: www.gardenvisit.com organizes information about public gardens in the U.S. and other countries and provides detailed histories of landscape styles and designers. We also recommend www.gardenweb.com.

Other books by Jamaica Kincaid

Her autobiographical first novel, *Annie John* (1985), focuses on a young girl growing up in Antigua, while *Lucy* (1990) follows a young woman who moves from the West Indies to the U.S. to work as an au pair. Kincaid's short stories are collected in *At the Bottom of the River* (1983). She returns to the Caribbean in her most recent novel, *The Autobiography of My Mother* (1996). Her works of nonfiction include *A Small Place* (1988), an angry critique of colonialism; and *My Brother* (1997), an account of her brother's death from AIDS. She published a children's book, *Annie, Gwen, Lilly, Pam and Tulip*, in 1989. *Talk Stories* (2001) collects eighty-five of the "Talk of the Town" pieces she wrote for the *New Yorker*. Finally, readers of *My Garden (Book):* will want to take a look at *My Favorite Plant: Writers and Gardeners on the Plants They Love* (1998), a collection of brief essays she edited by writers on their favorite plants.

Books about Jamaica Kincaid

There are a number of scholarly studies of Kincaid's fiction: *Jamaica Kincaid: Where the Land Meets the Body* by Moira Ferguson, *Jamaica Kincaid: A Critical Companion* by Lizabeth Paravisini-Gebert and Katherine Gregory Klein, *Jamaica Kincaid* by Diane Simmons, and *Jamaica Kincaid* edited by Harold Bloom.

If you like *My Garden (Book):*, you will like...

Vita's Other World: A Gardening Biography of V. Sackville-West by Jane Brown. A biography of the creator of Sissinghurst's famous gardens.

A Year at North Hill: Four Seasons in a Vermont Garden by Joe Eck and Wayne Winterrowd. The two landscape designers, both friends of Kincaid, chronicle a year in their Vermont garden.

The Meaning of Gardens: Idea, Place, Action edited by Mark Francis. A theoretical look at the social, economic, cultural, and political meanings of gardens.

The Writer in the Garden, edited by Jane Garmey. This collection of excerpts and essays includes well-known gardening writers like Henry Mitchell, Allen Lacy, Gertrude Jekyll, and Vita Sackville-West.

The Essential Earthman by Henry Mitchell. The first of several collections of Mitchell's *Washington Post* columns.

Video resources

Monet's Garden at Giverny (1999) is a documentary that takes viewers through Monet's famous garden and explains how he created it. The *Gardens of the World* series, narrated by Audrey Hepburn, includes entries on "Country Gardens," "Flower Gardens," and "Roses and Rose Gardens."

Internet resources

Find biographical information, photos, a map of Antigua, and a discussion of Kincaid's themes at www.cc.emory.edu/ENGLISH/Bahri/Kincaid.html. Read an interview with Kincaid from *Mother Jones* at www.mojones.com/mother_jones/SO97/snell.html. Comments about her inspiration for *The Autobiography of My Mother* are available at www.mg.co.za/mg/books/kincaid.htm. Read an interview with Kincaid at www.salon.com.

CHAPTER 5

May
Women and Family

CROWD-PLEASER
Amy and Isabelle by Elizabeth Strout

CLASSIC
Pride and Prejudice by Jane Austen

CHALLENGE
The Hours by Michael Cunningham

MEMOIR
And I Don't Want to Live This Life by
Deborah Spungen

POTLUCK
The Secrets of Mariko by Elisabeth
Bumiller

In her study of one Japanese woman and her family, Elisabeth Bumiller writes:

> It made particular sense to me to explore Japanese society through the experience of one family. More than most countries, Japan likes to think of itself as one large family, united by a unique, inscrutable Japaneseness.
>
> —*The Secrets of Mariko*

Bumiller is right to look to the family when trying to understand Japanese culture: studying the family as the basic unit of a society makes sense for most cultures. Our families are the sites of our most profound experiences; they expose us to the best and the worst that life has to offer. To come to terms with the people we become, we must look back to our families. As magazine articles and sociological studies attest, responsibility for the family remains the concern primarily of women in both traditional and nontraditional households. The works that we've chosen for this month highlight the rewards *and* the burdens of family life.

This month's selections emphasize the bonds between sisters, between mothers and daughters, between husbands and wives. They detail the multiple ways women negotiate families and families negotiate communities. *Amy and Isabelle* explores the often painful bond between mothers and daughters, their fierce love and surprising tenderness. The Classic selection, *Pride and Prejudice*, delineates the marriage market in early nineteenth-century England; Jane Austen humorously shows the five Bennet sisters seeking to establish new families of their own. Michael Cunningham's unconventional families in *The Hours* expose all that's right—and wrong—about family dynamics. In *And I Don't Want to Live This Life*, Deborah Spungen writes movingly of her daughter's mental illness and death and of the ways family life can go horribly wrong. Finally, this month's Potluck selection, *The Secrets of Mariko*, broadens our focus to examine how one family interacts with its culture and society.

May/Women and Family
Crowd-Pleaser
Amy and Isabelle by Elizabeth Strout, 1999, available in paperback from Vintage Books for $13.00

What is this book about?

Relationships between mothers and daughters provide a fertile field for novelists, perhaps even more fertile than relationships between star-crossed lovers. It is easy to see why: mothers and daughters, whether they like one another or not, are bound to spend years together. Love and anger, connection and separation, letting go and growing up characterize these relationships.

In Elizabeth Strout's take on the mother-daughter bond, Isabelle and Amy Goodrow live in a small, depressed New England mill town. Amy, a sixteen-year-old high school student, is quiet, shy, and has magnificent blonde hair. Her mother, Isabelle, is a secretary with a crush on her married boss and a sad, desperate ambition to be accepted by the middle-class women of her church. Isabelle's discovery of Amy's sexual relationship with her math teacher has created a seemingly irreparable rift between mother and daughter. Their disconnection and reconnection are painstakingly explored, as are the relationships among Isabelle's coworkers and Amy's friends. The complexity and intensity of Amy and Isabelle's relationship makes *Amy and Isabelle* an affecting read that will stay with you for a long time.

What should I know about the author?

Elizabeth Strout is originally from Portland, Maine. Readers familiar with New England will recognize Strout's description of the town of Shirley Falls as evocative of many regional mill towns. Strout currently lives in New York City with her husband and daughter. She teaches literature and writing at Manhattan Community College and writing at the New School. Her short fiction has appeared in the *New Yorker*. *Amy and Isabelle* is her first novel.

Questions for reflection and discussion

1. What do the town itself and the weather that summer add to the story? Strout spends a lot of time describing the physical layout of the town, what the buildings look like, what the river looks like, and the weather. Why might she do this? What do descriptions of the physical environment add to the story? What is the relationship between the weather and the unfolding of the plot?

2. Is Amy a convincing character? What does she do and say that seems realistic? Certainly few teens end up sexually involved with

their teachers. Discuss how Strout uses this sexual liaison to increase the conflict and distance between mother and daughter.

3. What sort of person is Isabelle? Why does she seem angrier with Amy than at Mr. Robertson? What does this reveal to us about Isabelle's life? Why doesn't Isabelle know what's going on with Amy, especially what's happening to her at school? What does our society expect from "good" mothers, and how does Isabelle rank against these expectations? What do you think of Isabelle? What would you have done?

4. Novels about mothers and daughters tend to explore the ways in which a deep and abiding love for someone can coexist with periods of intense dislike. How does the author demonstrate the connection between Amy and Isabelle? What are the sources of the dislike? Group members may want to explore and discuss their own relationships with their mothers or daughters. Do you share universal experiences?

5. Readers of *Amy and Isabelle* frequently note that the secondary characters (Fat Bev, Dottie Brown, Stacey Burrows) are more vividly portrayed than the main characters. Several readers have seen this as a flaw in the novel. Do you agree? Why or why not? Assuming, however, that Strout did this intentionally, *why* would she do it? What do the different types of characterization bring to the story?

If you like *Amy and Isabelle*, you will like...

The Good Mother and *Inventing the Abbots* by Sue Miller. Two painstakingly drawn stories of the best and worst of family life.

One True Thing by Anna Quindlen. The story of a daughter caring for her mother during her mother's final illness.

Anywhere but Here by Mona Simpson. The story of young girl accompanying her troubled, restless mother on a cross-country journey.

The Cape Ann and *The Empress of One* by Faith Sullivan. Two novels with overlapping characters depict mothers and daughters learning to survive during the Depression.

The Joy Luck Club and *The Bonesetter's Daughter* by Amy Tan. Explores mother and daughter love from the perspective of assimilated Chinese-American daughters trying to understand their immigrant mothers.

Video resources

In 2001, Oprah Winfrey produced a television movie of *Amy and Isabelle* starring Elisabeth Shue as Isabelle and Hanna Hall as Amy. Several of our further reading suggestions have been adapted into movies that explore the relationships between mothers and daughters. *Anywhere but Here* (Wayne Wang, 1999) stars Susan Sarandon and Natalie Portman. Also by Wayne Wang is *The Joy Luck Club* (1993). *One True Thing* (Carl Franklin, 1998) stars Meryl Streep, Renee Zellweger, and William Hurt. Leonard Nimoy's *The Good Mother*, with Diane Keaton and Liam Neeson, came out in 1988. The plot of *Tumbleweeds* (Gavin O'Connor, 1999) is very similar to that of *Anywhere but Here*; your group may want to compare the treatment of the mother-daughter bond in both films.

Internet resources

Interviews with Elizabeth Strout can be found at www. bookreporter.com, www.ivillage.com, and www.salon.com.

May/Women and Family
Classic
Pride and Prejudice by Jane Austen, 1813, several paperback editions available, including one from Bantam Classics for $4.95

What is this book about?

If you are a long-time devotee of Jane Austen and her work, you already know how much you are going to enjoy reading or rereading *Pride and Prejudice*. If you have never read Austen before, we envy your first-time experience. For those who love Austen, the only sour note to her work is that it is finite.

Published anonymously in 1813, *Pride and Prejudice* is the story of the five Bennet sisters, who range in age from fifteen to twenty-three. At the center of the plot are Mrs. Bennet's machinations to get her daughters married to eligible (read: wealthy) men. As she explores and exposes the complexities of family relationships, friendship, and love, Austen focuses most closely on Elizabeth Bennet, the second oldest. As the novel progresses, Elizabeth learns the personal meanings of the two title words: how her own pride has blinded her and fostered her prejudice.

From its beginnings in the early-to-mid eighteenth century, the novel as a genre has focused on the pursuit of romantic love. *Pride and Prejudice* is no exception, but its beauty lies in its fresh approach. What surprises first-time readers of Jane Austen is just how funny she is, with humor arising not only from the situation and story, but also from her language. We suggest that you mark favorite passages as you read and share them aloud with your book group.

What should I know about the author?

Jane Austen was born in 1775 to a clergyman and his wife; she had six brothers and one sister, Cassandra. Austen's fascination with the sisterly bond in her novels surely reflects her close relationship with Cassandra. She began writing as a child to amuse her family; her precocious early works already exhibit the detached, ironic tone she would later develop and perfect. Austen's life was short (she died at age forty-two) and, by our standards, a quiet one. She never married, and she lived with her family. She rarely traveled. When she did, she did not travel far, and her journeys were always to visit relatives. The two professions that attracted five of her six brothers no doubt sparked her interest in the clergy and the navy. While she always published anonymously, her works were quite popular during her lifetime; she counted the Prince Regent (later King George IV) among her biggest fans.

There are many biographies of Austen, but perhaps the best is Claire Tomalin's *Jane Austen: A Life*. David Nokes's *Jane Austen: A Life* offers an alternative view.

Questions for reflection and discussion

1. Austen, who never married, was very interested in what makes for a good marriage. To what extent is the Gardiners' marriage her ideal? Why is Elizabeth horrified by Charlotte's decision to marry Mr. Collins? Based on your understanding of Charlotte's position about marriage as well as Elizabeth's reasons for objecting, is Charlotte doing the right thing? Austen clearly wants us to believe that Elizabeth and Darcy, and also Jane and Bingley, will be happily married. She strongly suggests that people with good sense have good marriages. Based on the character traits of these two couples, what constitutes good sense for Austen, and what makes for a good marriage?

2. The Bennet estate has been entailed through the male line: without sons of his own, Mr. Bennet must relinquish his right to the estate at his death in favor of his cousin, Mr. Collins. Estates—land, inherited wealth, ancestral homes—are of paramount importance to Austen and her contemporaries. Other than the obvious reason of having plenty of money, why? What could be Austen's purpose in spending so much time describing the house and grounds at Pemberley? Elizabeth jokes that she falls in love with Darcy after she views Pemberley, but is this really a joke?

3. Austen presents a cautionary view of parenting in Mr. and Mrs. Bennet. How do they fail their children? You might review in volume two, chapter nineteen Elizabeth's own recognition of her parents' shortcomings and the evils that must therefore be visited upon their daughters. Despite their bad parents, Jane and Elizabeth turn out well; how would Austen explain this? *Pride and Prejudice* ends with four couples (Lydia and Wickham, Elizabeth and Darcy, Jane and Bingley, Mr. Collins and Charlotte) ready to start families of their own: what kind of parents do you expect them to be?

4. How does the title, *Pride and Prejudice*, relate to the strengths and weaknesses of Elizabeth and Darcy? Does Austen mean for us to assign one each of these traits to her characters? Austen suggests that they each have to overcome their pride and prejudice before they can marry, and readers have long debated whether this actually occurs. What evidence does the novel provide to support a stand on either side of this argument? If Jane Bennet represents the enviable absence of both pride and prejudice, why do readers overwhelmingly love Elizabeth better?

5. In *Jane Austen: Irony as Defense and Discovery*, Marvin Mudrick defines irony as the "discrimination between impulse and pretension, between being and seeming, between—in a social setting—man as he is and man as he aspires to be." Irony is Jane Austen's most important tool. Under which circumstances in *Pride and Prejudice* does she employ it best? How does her acerbic wit contribute to the comedy of her novel and to our enjoyment?

Other books by the author

If you like *Pride and Prejudice*, you are probably eager to read more of Jane Austen's work. Her other novels are *Sense and Sensibility*, *Emma*, *Mansfield Park*, *Persuasion*, and *Northanger Abbey*. Her juvenilia and unfinished works have also been published as *Catharine and Other Writings*. *Love and Freindship* [sic] should not be missed. *Jane Austen's Letters*, collected and edited by Deirdre Le Faye, are also a delight.

If you like *Pride and Prejudice*, you will like...

Jane and the Unpleasantness at Scargrove Manor by Stephanie Barron. Barron's mystery series stars Jane Austen herself as an amateur detective.

Queen Lucia by E.F. Benson. Benson also focuses on small village life in England. This is the first of five hilarious novels about the exploits of Lucia.

Evelina and *Cecilia: Memoirs of an Heiress* by Frances Burney. Burney was one of Austen's favorite authors.

The Semi-Attached Couple and the Semi-Detached House by Emily Eden. Eden's subject and voice are reminiscent of Austen's.

Bridget Jones's Diary by Helen Fielding. A loose updating of *Pride and Prejudice*.

Video resources

The last few years produced a flurry of dramatizations of Jane Austen novels. Most of the novels, including *Pride and Prejudice*, are available in multiple film versions. We recommend the much-admired 1996 BBC/A&E miniseries starring Colin Firth and Jennifer Ehle (Simon Langton). Other Austen adaptations we love include: *Emma* (Douglas McGrath, 1996) with Gwyneth Paltrow in the title role; *Clueless*, Amy Heckerling's update of Emma as a twentieth-century California girl (1995); the gorgeous *Sense and Sensibility* (Ang Lee, 1995) with Emma Thompson and Kate Winslet; *Persuasion* (Roger Michell, 1995); and *Mansfield Park*, inventively adapted by Patricia Rozema (1999).

Internet resources

If, after all this reading and video watching, you still haven't had enough of Jane Austen, consider joining the Jane Austen Society of North America. They publish an annual newsletter, host conferences, and throw a party every year on December 16 to celebrate Austen's birthday. You can find information online at www.jasna.org. This site, www.pemberley.com, provides a forum for discussion and much information on Austen and her novels. And don't miss the incredible wealth of links at lang.nagoya-u.ac.jp/~matsuoka/Austen.html.

Extra credit

Plan an outing to attend a Jane Austen conference. The Jane Austen Society of North America holds an annual meeting where important scholars present papers that are written for both academic and general readers. Locations change yearly, but upcoming

meetings are scheduled in Seattle; Toronto; Winchester, England,
and Los Angeles. Regional meetings and discussion groups are
held throughout the year by smaller, local groups; find out how
to join at www.jasna.org/region.html.

May/Women and Family
Challenge
The Hours by Michael Cunningham, 1998, available in
paperback from Picador for $13.00

What is this book about?

Michael Cunningham's Pulitzer Prize–winning masterpiece, *The
Hours*, treats the quiet despair of twentieth-century women's lives in
lyrical, moving prose. The intricately entwined plots converge on
Virginia Woolf's 1925 novel, *Mrs. Dalloway*, which Cunningham
reinterprets, revises, rewrites, and ultimately transcends. *The Hours*
begins with Woolf's suicide in 1941, but quickly flashes back to
1923, when Woolf was in the midst of writing *Mrs. Dalloway*, her
own masterpiece. Woolf shows up as a major character here, her creative process and daily life imaginatively brought to life in the chapters on "Mrs. Woolf." Woolf's struggles with the manuscript she
called, "The Hours" (later to become *Mrs. Dalloway*) are juxtaposed
with the stories of Laura Brown, a housewife and mother in mid-
twentieth-century Los Angeles who is reading *Mrs. Dalloway* and trying to make sense of her own life, and with Clarissa Vaughan, who,
in present-day New York City, is planning a party to celebrate the
award of the prestigious Carrouthers Prize to her friend Richard,
who is dying of AIDS. This is, in part, a book about family, about
the ways our families support and fail us, and the substitute families
we create. But this is also a book about the importance of books,
their power in creating community, their contribution toward
answering the question of how to live. *The Hours* is an immensely

rewarding read that will take on extra depth for those who have
already read *Mrs. Dalloway*.

Did you know...?

Named after newspaper publisher and owner Joseph Pulitzer
(1847–1911), the Pulitzer Prize is awarded yearly to works of fiction,
nonfiction, poetry, and biography that powerfully chronicle the
human condition. Unlike the Nobel Prize, which is awarded to
authors for their entire body of work, the Pulitzer Prize is awarded
for specific texts. Joseph Pulitzer owned the New York *World* newspaper and engaged in titanic struggles for supremacy with the other
nineteenth-century newspaper baron, William Randolph Hearst. The
Pulitzer Prize began a year after Pulitzer's death. The Columbia
School of Journalism supervises its administering committee. Two of
A Year of Reading's selections are Pulitzer Prize winners: *The Good
Earth* by Pearl S. Buck and *The Hours* by Michael Cunningham. Learn
more about Pulitzer and his prize at www.pulitzer.org.

What should I know about the author?

Michael Cunningham was raised in Los Angeles and now lives in
New York City. He earned his bachelor's degree at Stanford Univer-
sity and his M.F.A. at the University of Iowa's prestigious Writer's
Workshop. Cunningham won a Guggenheim Fellowship in 1993.
The Hours won both the Pulitzer Prize and the PEN/Faulkner Awards
for fiction in 1999.

Questions for reflection and discussion

1. Clarissa Vaughan's story is a reworking of Clarissa Dalloway's. If
   you have read *Mrs. Dalloway*, discuss the parallels and differences.
   Why use one work of art as an inspiration for another? What
   other novels can your group think of that "quote" extensively
   from an earlier work? *The Hours* was Virginia Woolf's working title
   for the novel that became *Mrs. Dalloway*. Why does Cunningham
   choose this title for his book? In what other ways does the title
   resonate?

2. Images of mothers and children permeate *The Hours*. Parenting is almost always figured as maternal, and friendship almost always as familial. To what extent is this a novel about the bond between mother and child? What role does the father have in parenting? Marriages also play out a maternal pattern. How does Cunningham imagine Virginia Woolf's relationship with her husband, Leonard? What does Virginia bring to the marriage? How does their relationship parallel Laura Brown's marriage to Dan and Clarissa Vaughan's relationship with Sally? Can the central role caretaking assumes in *The Hours* be linked to Cunningham's interest in the maternal? Is caretaking primarily a woman's role?

3. In *Mrs. Dalloway*, the lingering effects of World War I provide a backdrop for the action and lead to the suicide of a main character; in *The Hours*, World War I seems to be replaced by the AIDS crisis. How effective is this? What might Cunningham be trying to say about the nature of the AIDS crisis?

4. On the surface, Laura Brown's life would seem ideal for her time. Why isn't she happy? What do books, and in particular *Mrs. Dalloway*, offer her? Cunningham's belief in the centrality of books in forming our lives provides an opening for book group members to discuss the most meaningful books in their lives. What book has been your *Mrs. Dalloway*?

5. Virginia Woolf is not the only writer in *The Hours*; Richard has recently been honored with the Carrouthers Prize for his lifetime achievement in poetry. How does Cunningham characterize the writing process? What do we learn about writers' lives and patterns of thinking from this novel?

Did you know...?

The literary term for Cunningham's homage to Virginia Woolf is **pastiche**: a literary imitation of another writer's or work's style. According to Holman and Harmon's *Handbook to Literature*, writers use pastiche "for humorous or satirical purposes, perhaps as a mere literary exercise or *jeu d'esprit*, perhaps in all seriousness."

Other books by the author

Cunningham has written two other novels that speak to family issues: *Home at the End of the World* (1998), the story of two friends who create a new kind of family, and *Flesh and Blood* (1996), an epic family saga spanning three generations.

If you like *The Hours*, you will like...

Mrs. Dalloway by Virginia Woolf. Cunningham's inspiration and one of Woolf's finest novels.

Virginia Woolf by Hermione Lee. One of the most recent and best biographies of Woolf.

Mitz: The Marmoset of Bloomsbury by Sigrid Nunez. A fictional account of the Woolfs' lives in the 1930s, centered on Mitz, their pet marmoset.

The Blackwater Lightship by Colm Toibin. A lyrical Irish novel about a family rallying around their brother, who is dying of AIDS.

A Writer's Diary by Virginia Woolf. Excerpted from the volumes of her diary by her husband, Leonard Woolf, to illuminate her creative process.

DISCUSSION/REFLECTION STRATEGY

You might want to read the five books Cunningham selected as neglected masterpieces in July, 1999, for www.salon.com: Carol Anshaw's *Aquamarine*, Joe Brainard's *I Remember*, Samuel R. Delany's *Atlantis: Three Tales*, Lynn Freed's *The Mirror*, and Robert S. Jones's *Force of Gravity*. What connections can you make between Cunningham's own interests as a novelist and the books he likes to read?

Video resources

The film version of *The Hours* (Stephen Daldy, 2003) stars Meryl Streep and Nicole Kidman. Marleen Gorris adapted Woolf's *Mrs. Dalloway* in 1997.

Internet resources

Read an essay by Michael Cunningham about Virginia Woolf at http://www.salon.com/books/feature/2000/06/22/woolf/. Find out all there is to know about Virginia Woolf online at hubcap.clemson.edu /aah/ws/ vw6links.html.

May/Women and Family
Memoir
And I Don't Want to Live This Life by Deborah Spungen, 1983, available in paperback from Fawcett Books for $12.00

What is this book about?

In 1978, the death of twenty-year-old Nancy Spungen at the hands of her boyfriend, punk rocker Sid Vicious, became a media sensation. News outlets competed to provide lurid details and speculation; both *Saturday Night Live* and the *Tonight Show* mined the murder for jokes. With reporters camped out on her front lawn, obscene phone calls coming daily, and the knowledge that merchants were selling "Sid and Nancy" T-shirts, Nancy's mother Deborah wanted to scream at the world, "Nancy was my baby! She was my child!…No matter what she became, she didn't deserve to die this way—to be *treated* this way!…You don't understand her! She was *loved!*" This memoir is a powerful reminder that there are always people behind the headlines. Deborah Spungen vividly relates the story of Nancy's family. If you have ever lived with a mentally ill person, if you have ever loved some one bent on self-destruction, you will find much that is familiar in *And I Don't Want to Live This Life.*

What should I know about the author?

Deborah Spungen is a well-known victim's rights advocate. In 1980, shortly after her daughter's murder, she organized the first support group for homicide survivors in Philadelphia. In 1986, she launched

Families of Murder Victims, which provides counseling and advocacy services to over eighteen hundred crime victims each year. She cofounded the Student Anti-Violence Education Project, which provides an extensive violence prevention curriculum to children in Philadelphia schools. She has received several awards, including the 1995 Presidential Crime Victims Service Award.

DISCUSSION/REFLECTION STRATEGY

May is the ideal month to explore research on the **psychology of women and families**. Deepening your knowledge will broaden your understanding of the family dynamics central to so many novels and memoirs and give you new ways to discuss books. We recommend starting with these classic studies: Mary Field Belenky et al.'s *Women's Ways of Knowing: The Development of Self, Voice, and Mind*; Nancy Chodorow's *The Reproduction of Mothering: Psychoanalysis and the Sociology of Gender*; Carol Gilligan's *In a Different Voice: Psychological Theory and Women's Development*; Jean Baker Miller's *Toward a New Psychology of Women*; and Adrienne Rich's *Of Woman Born: Motherhood as Experience and Institution*.

Questions for reflection and discussion

1. Who was responsible for what happened to Nancy? This is not a question that can be answered definitively, but consider the actions of the following people: her mother, her father, her siblings, her doctors, her schools, herself. To what extent (if any) do these people bear responsibility for Nancy's troubled life and death? Deborah Spungen has some angry words for the state of Pennsylvania for its scarcity of facilities for troubled children and their families. Is her anger justified? Should states provide help for the mentally ill and their families? If so, what kind of help?

2. Is Deborah a reliable narrator? Were there any points in the text where you found yourself questioning her version of events? Notice that she is relating conversations from twenty years earlier and does not question her own memory of these things. There are numerous places in the book where Deborah repeats herself—frequently

mentioning that Nancy said she wanted to die, repeating the phrases, "we had no choice," or, "what choice did I have?" What do these repetitions suggest about Deborah's own ambivalence about how events unfolded? Would the same tale told by Frank, Suzy, or David have been substantially different?

3. In his memoir, *Parallel Time: Growing Up in Black and White*, journalist Brent Staples tells of trying to save, but eventually letting go of, his younger brother, who was shot to death in a drug deal gone bad. Staples relates that he had tried to get his brother out of the inner city, tried to get him educated, and tried to show him another way. He eventually realized that his brother had to live his own life and that Staples could not help him if he did not wish to be helped. Staples has said that when he tells this story, younger people admonish him for not doing more to help his brother, and older people just nod silently—they seem to understand his cutting his brother loose. Is this situation analogous to the Spungens sending Nancy to live in New York? Does the fact that they thought she was mentally ill make her situation different from that of Staples's brother?

4. Answering the following questions may require some research. Ask if there are any present or former punks in your reading group. (We bet there are.) Deborah Spungen is, not surprisingly, an unsympathetic observer of the punk scene. What was the punk movement? Is it possible that Sid and Nancy's behavior makes more sense within the punk subculture than it did in suburban Philadelphia?

5. Toward the end of the book, Deborah states, "I am not the same person I was before. My priorities have changed. Success has a new definition for me. Personal achievement—doing well in school and in business—used to be a major factor in my life. I was always driven to accomplish something. A big title and salary seemed important. They don't anymore." Yet Deborah is angered by the suggestion that Nancy's behavior was a rejection of the values she had grown up with. Is it fair to argue that Nancy's behavior is at least partly motivated by a rejection of her mother's values? Are people who systematically reject the values of the culture at large

more likely to be labeled "mentally ill" than those who don't? Do you think Nancy was mentally ill?

Other books by Deborah Spungen

Homicide: The Hidden Victims: A Guide for Professionals is a nonfiction work for mental health and criminal justice professionals.

If you like *And I Don't Want to Live This Life,* you will like...

I Never Promised You a Rose Garden by Joanne Greenberg. Classic high school reading in the 1970s. The story of a teen's three-year battle with mental illness and the doctor who helps her.

My Mother's Keeper: A Daughter's Memoir of Growing Up in the Shadow of Schizophrenia by Tara Elgin Holly. Holly's story is the reverse of Spungen's. She describes life with a mentally unstable mother.

Cherry by Mary Karr. A dark memoir of a difficult adolescence.

Lipstick Traces: A Secret History of the Twentieth Century and *In the Fascist Bathroom: Punk in Pop Music 1977–1992* by Greil Marcus. In these books, Marcus offers critical studies of the historical and art historical context of punk.

Extra credit

You may wish to deepen your understanding of the punk movement by actually listening to the music of the Sex Pistols. Their best album is generally considered to be *Never Mind the Bollocks, Here's the Sex Pistols*. When the album was released in 1977, *Rolling Stone* magazine said, "This band still takes rock and roll seriously, as a matter of honor and necessity, and they play with an energy and conviction that is positively transcendent in its madness and fever."

Video resources

The Filth and the Fury (Julien Temple, 2000), is an excellent documentary about the Sex Pistols with lots of performance footage. In 1980, Julien Temple directed *The Great Rock and Roll Swindle*, which is another documentary about the Sex Pistols, but not as well constructed as the more recent film. The 1995 series, *The History of Rock and Roll*, addresses the punk movement in volume nine. *Sid and Nancy* (Alex Cox, 1986) draws some of its material from Deborah Spungen's book and accounts of people who knew Sid and Nancy, but it should not be considered a factual account of their lives. Gary Oldman and Chloe Webb turn in astonishing performances in the title roles.

Internet resources

The Web is filled with all sorts of punk websites. We recommend www.worldwidepunk.com for its comprehensive listing of links and its excellent book reviews. Like the punk videos, punk websites contain profanity, disturbing images, and many references to drugs and sex.

May/Women and Family
Potluck
The Secrets of Mariko: A Year in the Life of a Japanese Woman and Her Family by Elisabeth Bumiller, 1995, available in paperback from Vintage Books for $14.00

What is this book about?

Journalist Elisabeth Bumiller spent fourteen months of the three years she lived in Tokyo interviewing and shadowing Mariko Tanaka. Bumiller's goal was to understand Japanese society by looking closely at the life of a representative woman and her family. With the help of an interpreter, Bumiller questioned Mariko about her marriage, her expectations for her children, her relationship with her elderly parents, her part-time job as a meter reader, her friends, and her community. She accompanied Mariko to work, to PTA meetings, to local festivals and fairs, to religious ceremonies, to adult education classes. *The Secrets of Mariko* is more than a study of one Japanese woman and her family, however; it is a biography of a culture viewed through the lens of Western values and expectations. Bumiller reveals much about the Japanese, but also much about Americans. *The Secrets of Mariko* is structured as "a year in the life," chronicling Mariko's changing relationships and activities over the course of 1991. Our understanding of Mariko mirrors the author's deepening understanding; by the end, we feel we know her, but we also realize she may have secrets we will never discover.

What should I know about the author?

Elisabeth Bumiller is a reporter for the *New York Times*. Before that, she wrote for the *Washington Post*. She spent four years in India with her husband, also a journalist; while in India, she researched her first book. After her husband was transferred to Tokyo in 1990, she reported on Japanese culture, society, and politics for the *New York Times*, as well as interviewing Mariko Tanaka for *The Secrets of Mariko*. Bumiller now lives in New York City with her family.

DISCUSSION/REFLECTION STRATEGY

Invite a guest speaker to talk to your book group about Japan. Contact the Asian studies or Asian history department at your local university. As you're reading, prepare questions for your speaker. What do you need to know about Japan in order to understand and enjoy *The Secrets of Mariko*? Your guest speaker may already be familiar with your book selection or may be willing to read it in order to facilitate discussion.

Questions for reflection and discussion

1. In her interviews with Bumiller, Mariko reveals much about herself as a daughter, wife, and mother. How would you characterize her in these roles? Does she see herself differently from how her family sees her? How does Mariko's relationship with her daughter, Chiaki, replay themes from her relationship with her mother, Ito? How do Japanese expectations for how a good daughter, wife, or mother should behave differ from American expectations?

2. Mariko's struggles highlight the problems a working mother faces in reaching a balance between her own needs and the needs of her family. How do Mariko's duties to her family conflict with her desires for herself? Are duty to family and self-development or self-expression mutually exclusive? How does Mariko try to strike a balance? Have other Japanese women solved this dilemma? Bumiller depicts feminism and the women's movement in Japan as a failure. She seems disappointed that Mariko is not more of a feminist and suggests that her life would be more fulfilling if she were. How useful it is to apply American standards for women's rights to Japan? What do you think of the author's desire to turn Mariko into a feminist? Is it fair?

3. Bumiller's discussion of the Japanese education system is especially fascinating. The Japanese are among the best-educated people in the world, but at what price? What ramifications do you imagine the cram schools have on family life? Bumiller suggests that the Japanese system of education expresses their value system; what does the American system say about American values? What can Americans learn from the Japanese? What might Japan learn from the American system?

4. Bumiller argues, "Mariko's story is a reminder that certain universal themes transcend borders." What "universal themes" might transcend cultural diversity and geographical location? What kind of "universal" message does Bumiller take from Mariko's life? Bumiller has been criticized for writing with an American bias, for judging the Japanese according to Western values. Do you agree with this criticism? Do the author's biases add or detract from the story she tells? Would Mariko find her attitudes and judgments offensive or puzzling? Is it possible for people of one culture to immerse themselves in another culture and eliminate cultural biases?

5. How does Mariko change over the course of her acquaintance with Bumiller? What effect does Bumiller have on the family's life? Bumiller realizes toward the end of *The Secrets of Mariko* that her book project may have far-reaching implications that she did not originally foresee; what do you think these are?

Other books by Elisabeth Bumiller

Elisabeth Bumiller has written a study of women in India, titled *May You Be the Mother of a Hundred Sons: A Journey among the Women of India*.

If you like *The Secrets of Mariko,* you will like...

Haruko's World: A Japanese Farm Woman and Her Community by Gail Lee Bernstein. Bernstein moved to Japan and lived with a family in order to write this study.

Broken Silence: Voices of Japanese Feminism edited by Sandra Buckley. Essays by and interviews with Japanese women who identify themselves as feminists.

Re-Imaging Japanese Women edited by Anne Imamura. Case studies about contemporary Japanese women.

The Accidental Office Lady by Laura J. Kriska. A memoir by an American who moved to Japan to work for the Honda corporation.

Too Late for the Festival: An American Salary-Woman in Japan by Rhiannon Paine. Paine lived in Japan and worked as a technical writer for Hewlett-Packard.

Video resources

Early Summer (Yasujiro Ozu, 1951) is about a young woman protesting an arranged marriage. *Tokyo Story* (1953), by the same director, looks at the conflict that erupts when an elderly couple visits their adult children. Yoshumitsu Morita's *The Family Game* (1983) is an award-winning comedy about the problems in a Japanese family.

Internet resources

Learn about Japanese culture at www.japaneseculture.about.com/mbody.htm. The site www.askasia.org/frclasrm/readings/

r000074.htm offers a look at working women in Japan since World War II. At www2.gol.com/users/friedman/writings/p1.html, you can read a scholarly article about the changing role of women in Japanese society over the past 150 years. Find a detailed and informative overview of Japanese women's lives at jin.jcic.or.jp/insight/html/focus05/focus05.html.

CHAPTER 6

June
Men and Family

CROWD-PLEASER
Before and After by Rosellen Brown

CLASSIC
The Rise of Silas Lapham by William Dean Howells

CHALLENGE
Native Speaker by Chang-Rae Lee

MEMOIR
A Heartbreaking Work of Staggering Genius by Dave Eggers

POTLUCK
The Lone Ranger and Tonto Fistfight in Heaven by Sherman Alexie

The silken texture of the marriage tie bears a daily strain of wrong and insult to which no other human relation can be subjected without lesion; and sometimes the strength that knits society together might appear to the eye of faltering faith the curse of those immediately bound by it. Two people by no means reckless of each other's rights and feelings, but even tender of them for the most part, may tear at each other's heart-strings in this sacred bond with perfect impunity; though if they were any other two they would not speak or look at each other again after the outrages they exchange.

—William Dean Howells, *The Rise of Silas Lapham*

The books we've chosen for June reflect the special commitment many of us make to husbands and fathers (or as husbands and fathers) this month. But as the passage from William Dean Howells's novel suggests, family life in these books is no breezily sentimental greeting card. The father in Rosellen Brown's timely *Before and After* struggles to make sense of an act of violence perpetrated by his son and to navigate the troubled waters of family and community life in the wake of this violence. Silas Lapham, the father and husband at the center of Howells's novel, enjoys a close but by no means carefree relationship with his wife and two daughters; his problem, in part, is how to balance family life with his professional life, how to apply the values of his home to his business. Chang-Rae Lee explores a similar theme in *Native Speaker*, where the protagonist, a spy, confronts a disintegrating marriage and a moral dilemma over his job, compounded by still-fresh grief after the death of his young son. In *A Heartbreaking Work of Staggering Genius*, Dave Eggers recounts the astonishing story of the death of both his parents from cancer within one five-week period and his own metamorphosis from son to brother to guardian of his eight-year-old brother, Toph. Finally, Sherman Alexie's collection of short stories features young Native American men who are all too often doomed to repeat the dismal histories of their parents. Despite the dark nature of much of this material, these are not bleak books. These authors treat men and family life even-handedly, finding the humor and the poignancy in men's struggles to commit and to relate.

June/Men and Family
Crowd-Pleaser
Before and After by Rosellen Brown, 1992, available in paperback from Delta for $12.95

What is this book about?

The Reiser family has lived in their small, peaceful town in New Hampshire for eleven years. For a variety of reasons, they are still outsiders. On the surface, the family seems fairly typical: the father sculpts and cooks, the mother has a pediatrics practice, the seventeen-year-old son goes to school and tests his parents' limits, and the thirteen-year-old daughter shifts between happy-go-lucky and teen angst.

The everyday life of this family is shattered, however, when a local teenaged girl is found bludgeoned to death in the snow, and Jacob Reiser, her boyfriend, is wanted for questioning. Authorities and family soon discover that Jacob has disappeared. Has he been kidnapped? Has he run away? Could he *possibly* have anything to do with the murder? *Before and After* charts the shifts in relationships and alliances that occur as this family is forced to confront the unthinkable. How do they now respond to one another? How can the family face their neighbors and friends? Alliances shift, and suddenly father and son are allied against not only the law, but also the mother. The outsider position of the family increases in the community, but now there are insiders and outsiders within the Reiser home.

What should I know about the author?

Rosellen Brown was born in 1939 in Philadelphia, but her childhood and adolescence were spent in Pennsylvania, California, and New York. She attended Barnard College and received an M.A. in English Literature from Brandeis. The seminomadic pattern begun in her youth followed her into adulthood. With her husband and two daughters, she has lived in Mississippi, New Hampshire, Texas, and Illinois. Brown states that she tends to experience geographical communities as an outsider and that she likes to project that experience onto her novel's characters. She is currently a faculty member of the Graduate Creative Writing Program at the School of the Art Institute of Chicago.

Questions for reflection and discussion

1. Note Brown's use of first- and third-person narrative techniques. Which character is allowed to speak directly to the reader? For which characters does Brown employ third-person point of view? Is there any one character that is heard from more often? Why do you think we are never presented directly with Jacob's point of view? What do the differing points of view bring to the overall impact of this story?

2. Can you accept Ben's version of himself? Why or why not? By what means does Brown give her reader the opportunity to see Ben more objectively? Note how Ben describes his relationship with Jacob. How do you think Jacob sees it? What elements of Ben's character and of his relationships with the other family members emerge unintentionally from Ben's narration?

3. How does Brown construct the character of Carolyn? How do we learn about who she is? Which details reveal her to us, e.g., what does her hand-washing say about her? Do the qualities making Carolyn a good doctor also make her a good parent? If Carolyn represents moral behavior and judgment in this novel, is morality dead or alive by the end of the book? This would be a good place in your discussion to talk about your responses to the ending. Do you believe that justice was served? Look at this question from many points of reference: the dead girl and her parents, Judith, Carolyn, Ben, Jacob.

4. What is Carolyn's relationship with her son like prior to this murder and afterward? The scene where Ben tells Jacob what Carolyn has said to the grand jury is crucial to understanding the family dynamic. What is your response when Jacob does not reject Carolyn after her appearance before the grand jury, but rather embraces and tries to comfort her? What does Carolyn mean when she says to Jacob, "How could I have doubted you for a minute? Who did I think you were?"

5. Do you think Judith is the strongest member of the family? If you believe she is strong, what kind of strength does she have: morality, self-assuredness, resilience? Do you trust her version of events and relationships?

Other books by Rosellen Brown

Half a Heart features a comfortably middle-class white woman who is reunited with the daughter she left with the child's black father many years earlier. *Tender Mercies*, like *Before and After*, examines relationships in the aftermath of tragedy—in this case, a boating accident. Brown has published two other novels, *Civil Wars* and *The*

Autobiography of My Mother, a book of short stories titled *Street Games*, and three books of poetry.

If you like *Before and After*, you will like...

A Crime in the Neighborhood by Suzanne Berne. A murder in the neighborhood, a father's defection from his family told from the perspective of ten-year-old Marsha.

A Map of the World by Jane Hamilton. A tragedy occurs when a neighbor's daughter drowns in the Goodheart's pond.

Intimacy by Hanif Kureishi. Breakup of a marriage causes the husband/father to question exactly what it means to be both at the same time.

The Deep End of the Ocean by Jacquelyn Mitchard. Story of parents' worst nightmare when a son disappears almost before his mother's eyes.

Living to Tell by Antonya Nelson. Bumbling heroes, insomniacs, ugly secrets, ugly babies—all in a well-told tale.

Video resources

As divided as people may be in their opinions about the book, the film version of *Before and After* (1996) has everyone agreeing—it's bad. Though starring Meryl Streep and Liam Neeson with Barbet Schroeder as director, the movie never rises above melodrama with an all-too-neat happy ending. Both *The Deep End of the Ocean* (Ulu Grosbard, 1999) and *A Map of the World* (Scott Elliott, 2000) have been made into movies, with *A Map of the World* receiving very favorable critical and viewer response.

Internet resources

Read Don Lee's profile of Rosellen Brown in *Ploughshares: The Literary Journal of Emerson College* at www.pshares.org. Listen to an interview with Rosellen Brown on writing and mothers at www.npr.org.

Extra credit

How do authors come up with the ideas for their novels? Rosellen Brown has said that the seed for her novel came from a short article in a local newspaper about the brutal death of a young woman. She saved the article and several years later, wrote *Before and After*. Think like an author this month and find your own seeds for fiction. Each member should peruse the newspaper, keeping a file of articles that could become a story in the hands of a writer. Plan to share your files during your book group meeting.

June/Men and Family
Classic
The Rise of Silas Lapham by William Dean Howells, 1885, several paperback editions available, including one from Penguin for $10.95

What is this book about?

William Dean Howells's fine novel is a hybrid: part domestic family saga, part novel of manners, part pioneering novel of business life. It was the first to treat a character new to the American scene: the businessman. The novel's title suggests a rise in fortune. Silas Lapham, however, has already made his fortune. The novel's first scene shows him being interviewed for the "Solid Men of Boston" series in the local paper, in his element at his paint factory. Silas's speeches to the journalist illustrate his character: an appealing mixture of boastfulness, pride, down-home sensibility, and humility. He and his wife grew up in rural Vermont: having money isn't something they're entirely used to. As country people transplanted to the city, they've lived simply, never bothering to mix in Boston society because they're happier at home with their two daughters than out at fancy dinners. It has never occurred to Silas to use his wealth to buy an entrée to the upper echelon of Boston society. But when the novel opens, he is about to consider just that.

As the newspaper article makes clear, Silas Lapham has made it in the business world, but he occupies no position whatsoever socially. His two daughters, Penelope and Irene, are old enough to marry, but know no likely suitors. A chance meeting between Mrs. Lapham and an aristocratic Boston socialite, Mrs. Corey, introduces them to one: Tom Corey, ambitious and eager to find meaningful work, intrigued by Penelope's arch irony and captivated by Irene's sweetness and beauty. The drama of this novel unfolds partly through the interactions between the *arrivistes* Laphams and the Coreys, an old Boston family, and partly through the expectation aroused by the title—every rise must have its fall.

Did you know...?

The term **literary realism** refers to both a writing style and a subject matter. William Dean Howells called it "the truthful treatment of material." Realist writing attempts to present everyday life as it really is in an accurate, objective manner. It typically takes the middle classes for its subject. Realist writers often use dialogue or dialect to convey people's real speech patterns. Characterization, rather than plot, becomes the focus of the realist novel. Besides Howells, Henry James and Mark Twain are the best known American realists.

What should I know about the author?

William Dean Howells was born in Ohio in 1837. He began his writing career as editor of the *Ohio State Journal*. The year 1860 was pivotal: he met his future wife and published a campaign biography for Abraham Lincoln titled *Lives and Speeches of Abraham Lincoln*. Howells began publishing more widely and traveled to Boston and New York, where he met important literary figures. In 1861, he was appointed U.S. Consul to Venice, where he lived for four years. When he returned to America, Howells accepted a post as assistant editor at *Atlantic Monthly*; he would later wield enormous influence as its editor. He wrote prolifically until his death in 1920.

Questions for reflection and discussion

1. *The Rise of Silas Lapham* opens with an interview. The interviewer and the reader are in similar positions—each needing to find out what Silas Lapham is like. Why do you think Howells structures the first chapter in this way? How does the interview convey information about Lapham's character? What is your opinion of him by the end of the first chapter? Does Howells want him to be a sympathetic character? Bartley Hubbard obviously views him ironically. Does your opinion follow Hubbard's?

2. Writers have long made use of the country versus city theme. When Silas tries to ingratiate himself with the Coreys, his scornful wife must remind him, "We're both country people, and we've kept our country ways." What country ways have the Laphams retained? What are the city or society ways to which they aspire? Why would this theme of country versus city have such lasting appeal for novelists? How does Howells make it clear to the reader that the Coreys belong in quite another class? The Coreys condemn the Laphams, but does Howells? One tenet of literary realism is that the narrator presents material through an objective, neutral voice. Do we ever see Howells abandoning neutrality?

3. Howells is obviously interested in investigating the connection between the personal life of the family and the public life of business. Persis and Silas built their paint factory together, though by the time the novel opens, Persis is no longer involved in the daily workings of the business. What was Persis's role in the business? How were things different at the factory when Persis followed its daily workings? If Persis had stayed involved, would Silas have been able to maintain his business and keep his fortune? The personal and professional is further complicated by Tom Corey, who works for Silas, but is also a potential son-in-law. Silas says repeatedly that "the two things won't mix." But why not? Why does Persis caution him about overinvolving Tom?

4. The unfolding relationship between Tom Corey and the Lapham sisters provides the novel with structure and suspense. When did

you realize that Corey is interested in Penelope, not Irene? If you go back and look at their scenes together, at what point does Corey himself realize he's more interested in Penelope? Why do the Laphams—and the Coreys—all make the mistake of assuming Corey prefers Irene? How unconventional is Howells's decision to make the not-so-pretty sister the more desirable one?

5. *The Rise of Silas Lapham* is considered an important realist novel. What aspects of its style, subject matter, or technique point to literary realism? Why might American writers in the late nineteenth century have become so interested in realism? What are other options? Are most novels written today still realist in style? If this style of novel is the preferred one with your group, your members might discuss its appeal and also what it is about other types of novels that do not appeal. Consider science fiction, horror, western, romance.

Other books by William Dean Howells

Howells was extraordinarily prolific and influential. You can find a detailed bibliography of all of his works at the website for the William Dean Howells Society (listed below). Readers of *Silas Lapham* can learn more about the marriage of journalist Bartley Hubbard in *A Modern Instance* (1882), one of the first novels to investigate the new social issue of divorce. *A Hazard of New Fortunes* (1890), set in New York and examining life among all the social classes, is considered by many to be his finest novel.

Books about William Dean Howells

As a major proponent of literary realism, Howells is the focus of many critical studies. Kenneth Eble's *William Dean Howells* (1982) is published as part of the Twayne series of critical studies which are generally short, accessible accounts of a writer's life and works. Find out what literary scholars now think about *The Rise of Silas Lapham* in *New Essays on The Rise of Silas Lapham*, edited by Donald E. Pease. The standard biography is Kenneth S. Lynn's *William Dean Howells: An American Life*.

If you like *The Rise of Silas Lapham*, you will like...

Democracy: An American Novel by Henry Adams. Set in Washington in the 1870s, this novel proves that politics have always been corrupt.

The Bostonians by Henry James. Set in the same city as *The Rise of Silas Lapham*, this James novel takes the women's rights movement as its subject.

The Silent Partner by Elizabeth Stuart Phelps. Fascinating novel about a woman factory owner written by a contemporary of Howell.

The Adventures of Huckleberry Finn by Mark Twain. Twain was one of Howells's closest friends.

The House of Mirth and *The Age of Innocence* by Edith Wharton. Wharton's masterpieces minutely dissect upper-class New York society.

Extra credit

Learn more about working conditions at the factories that sprang up across New England in the nineteenth century by scheduling a visit to Lowell, Massachusetts, where you can tour textile mills. The Lowell National Park website provides information at www.nps.gov/lowe/.

Video resources

Several of the further reading suggestions above have been made into movies, with Henry James and Edith Wharton being especially well served by Hollywood. *The Bostonians* (James Ivory, 1984) stars Christopher Reeve and Vanessa Redgrave. Jane Campion's gorgeous *Portrait of a Lady* (1996) stars Nicole Kidman as Isabel Archer. The critically acclaimed *Wings of the Dove* (Iain Softley, 1997) stars Helena Bonham Carter. *Washington Square* (Agnieska Holland,

1997) is also worth a look. Fifteen years after making *The Bostonians*, Merchant-Ivory returned to James with an adaptation of *The Golden Bowl* (James Ivory, 2000). *The Age of Innocence* (Martin Scorsese, 1993) was well received by critics. *The House of Mirth* (2000) was brilliantly adapted by Terence Davies, with Gillian Anderson delivering a fine performance as Lily Bart.

Internet resources

William Dean Howells has his own society. They maintain a fantastic scholarly site with tons of information and links at www.gonzaga.edu/faculty/campbell/howells.

June/Men and Family
Challenge
Native Speaker by Chang-Rae Lee, 1995, available in paperback from Riverhead Books for $12.95

What is this book about?

Native Speaker opens with the list Henry Park's wife, Lelia, hands him as she leaves him: "You are surreptitious, B+ student of life, first thing hummer of Wagner and Strauss, illegal alien, genre bug, Yellow peril: neo-American, great in bed, overrated, poppa's boy, sentimentalist, anti-romantic, _____ analyst (you fill in), stranger, follower, traitor, spy." Widely quoted in reviews of the novel, the list sets up the main themes of the novel. Identity and alienation, culture and family predominate. But the most damning entry never makes it onto the list. Instead, Henry finds what he considers the key written on a scrap: *"False speaker of language."*

Korean-American Henry Park is a spy. His job is often prosaic—watching people, researching their lives, writing reports about them. But its consequences can be far-reaching and devastating—to the individual and, we discover, to the community. Conflicting loyalties emerge after Henry is hired to infiltrate the campaign headquarters of John Kwang, a successful Korean-American businessman who plans to run for mayor. Spying is not something Henry does, but rather something that he is. "To be a true spy of identity, you must be a spy of the culture." The professional bleeds into the personal, the personal—to Henry's boss's displeasure—into the professional. Henry has been practicing all of his life for this particular job.

But *Native Speaker* cannot really be described as a spy novel. Intricately plotted and structured, written in extraordinarily evocative language, it examines questions of family and culture, community and identity.

What should I know about the author?

Born in 1968 in Seoul, Lee immigrated to the United States at age three. His family settled in Westchester County, New York, where his father learned English and practiced as a psychiatrist. Lee attended Yale University and worked on Wall Street before pursuing his "love of writing" with an M.F.A. from the University of Oregon. After earning his degree, he taught in the creative writing program at the University of Oregon. He now lives in New Jersey with his wife and daughter.

Questions for reflection and discussion

1. *Native Speaker* depicts many marriages: Henry's parents, Jack and Sophie, John Kwang and May, Alice and Stew, and of course, Henry and Lelia. In fact, the novel is organized around the disintegration of their marriage and their slow, painful reconciliation. What models of marriage do these couples provide for Henry and Lelia? What's wrong with Henry's and Lelia's marriage? How is Henry failing her? Is Lelia failing Henry in any way? Do you sympathize with one more than with the other? What is worth saving in this relationship?

2. Fatherhood and family relationships are a central theme in *Native Speaker*. Think about Henry's relationships as father and as son, including relationships with father figures like Jack, Luzan, and John Kwang. Dennis Hoagland's intelligence agency and John Kwang's campaign headquarters are also largely structured as

family relationships. Why is family so important in this novel about language, identity, culture, and assimilation? How would you characterize the different father/son pairings?

3. Henry tells Lelia, "When I was a teenager, I so wanted to be familiar and friendly with my parents like my white friends were with theirs. You know, they'd use curses with each other, make fun of each other at dinner, maybe even get drunk together on holidays." Lelia replies, "It's not so goddamn wonderful, you know." How does Henry characterize his parents' parenting style? How is this different from an American style of parenting?

4. Although Lelia insists on sending their son to Korean school, Henry wants Mitt to grow up "univocal" in the hopes that this will give Mitt "the authority and confidence that his broad half-yellow face could not." In this novel, language *is* identity: what you speak and how you speak it is who you are. But Henry considers himself a native speaker of no language. How does his identity develop or evolve based on the languages he does and doesn't speak? How can he form a cultural identity as a Korean-American when he can't speak Korean fluently or comfortably? How many of the items on Lelia's list are related to Henry's issues with language? Is Henry right in believing Mitt will have a better chance if he doesn't try to bridge two cultures?

5. Why do you think Chang-Rae Lee makes Henry Park a spy? We usually think of spy literature as exciting and suspenseful, but Henry's job is anything but alluring. How would it change the book for Henry not to be a spy? How does his work help us understand his position as a nonnative speaker in between cultures?

Other books by Chang-Rae Lee

Some of the themes from *Native Speaker* recur in Lee's widely acclaimed second novel, *A Gesture Life* (1999), about an elderly Japanese immigrant looking back on his World War II experiences.

If you like *Native Speaker,* you will like...

Donald Duk: A Novel by Frank Chin. Story of a twelve-year-old Chinese-American boy and his struggles for identity.

Chinhominey's Secret by Nancy Kim. Debut novel about a Korean-American family and the prophecy that has followed the family for twenty years.

China Men by Maxine Hong Kingston. Combination of memoir, myth, and fiction about four generations of the men in Kingston's family.

Yellow by Don Lee. A debut collection of short stories about Asians living in white America.

China Boy by Gus Lee. A novel about the struggles of a Chinese-American boy growing up in the 1950s in an African-American neighborhood in San Francisco.

DISCUSSION/REFLECTION STRATEGY

Any of this month's selections can be paired with a video for a discussion of relationship between fathers and sons. Choose one or two films to watch and see what themes emerge that resonate with those of your book selection. We recommend *Parenthood* (Ron Howard, 1989), *October Sky* (Joe Johnston, 1999), *A River Runs Through It* (Robert Redford, 1992), *Kramer vs. Kramer* (Robert Benton, 1979), and *The Great Santini* (Lewis John Carlino, 1979). Both *EdTV* (Ron Howard, 1999) and *The Truman Show* (Peter Weir, 1998) are about "reality" television, but each includes touching explorations of the father/son theme. Finally, Thomas Vinterberg's 1998 film from Denmark, *Festen* (or *The Celebration*), is an exceptionally powerful film about a young man returning home for his father's birthday party and simply telling the truth.

Video resources

First Person Plural, a documentary by Deann Borshay Liem, who was adopted from Korea by an American couple in 1966, narrates her trip back to Korea to find her birth family. Find out more at www.naatanet.org, which is the National Asian American Telecommunications Association website. *Yellow* is a feature film written and directed by Chris Chan Lee (1998) about a group of adolescent Korean-American males coming of age in Los Angeles.

Internet resources

Find a reader's guide to *Native Speaker*, including detailed discussion questions, at www.penguinputnam.com/static/rguides/us/native_speaker.html. Read an interview with Lee at www.nytimes.com/books/99/09/05/reviews/990905.05garnet.html. Listen to Lee read from *A Gesture Life* at www.wcpn.org/schedule/schedules/2001/book-club.html. Visit a website on Maxine Hong Kingston for informative links on Asian-American literature and history at falcon.jmu. edu/~ramseyil/kingston.htm.

June/Men and Family
Memoir
A Heartbreaking Work of Staggering Genius by Dave Eggers, 2000, available in paperback from Vintage Books for $14.00

What is this book about?

Dave Eggers was twenty-one when his parents died of cancer within five weeks of one another. Though he had help from his two older siblings, Eggers became the primary caretaker of his younger brother, eight-year-old Toph. This memoir covers the period of Eggers's twenties as he raises his brother and tries to establish himself as a magazine publisher.

A Heartbreaking Work of Staggering Genius consists of deeply moving accounts of sad occurrences—Eggers description of his mother's last weeks will be painful and familiar to anyone who has ever taken care of the terminally ill—and hysterically funny renderings of conversations and situations among the Bay Area twentysomethings of the 1990s. But what makes this a "work of staggering genius" is that

Eggers does not merely alternate between comedy and drama: he shows comedy and tragedy as two sides of the same coin. Life is present in all its messiness.

The book not only challenges the conventional dichotomy between the sad and the funny, it also challenges the expectations we have of memoirs. We expect them to be faithful, if somewhat biased, renderings of what happened in someone's life. Within the prefatory sections (which should not be missed), Eggers calls into question the issue of truthfulness in memoirs. Names and identifying characteristics need to be changed to protect privacy, conversations need to be reconstructed, and timing of certain events changed in order to make the narrative readable. Eggers is not only writing a memoir, he is writing about writing a memoir.

What should I know about the author?

Dave Eggers was born in 1971 and grew up in Lake Forest, Illinois, with his parents and three siblings. Since leaving Lake Forest, he has worked as a cartoonist, an office temp, a graphic designer, and a freelance writer. In 1993, he cofounded the short-lived *Might Magazine* in San Francisco. Eggers currently edits *McSweeney's*, an online journal which also publishes contemporary fiction. *A Heartbreaking Work of Staggering Genius* is his first book.

Questions for reflection and discussion

1. Does Dave Eggers come across to you as a reliable narrator? This is a tricky question since in the preface to the book Eggers candidly rejects literal truth as the basis of this (or any) memoir. How does this rejection of complete truth affect your trust in the narrator? Does wondering about the veracity of the author affect your reading of the text?

2. Does the life lived by the Eggers children after the death of their parents reject or uphold the values and standards set by their parents? How did the Eggers live before the parents became ill? What does Dave Eggers tell us about how the children were brought up? Does Eggers think they were a happy family? What effects did the

father's alcoholism have on his family? How does Eggers structure his own parenting of Toph? Does he reject how he was parented, or does he try to retain some of what his parents gave him?

3. At several points in the text, Eggers uses the image of a "lattice" to illustrate his sense of community. Why does he think this image is important? What are his hopes and dreams for his network of friends, acquaintances, and other people of his own age? How does MTV's show *The Real World* fit into Eggers's dream of community? Why is it important to him to audition for the show?

4. List the rhetorical strategies (or gimmicks—if they annoy you) Eggers employs in this book. What does he do that one does not find in traditionally structured narratives? Do you find his self-consciousness liberating or frustrating? How did reading the preface(s) affect your reading of the book? Will reading the preface to this book alter how you approach other memoirs? Is it ever possible to take these conventions (the reconstruction of dialogue, the coherent narrative flow) at face value?

5. The 2001 paperback edition of the book contains an addendum titled "Mistakes We Knew We Were Making," in which Eggers expands on the issues raised in the preface to the book. In an extended passage, Eggers objects to the fact that people call his book, or portions of it, ironic. He defines irony as "the use of words to express something different from and often opposite to their literal meaning." He then argues that there are few instances in his book that meet that definition. It is not necessarily ironic to employ humor when recounting difficult stories. Is this true? Is Eggers's definition of irony correct? Is it, perhaps, too narrow? Do you think the book has an ironic tone? Your group may want to explore why Eggers felt a need to justify himself to his original readers in this addendum.

Other works by Dave Eggers

A Heartbreaking Work of Staggering Genius and *You Shall Know Our Velocity* are Egger's only books so far. For other written material by him see the Internet Resources section below.

If you like *A Heartbreaking Work of Staggering Genius,* you will like...

My Misspent Youth by Meghan Daum. Essays by a writer in her twenties who has already published in prestigious magazines like the *New Yorker* and *Harper's.*

Fraud by David Rakoff. Self-conscious, wide-ranging essays.

Me Talk Pretty One Day and *Barrel Fever* by David Sedaris. Biting, hilarious essays and stories about family life by the frequent NPR contributor.

A Supposedly Fun Thing I'll Never Do Again: Essays and Arguments by David Foster Wallace. Witty, self-analytical essays.

Video resources

Ordinary People (Robert Redford, 1980) takes place in Eggers's hometown, Lake Forest, Illinois, and chronicles the anger and despair suffocating a middle-class family. Another tale of violent emotions simmering beneath the surface of middle-class respectability is Ang Lee's 1997 film *The Ice Storm.*

Internet resources

An interview with Dave Eggers can be found at www.salon.com in which he specifically addresses his relationship with Toph and his thoughts on parenting. The site also includes book reviews written by Eggers. www.mcsweeneys.net is Dave Eggers's online quarterly review of literature.

June/Men and Family
Potluck
The Lone Ranger and Tonto Fistfight in Heaven by Sherman Alexie, 1993, available in paperback from Harper-Perennial for $13.00

What is this book about?

Set on the same Spokane Indian Reservation where Alexie himself grew up, the stories collected in *The Lone Ranger and Tonto Fistfight in Heaven* feature a diverse cast of characters and a range of styles. Some stories are realistic, while others are dreamlike, even mystical. The "I" of one chapter is not always the "I" of another chapter. What ties this collection together is setting. Each story deals with life on the rez—how men, women, and children cope with the rampant alcoholism, high unemployment, inferior schools, unwholesome diets, and general despair that characterize reservation life. "Why should we organize a reservation high school reunion?" Victor asks. "My graduating class has a reunion every weekend at the Powwow Tavern." You might expect such subject matter to lead to extremely bleak fiction. As Alexie notes, "It's hard to be optimistic on the reservation." But Alexie's sense of humor and spirit cannot be overcome even by the dismal circumstances that fuel his fiction. These are very funny, even laugh-out-loud, stories.

Extra credit

Attend an author reading and book signing. Local bookstores host authors on tour to promote recently published books, while universities invite authors to lecture. Many public libraries also host author events. Call bookstores, universities, and libraries near you and ask to be placed on the mailing list for upcoming events, or check out publishers' websites for your favorite authors to find out if and when they're on tour. Your local newspaper runs announcements of readings in the current events section. Authors' websites are also a good source for more information. Sherman Alexie's website, for example, lists every date and place where you can find Alexie for the next year!

What should I know about the author?

Sherman Alexie, born in 1966 to a Spokane mother and a Coeur d'Alene father, did not grow up planning to be a writer. In fact, he claims never to have read a book by a Native American writer until he was twenty-one and in college. He grew up on the Spokane Indian Reservation in Washington, and, like one of his characters in *The Lone Ranger and Tonto Fistfight in Heaven*, left the reservation to attend a white high school where he played basketball. He attended Washington State University in Pullman and planned to pursue a career in medicine until he discovered poetry in a poetry workshop. He published *The Business of Fancydancing*, a poetry collection, just one year after graduating from college; his success as a writer encouraged him to win a battle against alcoholism. Since then, he has written prolifically—poetry, short stories, novels, films, music, essays, columns—and collected dozens of awards. He currently lives in Seattle with his wife and child, but he spends much of the year traveling across the country and lecturing.

Questions for reflection and discussion

1. Alexie has been praised by readers and reviewers for his tough, honest look at contemporary life on Indian reservations. What is life on the rez like? How does Alexie write about the family? What images or scenes stick out for you? Alexie confronts serious social problems in his fiction. Does he suggest solutions? His memorable formula is "Survival = Anger + Imagination." Is there more anger or imagination at work in *The Lone Ranger and Tonto Fistfight in Heaven*? How does this combination ensure survival? We see Alexie using his imagination, but how do his characters use their imaginations to survive?

2. Alexie depicts modern Indian life as being steeped in ancient native traditions and beliefs. The importance of storytelling becomes central in the stories about Thomas Builds-the-Fire, while a number of Alexie's alter egos want to be warriors. Dancing is a recurring motif, as are dreams and visions. How do Indians on the reservation preserve their culture? How does Alexie use his tribe's culture to craft and produce fiction? The character of Thomas Builds-the-Fire is especially interesting. Thomas tells stories compulsively, but no one will listen. What kind of comment is this on the artist's role?

3. "Indians need heroes to help them learn how to survive." Several of the stories in *The Lone Ranger and Tonto Fistfight in Heaven* explore

the search for heroes in musicians, basketball players, local Indians who accomplish amazing feats. Are there any fathers among the heroes? Why are heroes so important on the reservation? Why is it so hard for Victor and the other characters to find heroes? You might look closely at "The Only Traffic Signal on the Reservation Doesn't Flash Red Anymore." What role models does our culture provide for Native American children? Should white Americans teach their children about Native American history and heroes? What does the title suggest about this issue?

4. Why do you think Alexie calls himself and his people "Indians" rather than "Native Americans"? Targeted to a mixed audience of whites and Native Americans, *The Lone Ranger and Tonto Fistfight in Heaven* comments frequently on the history and current state of white-Indian relations. Which of the many comparisons between how things happen on the reservation and how they happen "in the outside world" most struck you? Elsewhere, Alexie has compared the white European treatment of Native Americans to the Holocaust and called it genocide. How can centuries of abuse, mistreatment, and mass murder ever be rectified? Do you think it's possible for whites and Indians ever to bridge the gap that divides them in *The Lone Ranger and Tonto Fistfight in Heaven?*

5. Because Alexie employs such diverse styles to tell these stories, this book is a great choice for book groups to begin a study of the short story. Which stories are your favorites? Do you prefer first-person narration or third? Stories with an organizational "hook," like "Jesus Christ's Half-Brother Is Alive and Well on the Spokane Indian Reservation" or "Indian Education"? Straightforward, realistic stories or mystical stories? As in most collections, the quality does vary from story to story. What marks a story as one that will stand the test of time? What patterns emerge about your own reading tastes based on your preferences in short stories?

Other books by Sherman Alexie
Alexie's astonishing productivity has led Bruce Barcott, writing in *The Salon.com Reader's Guide to Contemporary Authors*, to dub him a "one-man cultural industry." His poetry collections include: *The Business of*

Fancydancing: Stories and Poems (1992), First Indian on the Moon (1993), The Summer of Black Widows (1996), The Man Who Loves Salmon (1998), and One Stick Song (2000), which also includes prose pieces. He is best known for his fiction: Reservation Blues (1995), which stars some of the characters from The Lone Ranger and Tonto Fistfight in Heaven; the controversial Indian Killer (1996), a thriller about a serial killer whose signature is to scalp his victims; and The Toughest Indian in the World (2000), a collection of short stories.

If you like *The Lone Ranger and Tonto Fistfight in Heaven*, you will like...

The Remains of River Names by Matt Briggs. Interlinked stories about a family in the Pacific Northwest.

Jesus' Son by Denis Johnson. A collection of linked stories narrated by a heroin addict. Made into an excellent film starring Billy Crudup.

Green Grass, Running Water by Thomas King. Linked stories with each chapter starring a different character.

Walking the Rez Road by James Northrup. This collection follows a group of characters who live on a Chippewa reservation in Minnesota.

Grand Avenue by Greg Sarris. Stories centering on one community in California, written by a Native author.

Did you know...?

The film adaptation of *Smoke Signals* was billed as the first Native American film written, directed by, and starring Native Americans. But *Smoke Signals* is not the only film dealing with life on the rez. *Smoke Signals* has been compared to *Dance Me Outside* (Bruce McDonald, 1995), which also stars Adam Beach and focuses on young men coming to terms with reservation life. Alexie adored *Powwow Highway* (Jonathan Wacks, 1989), a buddy on-the-road movie, when he first saw it, though he now considers it shamefully stereotypical. *Dances with Wolves* (Kevin Costner, 1990) has been much maligned for presenting such a cuddly view of the Lakota Sioux, but Costner and company are to be commended for using Native Americans in Native parts and for insisting on the use of the Lakota language. Graham Greene, familiar to viewers of *Dances with Wolves*, stars in *Medicine River* (Stuart Margolin, 1993) and in *Thunderheart* (Michael Apted, 1992). Read Alexie's hilariously pointed critique of Hollywood Indians at www.fallsapart.com/tonto.html.

Video resources

Alexie wrote the screenplay for the critically acclaimed film, *Smoke Signals* (Chris Eyre, 1998), basing the script on "This Is What It Means to Say Phoenix, Arizona," a short story in *The Lone Ranger and Tonto Fistfight in Heaven*. The film won the coveted Sundance Film Festival Audience Award in 1998. He has just completed directing a digital film based on his first published work, *The Business of Fancydancing*. Read about Alexie's other film projects at his official website, the address for which is listed below.

Internet resources

Eager to promote himself and his work, Sherman Alexie is all over the Web. The Official Sherman Alexie Website is a must-visit; the site organizes an incredible wealth of information by and about Alexie: www.fallsapart.com. Listen to Alexie read from *The Toughest Indian in the World* at www.salon.com/audio/2000/10/05/alexie/. Learn more about Alexie's tribes, Spokane and Coeur d'Alene, at www .spokanetribe.com and www.rootsweb.com/~idreserv/cdhist.html. Alexie contributed a series of "What I'm Reading Now" columns at www.contentville.com.

CHAPTER 7
July
Women's Journeys

CROWD-PLEASER
On Pilgrimage by Jennifer Lash

CLASSIC
Travels in West Africa by Mary Kingsley

CHALLENGE
Passionate Nomad by Jane Fletcher
Geniesse

MEMOIR
*Beyond the Sky and the Earth: A Journey
into Bhutan* by Jamie Zeppa

POTLUCK
Talking to High Monks in the Snow
by Lydia Minatoya

To my taste there is nothing so fascinating as spending a night out in an
African forest, or plantation; but I beg you to note I do not advise anyone to
follow the practice. Nor indeed do I recommend African forest life to anyone.
Unless you are interested in it and fall under its charm, it is the most awful
life in death imaginable. It is like being shut up in a library whose books you
cannot read, all the while tormented, terrified, and bored. And if you do fall
under its spell, it takes all the colour out of other kinds of living.

—Mary Kingsley, *Travels in West Africa*

The selections for July prove that travel writing is alive and well. Travel memoirs became popular when all travel was hard travel, and there was little access to pictures of different places. Though traveling is easier than it has ever been and we are saturated with images from around the globe, the travel memoir retains its appeal. Why? Maybe because good writing is about both the physical journey and the inner journey—not only where travelers go, but how they are changed by the experience.

Jennifer Lash travels over well-worn paths in her pilgrimage to religious sites in France and Spain, using her journey to facilitate physical and spiritual healing after undergoing cancer treatment. The formidable Mary Kingsley, Victorian gentlewoman and African explorer, describes rainforests, friendly cannibals, and what it is like to wade through leech-filled swamps in *Travels in West Africa*. Jane Fletcher Geniesse's biography of Freya Stark is a fascinating look at another intrepid solo traveler. Jamie Zeppa traveled to Bhutan to teach English, intending to stay for two years, but remaining for eight. Lydia Minatoya's account of living in Okinawa and traveling in China and Nepal shares with Zeppa's story a humorous and touching look at negotiating cultural difference. But Minatoya, unlike Zeppa, is returning to the land of her parents, looking for the places they lived, and hoping to find herself.

July/Women's Journeys
Crowd-Pleaser
On Pilgrimage: A Time to Seek by Jennifer Lash, 1999, available in paperback from Bloomsbury for $15.95

What is this book about?

No longer a practicing Catholic, but desiring to observe practices of faith, novelist Jennifer Lash set out on a pilgrimage across France, following the ancient path to Santiago de Compostela in Spain. Battling cancer, Lash was not on a pilgrimage of thanksgiving, as her fellow pilgrims were, but rather on "a quest, a general, rather random voyage of discovery." What she wanted to discover was hazy even to herself.

Embarking on a pilgrimage, she thought, and taking time to observe would surely lead to discovery. What Lash ultimately learns and articulates about the struggle to believe was well worth the journey.

Near the end of her pilgrimage, Lash visits a Buddhist monastery in France and finds herself drawn to Buddhist tenets of mindfulness, practice, and diligence. And no wonder: she had been practicing her faith mindfully and diligently throughout her journey. Lash lodges in monasteries and cloisters, visits saints' homes, views relics, converses with holy men and women, describes holy sites, meditates in cathedrals. In Lash, readers will find a travel writer with keen powers of observation and a lively curiosity. *On Pilgrimage: A Time to Seek* recounts no great leap of faith and no epiphany. Rather, this is a book that encourages believers and nonbelievers to meditate on the power of faith to sustain, on the power of connection with fellow seekers to transform.

What should I know about the author?

Born in England in 1938, Jini Fiennes (pronounced Fines), as Jennifer Lash was known to friends and family, published her first novel in 1961. Two more novels appeared, but then the demands—and joys—of family life superseded. She gave up writing fiction for fifteen years. Lash's difficult childhood would furnish her with dark material for her fiction, but her own marriage and family life were happy. She and her husband led a peripatetic life, moving fifteen times in as many years. Their seven children would grow up to be enormously accomplished: actors Ralph Fiennes and Joseph, film director Martha, actor and producer Sophie, and composer Magnus. Only Jacob, a gamekeeper, and adopted son Mike Emery, an archaeologist, are not in the film business. Fiennes died of cancer in 1993, shortly after the publication of *On Pilgrimage*.

Questions for reflection and discussion

1. *On Pilgrimage* is subtitled *A Time to Seek*. It's clear why, after diagnosis and treatment of cancer, this would be the right time for Lash to embark on a pilgrimage. But what is she seeking? What does she think she can find on a pilgrimage that she can't find at home?

When she does return home, she finds herself depressed, in "the most disorienting dark." What do you make of this reaction, and what might Lash have done to preserve some of the spirit of her pilgrimage at home?

2. "Being with people whose whole lifestyle is a demonstration of their certainty and focus can be unnerving if you are unsure yourself," Lash writes. Does she want to become sure of something on this journey? Why is it ironic for a woman who describes herself as not an "ardent believer" to structure a journey around organized religion? What are her criticisms of Catholicism? Does she too readily assume that the nuns she stays with have found the answers?

3. Your group may use *On Pilgrimage* to launch a discussion about differences in religious belief and faith among group members. Were you raised in a religious household? What were your parents' beliefs? Did you attend services in a place of worship? Would you describe your faith as strong? Is it difficult to live without strong religious beliefs? What does faith mean to you?

4. Lash discovers that many of the important sites of pilgrimage have become distressingly commercialized. Why is it a problem for a pilgrimage to be too well-organized? Why do you think sites of pilgrimage attract so many tourists? Lash makes some interesting distinctions between tourists and pilgrims. Why do you think she scoffs at one and welcomes the other?

5. After experiencing cancer, Lash realizes, "I had for some time been voting myself out of life. I had been diving for the dark. Feeling driven, of course; but there is always choice. Considering *Death* had meant considering *Life*. I knew that now, I had made a firm decision towards life, not for length of time, that wasn't the point, but to find fresh ways of liberating its quality." Why isn't "length of time" the point for Lash? Do we need a life-threatening illness to make us reconsider the way we're living? What fresh means of liberation has Lash discovered at the end of her journey? What qualities in your life need liberating?

Other books by Jennifer Lash

Lash is the author of seven novels: *The Burial* (1961), *The Climate of Belief* (1962), *The Prism* (1963), *Get Down There and Die* (1977), *The Dust Collector* (1979), *From May to October* (1980), and critically acclaimed *Blood Ties* (1998). Her novels typically explore dark themes, such as dysfunctional families and mental illness.

If you like *On Pilgrimage*, you will like...

Ultimate Journey: Retracing the Path of an Ancient Buddhist Monk Who Crossed Asia in Search of Enlightenment by Richard Bernstein. Bernstein journeys in the footsteps of a seventh-century Chinese monk, whose spiritual quest lasted fifteen years.

The Pilgrimage Road to Santiago: The Complete Cultural Handbook by Linda Kay Davidson and David M. Gitlitz. Comprehensive guide to art, shrines, and historical sites along the famous Christian pilgrimage road to Santiago, Spain.

Walking the Bible: A Journey by Land Through the Five Books of Moses by Bruce Feiler. Feiler's personal journey through the physical and spiritual geography of the Holy Land.

Pilgrimage Stories: On and Off the Road to Santiago by Nancy Frey. Told from the perspective of modern-day pilgrims—both as a narrative of their quest and as an exploration of how their lives were affected by their journeys.

A Woman's Path: Women's Best Spiritual Travel Writing edited by Lucy McCauley, Amy Carlson, and Jennifer Leo. Inspiring stories of women who discover self-truths and inner peace through their travels.

Video resources

While none of Lash's works have been filmed yet, you may be interested in viewing *Onegin* (1999), something of a Fiennes family affair: directed by Martha Fiennes, starring Ralph Fiennes (look also for

Sophie Fiennes in a small part), with music composed by Magnus Fiennes. A documentary on some of the sites Lash writes about might also be informative. Look for *In Search of History: Lourdes* and *Lourdes: Pilgrimage and Healing* (2000).

Internet resources

Don't miss Jennifer Lash's page at members.aol.com/SFSibley/ JiniLnks.htm. It contains links to information about Lash, including brief biographies, interviews, articles, reviews, obituaries, and interviews with her children. Of special interest to readers of *On Pilgrimage* are the photos Lash took while on her pilgrimage. Check out the family photographs and articles about the publicity tour undertaken by Ralph, Sophie, and Joseph Fiennes to promote their mother's posthumously published novel, *Blood Ties*, at www.angelfire.com/biz5/ beeswing/lashindex.html.

July/ Women's Journeys
Classic
Travels in West Africa by Mary Kingsley, 1897, available in paperback from the Phoenix Press for $16.95

What is this book about?

Mary Kingsley traveled to the western coast of central Africa twice during the 1890s. With little money and no traveling companions, she went to complete her father's research on the spiritual practices of African tribes of the west coast and to collect fish and reptile specimens for the British Museum. Her travels were difficult and make for fascinating reading. She had to contend with extremes of heat and cold, snakes, leeches, swamps, boat trips through rapids, and armies of mosquitoes. She met with European missionaries, traders, bureaucrats, military personnel (the English, French, and Germans had colonized most of West Africa), local chieftains, cannibals, and traders. Kingsley did all of this while dressed in the full regalia of respectable Victorian womanhood—voluminous skirts, long-sleeved blouses, stockings, boots, and hats.

Mary Kingsley recounts her story with energy and wit. She is especially good when describing the spiritual beliefs of the Africans she encounters since she respects the people and refuses to categorize them as either savages in need of salvation or as child-like and in need of protection.

What should I know about the author?

Mary Kingsley lived from 1862 until 1900. She was the daughter of George Kingsley, who trained as a doctor but spent most of his life as an explorer and traveler. Mary Kingsley's mother did not accompany her husband on his travels, instead remaining in London to raise their children and maintain the family home. Kingsley did not have any formal education, but read a great deal on her own, especially the books on travel that formed the basis of her father's library. She nursed her parents through their final illnesses; she set out for Africa soon after their deaths. *Travels in West Africa* was a popular success, and Kingsley became a sought-after lecturer when she returned to England. She traveled to Cape Town during the Boer War intending to nurse soldiers, but caught a fever and died on June 3, 1900.

Questions for reflection and discussion

1. Why does Mary Kingsley say she is going to Africa? Does her early life at home suggest other reasons for going? Do you think she has goals and desires that she does not express?

2. What objections does Mary Kingsley have toward missionaries? Does she have any sympathy with their goals or methods? Why or why not? Do you agree with her assessment of them? Why does she exempt the Jacots from this criticism? Why does she prefer the company of traders? Discuss this quotation: "If the aim of life were happiness and pleasure, Africa should send us missionaries instead of our sending them to her—but, fortunately for the work of the world, happiness is not."

3. *Travels in West Africa* is filled with wonderful stories. What are your favorite anecdotes from Kingsley's tale? What most surprised you

about what she says and does? What were some of the more frightening moments she experienced? What do you think of her style of writing? Do you find her funny? How does her literary style affect your reading of her memoir? Do you find her an inspirational figure?

4. There are several anecdotes in the book that mark Mary Kingsley as a person from a particular place and time. For example, she refuses to change her style of dress; she wears in western Africa the same things she wears in England. She drinks tea every day. She refuses to walk in front of a man during a particular trek for fear that he will see that she has used a shoe lace as a "stay-lace." The note sent to her by the trader who thought she was a man embarrasses her. Yet she is traveling under difficult circumstances with little money and no friends. She endures physical hardship and is a demanding and effective boss to the native men she employs. Are these different aspects of her personality contradictory? What accounts for her ability to do all these things? Why is she not afraid?

5. One of the pleasantly surprising aspects of *Travels in West Africa* for the modern reader is Kingsley's refusal to consider all inhabitants of the vast continent of Africa as alike. Though she sometimes says things that make us wince (for example, when she discusses the inferiority of native languages), she recognizes the distinctions among tribes and among individuals. Why does she especially like the Fan tribesmen? What characteristics do they exhibit that she admires? In the chapter, "Stalking the Wild West African Idea," Kingsley exhorts all those who wish to understand the cultures of African to put aside their own ideas about religion and opinions about life. Why does she think this is important, and does she live up to her own ideal?

Books about Mary Kingsley

Kingsley's short life has been treated in two recent biographies: *Mary Kingsley: Imperial Adventuress* by Dea Birkett and Katherine Frank's excellent *A Voyager Out: The Life of Mary Kingsley*. Caroline Alexander recreated Kingsley's journey one hundred years later in *One Dry Season: In the Footsteps of Mary Kingsley*.

If you like *Travels in West Africa,* you will like...

The Lake Regions of Central Africa by Richard Francis Burton. The famous explorer describes one of the many areas to which he journeyed.

Out of Africa by Isak Dinesen. The classic account of Africa's lure. Isak Dinesen is the pen name of Karen Blixen.

Looking for Lovedu: Days and Nights in Africa by Ann Jones. A recent account of a journey across the African continent.

Africa Solo: A Journey Across the Sahara, Sahel, and Congo by Kevin Kertscher. The author crosses Africa, mostly alone.

Malaria Dreams: An African Adventure by Stuart Stevens. A hilarious account of Stevens's misadventures in Africa.

Histories of Africa

King Leopold's Ghost by Adam Hochschild. A riveting and horrifying account of the Belgian occupation of Central Africa.

Hearts of Darkness: The European Exploration of Africa by Frank McLynn. Addresses European exploration and colonization of the continent as a whole.

The Scramble for Africa: White Man's Conquest of the Dark Continent from 1876 to 1912 by Thomas Pakenham. Studies the European conquest of Africa.

Video resources

The African Queen starring Katherine Hepburn and Humphrey Bogart (John Huston, 1951) is a must-see. Though Hepburn plays a missionary in Africa, her personality and conviction in the rightness of her behavior is suggestive of Mary Kingsley. Clint Eastwood's *White Hunter Black Heart* is a fictionalized version of the filming of *African Queen* (1990). *The Ghost and the Darkness* (Stephen Hopkins, 1996) stars Val Kilmer and Michael Douglas as big cat hunters in nineteenth-century Africa. Check libraries for *Mary Kingsley* from the series, *Ten Who Dared*, produced by Ambrose Video.

Internet resources

One hundred years after Mary Kingsley made her first journey, researchers from Cornell University followed in her footsteps. Photographs of Kingsley, the region traveled, the Cornell scientists, and the three species of fish named after Kingsley are pictured on a website: www.nbb.cornell.edu/neurobio/hopkins/mkingsley.html.

July/Women's Journeys
Challenge
Passionate Nomad: The Life of Freya Stark by Jane Fletcher Geniesse, 1999, available in paperback from Random House for $14.95

What is this book about?

The extraordinarily intrepid explorer and travel writer, Freya Stark, was also extraordinarily long-lived. In her one hundred years (1893–1993), she traveled the world; hobnobbed with writers, statesmen, and royalty; advised heads of state; and won rave reviews for the memoirs she wrote about her adventures.

The solitary travels that would bring Stark fame and fortune didn't begin until she was in her mid-thirties; she didn't publish her first book until she was forty-one. Stark had always traveled: she spent a "nomadic youth," as her biographer puts it, accompanying her unhappy parents around Europe. She devoted her twenties to living as a dutiful daughter and trying to find a husband. But when her attempts at love failed, Stark decided to recreate herself as an explorer. She added Arabic to an already impressive list of languages and set out for Lebanon. She spent the next fifty years criss-crossing the Middle East, venturing where no European woman—and sometimes no European man—had ever been before, discovering cities and ruins, and writing bestselling accounts of her adventures. Jane Fletcher Geniesse's ably researched and elegantly written biography details Stark's expeditions and provides background on the fascinating women and men she knew. But Geniesse also delves below the surface to create a portrait of a complex and contradictory woman.

Did you know...?

Lady Mary Wortley Montagu, who lived from 1698 to 1762, was the first British woman to travel to the Middle East and write about it. In 1716, when her husband was appointed ambassador to Turkey, Lady Mary took the unusual step of accompanying him to his post in Constantinople. She studied the language, visited the sites (usually in disguise), and corrected glaring errors in previous (all male) travelers' accounts of life in the harem. She also learned from the Turks about smallpox inoculation, which was then considered quite controversial; disfigured from the disease herself, she had her daughter inoculated. She wrote up her travels as a series of letters to friends and family back home in England. These delightful letters were published posthumously in 1763 as *The Turkish Embassy Letters*. Learn more about Lady Mary in Isobel Grundy's thorough biography, *Lady Mary Wortley Montagu*.

What should I know about the author?

Born in Ohio in 1936, Jane Fletcher Geniesse attended Radcliffe College and Columbia University. She has published widely in journals and magazines, including *House Beautiful*, *Architectural Digest*, and *Ladies' Home Journal*. She worked as a freelance reporter for several newspapers, including the *Washington Post* and the *New York Times*. Geniesse has written one novel, *The Riches of Life*. *Passionate Nomad* is her first biography.

Questions for reflection and discussion

1. According to her biographer, Stark was not a feminist. She always felt more comfortable in the company of men and often treated women contemptuously. Why do you think Stark showed little interest in women's issues? Why did she find men more interesting?

Do you think of Stark as a feminist despite her biographer's claims? What causes some women (and men) to become feminists and some not? In your group, how many of you self-identify as feminists? What does the word mean to you?

2. "A host of nineteenth-century travelers awash in mid-Victorian romanticism had hurried East to escape what in their view was the West's soulless commercialism. They usually returned to compose paeans to the desert tribesman as the last repository of chivalry and honor." Her biographer dissociates Stark from this attitude, but is she exempt from condemnation? Jane Fletcher Geniesse's caustic treatment of the East's allure aside, what do you think has drawn so many travelers to the Middle East? What does Stark seek in the Middle East? What place above all others have you always wanted to visit? Why does this place attract you?

3. Jane Fletcher Geniesse remarks frequently on the pain Stark's lack of beauty caused her, but provides little documentary evidence that Stark was obsessed with her appearance. How can we tell if this is Stark's obsession or her biographer's? What biases emerge in this book? The use of source material is an important part of writing a biography. How can we tell when a biographer uses her source material responsibly? Do you think Geniesse likes Freya Stark? Is it necessary to like your subject in order to write about her?

4. The desire for travel and escapade may not have been unusual in a woman of Stark's generation, but acting on the desire certainly was. What was it about Freya Stark that gave her the determination to travel? Which of her successes was particularly striking? She lived a long and varied life. Which period most interested you? You may want to think also about Jane Fletcher Geniesse's writing. By which periods does she seem most inspired?

5. Critics frequently commented that Stark's books transcended the travel genre and properly belonged to the larger category of literature. What do you think of this claim? What kinds of writing are literature, and what kinds aren't? Like travel writing, biography is also a genre that is frequently considered as a subcategory of literature.

Why is biography not considered literature? Can biography also "transcend" its genre? How? What about this particular book? Does it transcend its genre?

DISCUSSION/REFLECTION STRATEGY

Because most biographies are long, they do require a special commitment from readers. You might start with a biography of a favorite writer; you'll find good biographies of Jane Austen, Charlotte Brontë, and Virginia Woolf. Or read a biography of a writer in conjunction with one of her works. We like Margot Peters's *May Sarton* paired with Sarton's *Journal of a Solitude*. Compare the biography with the autobiography: read *Passionate Nomad* along with a volume of Stark's autobiography. Or plan a biography night to investigate different art forms. Read Roxana Robinson's *Georgia O'Keeffe: A Life* and bring a volume of O'Keeffe's paintings to your book group meeting. Listen to Billie Holiday while discussing Farah Jasmine Griffin's *If You Can't Be Free, Be a Mystery: In Search of Billie Holiday*.

Books by Freya Stark

Many of Stark's works are still in print; as you read *Passionate Nomad*, you will no doubt compile a list of titles that interest you. Our favorites include *The Valleys of the Assassins* and *Alexander's Path*. Stark wrote her autobiography in four volumes: *Traveller's Prelude, Beyond Euphrates, The Coast of Incense*, and *Dust in the Lion's Paw*. Malise Ruthven has edited several collections of Stark's travel photographs including *Freya Stark in South Arabia* and *Freya Stark in Persia*.

If you like *Passionate Nomad,* you will like...

Crossing Borders: An American Woman in the Middle East by Judith Caesar. A Western woman's view of the political forces and issues of Saudi Arabia and Egypt.

A Passage to Egypt: The Life of Lucie Duff Gordon by Katherine Frank. In 1861, at age forty, Gordon left her husband and children behind and traveled to South Africa, seeking a cure for tuberculosis.

Amazing Traveler Isabella Bird: The Biography of a Victorian Adventurer by Evelyn Kaye. Bird broke free of nineteenth-century social norms for women, traveled the world, and wrote about her adventures in Colorado, Japan, and Tibet, just to list a few.

Desert Queen: The Extraordinary Life of Gertrude Bell: Adventurer, Advisor to Kings, Ally of Lawrence of Arabia by Janet Wallach. A recent biography of an explorer whose knowledge of the Middle East influenced policy-makers and statesmen.

Video resources

For discovering the allure of the desert and the majesty of the endless expanse of sun and sky, you cannot do better than David Lean's epic *Lawrence of Arabia* (1962). Considered by many to be one of the finest films ever, Lean's biography of the British soldier and explorer, T.E. Lawrence, retains its power after all these years. The film is worth watching for its cast alone: Peter O'Toole, Alec Guinness, Anthony Quinn, and Omar Sharif.

Internet resources

The site, www.journeywoman.com, offers guidance and resources for women travelers. Find out more about the Society for Women Geographers at www.iswg.org/.

July/Women's Journeys
Memoir
Beyond the Sky and the Earth: A Journey into Bhutan by Jamie Zeppa, 1999, available in paperback from Riverhead Books for $13.95

What is this book about?

In 1988, Jamie Zeppa was twenty-three years old, living in Canada, and planning to enter graduate school to study English literature. Instead, she applied for a two-year appointment as an English language teacher in Bhutan, a small nation in the Himalayas. She left her home, her fiancé, her graduate school plans, and her grandfather.

Dealing with everyday life in Bhutan meant living without electricity, running water, and central heating. Zeppa spent the first several weeks eating nothing but cookies she had brought with her because she did not know how to make herself food. Life in Bhutan meant coping with rats, walking for hours to visit friends, learning to cook on kerosene stoves. But it also meant teaching English to wonderful second graders and later college students, sharing village life, discovering Buddhism, being surrounded by the tallest mountains in the world, and letting go of fear.

Jamie Zeppa's two years in Bhutan stretched to nine, as she fell in love with Bhutan and the people in it. *Beyond the Sky and the Earth* tells of a long journey to Bhutan and an even longer journey to love and fulfillment.

What should I know about the author?

Jamie Zeppa was born in 1964 in Sault Ste. Marie, a northern Ontario steel town. She was raised by her paternal grandparents. She studied English literature at Carleton University in Ottawa and York University in Toronto. In 1989, she left Canada for Bhutan, where she lived until 1998. After teaching English, Zeppa worked for the World Wildlife Federation as a communications officer and the Canadian Cooperation Office as a language and writing instructor in the capital of Bhutan.

Zeppa has said that she wanted to be a writer ever since she read *Harriet the Spy* in fifth grade. In 1996, she won a Canadian Literary Award for an essay that became the basis for *Beyond the Sky and the Earth: A Journey into Bhutan*. She lives in Toronto and is working on a novel.

Questions for reflection and discussion

1. Jamie Zeppa encounters enormous difficulties when she first moves to Bhutan: there are rats to contend with, she cannot use her stove, and the language barrier is immense. To what extent are her problems a result of her fears? How does she change during the first few months in Bhutan? What does she grow to love in Bhutan?

2. In a way, returning to Canada was like arriving in Bhutan all over again. There is noise to contend with, technology thwarts her, and she finds it hard to talk to people. How has she changed? What aspects of life in the West does she find anxiety-provoking? What happens to her relationships with people in Canada? What is the significance of the woman remarking that she never takes the bus? Why does Zeppa include this anecdote? Why does she want to return to Bhutan?

3. Zeppa's journey is both physical and spiritual. Over time in Bhutan, she studies and embraces Buddhism. Why does Buddhism appeal to her? What is "mindfulness?" How does practicing meditation help her to become fully at home in Bhutan? Explain the Buddhist idea that desire causes suffering. How does acknowledging this change Zeppa? What challenges does she face in attempting to overcome desire?

4. A theme running through *Beyond the Sky and the Earth: A Journey into Bhutan* is that of trying to resolve conflicting values or ideals. Zeppa wants to honor the Bhutanese way of doing things, she does not want to patronize or condescend to her students or fellow villagers, but she is also faced with situations she thinks are wrong, e.g., corporal punishment in school, gender inequalities, freedom of speech issues. How does she articulate her dilemmas, and what does she do about them? Do you agree with what she did (or did not) do?

5. Describe Jamie Zeppa's relationship with Tshewang. What is the moral dilemma confronting Zeppa? Why does she hesitate to get involved with him? Does she do "the" right thing? Or "a" right thing? What do they like about one another? What do they share? Does the book's postscript change your opinion about what they did? We tend to think of love relationships that end as having failed or been wrong somehow. But is this fair? Can a relationship come to an end but still have been a positive expression of love?

Extra credit

There are few authors who would not be overjoyed to hear from people who admire their work. Getting in touch with authors is fairly easy. They can always be written to in care of their publisher. Most publishers have websites that provide the publisher's address and, in some cases, the author's email. If the author you admire teaches at a college or university, check the university web site for email links or information about what the author is up to. Some authors even have their own site (for example, www.neil-gaiman.com), letting fans know about upcoming readings and tours. Readings and book signings are a great way to meet your favorite author. To find out about traveling authors, check www.publishersweekly.com. The online version keeps up to date with book tour information.

If you like *Beyond the Sky and the Earth: A Journey into Bhutan,* you will like...

Mango Elephants in the Sun: How Life in an African Village Let Me Be in My Skin by Susana Herrera. Herrera traveled to Cameroon as a Peace Corps volunteer. Her memoir blends an account of teaching English in the village with an account of growing up in America.

Dear Exile: The True Story of Two Friends Separated (for a Year) by an Ocean by Hilary Liftin and Kate Montgomery. A memoir in the form of letters exchanged between Liftin, a New Yorker, and Montgomery, who travels to Kenya as a Peace Corps volunteer.

The House on Dream Street: Memoir of an American Woman in Vietnam by Dana Sachs. An account of contemporary life in Vietnam.

Iron and Silk by Mark Salzman. Salzman blends his story about teaching English to Chinese students with a story about his own martial arts studies.

Living Poor: A Peace Corps Chronicle by Moritz Thomsen. Unsparing look at difficult living conditions in Ecuador.

Video resources

The Cup is billed as "the first full-length feature film made in the Tibetan language." Made by Bhutanese director Khyentse Norbu, *The Cup* tells the story of young Buddhist monks in the Himalayas who become obsessed with soccer. This delightful movie was filmed in an actual Himalayan monastery and features real monks as the actors.

PBS produces a series called *The Living Edens*, which includes an episode titled *Bhutan: The Last Shangri-La*. Also available is *Mystic Lands: Bhutan*.

Internet resources

A good place to start online research on Bhutan is the country's official website, www.kingdomofbhutan.com. See www.bootan.com for travel and tourism information with some great pictures and www.taktsang.org for discussion forums and links to various Buddhist websites. The PBS video series *The Living Edens* has a companion website at www.pbs.org/edens/bhutan.

Did you know...?

The mythical city of **Shangri-La,** where the streets are paved with gold and people live forever in eternal youth, became well known in the West through James Hilton's novel, *Lost Horizon*. Hilton based his story on Himalayan folk tales about the elusive city appearing to mortals only at certain times. Frank Capra's 1937 film version starring Ronald Colman and Jane Wyatt is chock-full of over-the-top sentimentality—but is still fun to watch. For a nonfiction look at the same territory, the History Channel produced a video called *In Search of History: Tibet's Lost Paradise: Shangri-La*.

July/Women's Journeys
Potluck
Talking to High Monks in the Snow: An Asian-American Odyssey by Lydia Minatoya, 1991, available in paperback from HarperPerennial Library for $13.00

What is this book about?

The best travel narratives are as much about the traveler's inward journey as they are about the places visited and people met. Recitations of sights, sounds, and meals will be meaningless to the reader unless the author conveys why she is traveling in the first place and what effect that travel has on her.

Lydia Minatoya's memoir of her time spent in Japan, China, and Nepal succeeds as both description and introspection. Whether she is describing the sea and sky surrounding Okinawa, the mammoth and complex industrial parks in China, or mountain villages in Nepal, her voice is sure and true. In addition to landscape, Minatoya deftly draws portraits of American expatriates in Japan, Chinese bureaucrats, Nepalese village women, and her Japanese relatives. But when Minatoya turns her attention to growing up in Albany, watching her parents live with racism, listening to what they say and do not say about the relocation camps, learning the family secrets about her grandmother, and coping with the loss of her job, the reader realizes the extent of her power. Minatoya delineates the intricacies of the inner landscape as well as she describes the outer. Though the anecdotes in *Talking to High Monks in the Snow* are many and varied, the author's sensitive voice unites them all into a story that resonates far beyond the confines of her individual life.

Did you know...?

Talking to High Monks in the Snow: An Asian-American Odyssey won the 1991 PEN/Jerard Fund Award. The **PEN Foundation** describes itself: "As a major voice of the literary community the organization seeks to defend the freedom of expression wherever it may be threatened, and promote and encourage the recognition and reading of contemporary literature." The acronym PEN stands for the poets, playwrights, essayists, editors, and novelists who constitute its membership. The PEN American Center is just one of the 130 centers which make up PEN International. Find out more at www.pen.org.

What should I know about the author?

Lydia Minatoya grew up in Albany, New York, and received a Ph.D. in psychology from the University of Maryland. She has taught psychology and counseling in the United States and Japan and has taught English in China. She currently lives in the Seattle area with her husband and two children. She is a counselor at North Seattle Community College.

Questions for reflection and discussion

1. Lydia Minatoya's parents met at a Japanese internment camp. Why were Japanese-Americans put into camps? What had Minatoya's parents' lives been like before World War II? How did her parents speak of the time in the camp? Compare Minatoya's mother's reluctance to speak of her wartime experiences with the story Dr. Kinjo tells about Mrs. Kinjo and the Battle of Okinawa.

2. Consider the difference between tourism and traveling. Tourism means visiting places for the purpose of recreation; traveling means visiting or living in other places for other, perhaps deeper, purposes. Is Minatoya a tourist or a traveler? Why does she travel? What is she leaving behind? What is she looking for? How does her own story relate to the tale of Momotaro the Peachboy?

3. Minatoya travels to Japan, China, and Nepal. What does she do in each place? What are some of the memorable episodes in each location? Discuss some of the noteworthy people Minatoya meets: Dr. and Mrs. Kinjo, the elderly patriarch of her family, the university instructor Clark, Ms. Zhang, the elderly Chinese professor, Dr. Auntie Liu, Pam in Nepal, Major Rai. What does she learn from these people?

4. Throughout her memoir, Minatoya pieces together the story of her maternal grandmother. What did she do? What happened to her? The end of the book reveals a shocking secret about the grandmother that neither her daughter nor granddaughter had known. What was it? Compare the mother's reaction to learning this secret with Minatoya's father's reaction at learning that he had been underpaid for years. What do their respective responses reveal about their attitudes toward life? How did you react to the secret?

5. The title, *Talking to High Monks in the Snow*, comes from the book's epigraph, which is a quotation from Chen Jiru. Why does Lydia Minatoya choose this excerpt both to begin her book and provide its title? How does the memoir mirror the tone, form, and content of the epigraph?

Did you know...?

The term *issei* refers to first-generation immigrants to the United States from Japan. The American-born children of issei are called *nisei*. The children of nisei (the grandchildren of issei) are referred to as *sansei*. Though, of course, there are always differences among individuals, it is a staple of Japanese-American memoirs and literature that nisei are anxious to assimilate to American culture. Note the episode in Minatoya's book where her cousin insists she is a "California girl" and not Japanese. Sansei tend to be more interested in their Japanese heritage, connecting with their grandparents to learn about ancestry and culture.

Other books by Lydia Minatoya

The Strangeness of Beauty is a novel about three generations of Japanese women.

If you like *Talking to High Monks in the Snow*, you will like...

36 Views of Mount Fuji: On Finding Myself in Japan by Cathy N. Davidson. Wonderful travel narrative by a professor who teaches English at a Japanese women's college.

Out of the Frying Pan: Reflections of a Japanese American by Bill Hosokawa. A memoir of wartime incarceration in the internment camps.

Polite Lies: On Being a Woman Caught Between Cultures and *The Dream of Water: A Memoir* by Kyoko Mori. A collection of essays and a memoir about making sense of Japanese culture twenty years after leaving it.

Turning Japanese: Memoirs of a Sansei by David Mura. A detailed reflection on issues of identity and culture by the Japanese-American poet.

Nisei Daughter by Monica Sone. The author grew up in Seattle before World War II; her family was sent to an internment camp during the war.

Extra credit

The internment of Japanese-Americans in relocation camps during the Second World War is one of the sadder episodes in American history. Learn more about this in *Farewell to Manzanar: A True Story of Japanese-American Experience During and After the World War II Internment* by Jeanne Wakatsuki Houston and James D. Houston and *Desert Exile: The Uprooting of a Japanese-American Family* by Yoshiko Uchida. The photographer, Joan Myers, photographed the remains of the camps during the 1980s. Her beautiful, haunting pictures can be found on the Web at www.joanmyers.com and in the book *Whispered Silences: Japanese-Americans and World War II* by Gary Y. Okihiro and Joan Myers.

Video resources

Two fine documentaries available from PBS are *Ancestors in the Americas* by filmmaker Loni Ding and *Children of the Camps*. *Ancestors in the Americas* provides a comprehensive view of the history of Asians in North America from the eighteenth century through the twentieth. *Children of the Camps* tells the story of the children interned in relocation camps during the 1940s. Check your local library for the videos or go to www.pbs.org for ordering information (and for a companion website). *Come See the Paradise* (Alan Parker, 1990) is a feature film about the internment camps starring Dennis Quaid.

Internet resources

Read a review of this book in *Ploughshares: The Literacy Journal of Emerson College* at www.pshares.org. Visit the companion website to the documentary film, *Ancestors in the Americas,* at www.pbs.org/ancestorsintheamericas for information about the history and legacy of Asians in North America. Be sure to visit the digital exhibitions at the website of the Japanese American National Museum at www.janm.org.

CHAPTER 8
August
Catastrophic Reading

CROWD-PLEASER
The Fireman's Fair by Josephine
Humphreys

CLASSIC
A Night to Remember by Walter Lord

CHALLENGE
Matigari by Ngugi wa Thiong'o

MEMOIR
The Last Voyage of the Karluk by William
Laird McKinlay

POTLUCK
*Fire on the Mountain: The True Story of the
South Canyon Fire* by John Maclean

On television a psychiatrist was talking about post-traumatic stress, predicting an increase in depression, divorce, and crime. 'Folks might not even realize they're under stress,' the shrink said. 'They might say they're doing just fine, but we have to realize that some storm damage, the strain it's put on our community, is invisible at this point. We may not know the full extent of it for quite some time.'

—Josephine Humphreys, *The Fireman's Fair*

Radio, television, and now the Internet bring catastrophe into our homes. We watch forests burning, bombs dropping, hurricanes hitting, and the towers collapsing. The raw intensity of the images can leave us paralyzed with fear. By engaging our minds and hearts, however, literature about catastrophes can help us move beyond terror.

Our selections for August offer a twist on the beach-read. These are fast, suspenseful, "can't-put-it-down" reads, but they also linger in the imagination and demand quiet reflection. Josephine Humphreys's novel, *The Fireman's Fair*, asks: how does a community heal after a hurricane? Walter Lord's classic narrative about the sinking of the *Titanic* traces the individual stories behind the disaster. Ngugi wa Thiong'o's fable-like novel, *Matigari*, focuses on what can only be considered a century-long catastrophe of war, corruption, famine, and drought in Africa. William Laird McKinlay, schoolteacher turned meteorologist, remembers the disasters that befell Vilhjalmur Stefansson's ill-prepared 1913 Arctic expedition. Finally, John N. Maclean investigates the disastrous 1994 South Canyon fire in Colorado, which burned for ten days and took the lives of fourteen firefighters. These are works that strive to show the fault lines that are left after seismic shifts and to explore the lasting effects of large-scale catastrophe on the individual psyche and the fabric of the community.

August/Catastrophic Reading
Crowd-Pleaser
The Fireman's Fair by Josephine Humphreys, 1991, available in paperback from Penguin for $13.00

What is this book about?

Rob Wyatt, the protagonist of Josephine Humphreys's third novel, is an improviser, an observer, coasting through life, unable to commit. He laments that his thirty-two years have only "added up to a picture of failed dreams and petty pleasures and lack of action." He has just survived a hurricane, but he hates his job, is in love with his boss's wife, and worries that his parents' marriage is about to implode. Enter Billie Poe, nineteen years old, the "bearer of hope," as Humphreys once called her in an interview. Billie seems fragile, even damaged—and with her past, she should be. But she reveals a core of steely strength and sets Rob on the path toward healing. The aftermath of Hurricane Hugo provides plot and metaphor; there is literal and metaphorical storm damage to be assessed, there are literal and metaphorical storms to be weathered.

Humphreys compels our interest in *The Fireman's Fair* through the strong voice and inner life of Rob himself, through the interactions and developing story line among a cast of believable characters, and through her precise yet lyrical writing style.

What should I know about the author?

Josephine Humphreys, born in 1945, was raised in Charleston, South Carolina, the setting for *The Fireman's Fair*. She left the South to go to graduate school (she has a master's degree from Yale and worked on her doctorate at the University of Texas at Austin), but returned to teach English, raise her two children and, ultimately, write. Her first novel, *Dreams of Sleep*, was published in 1984. Humphreys cites Louisa May Alcott's *Little Women* and everything by Reynolds Price as the most influential books she's read. *The Fireman's Fair* is dedicated to Price, her mentor.

Questions for reflection and discussion

1. What makes a work of literature "southern"? The author or the subject matter? Humphreys herself is southern, and the setting for *The Fireman's Fair* is South Carolina, but is this enough to qualify a work as southern? What strikes you as particularly southern about *The Fireman's Fair*? Based on the definition below of regionalism, is *The Fireman's Fair* a work of regionalism?

2. Humphreys had finished her novel when Hurricane Hugo hit Charleston; she spent three months rewriting in order to set her story in the hurricane's aftermath. How does the hurricane contribute to the plot? What kinds of stresses does the hurricane reveal? How does it function as a metaphor? Why would Humphreys choose to open the novel *after* the hurricane is over? Finally, what is the hurricane's relation to the Fireman's Fair of the title? Why begin with a hurricane and end with a fair? What would this novel be without the hurricane?

Did you know...?

Southern literature can be classified as a type of **regional literature**. Regionalism refers to "fidelity to a particular geographical section; the accurate representation of its habits, speech, manners, history, folklore, or beliefs. A test of regionalism is that the action and personages of a work called regional cannot be moved, without major loss or distortion, to any other geographical setting" (Holman and Harmon, *A Handbook to Literature*). Southern fiction typically focuses on themes and motifs like the land, family relationships, race, secrets, religion, and sin. Classic southern authors include William Faulkner, Tennessee Williams, Flannery O'Connor, Ellen Glasgow, and Eudora Welty.

3. Several reviewers note that Billie Poe belongs to a type of character Humphreys also utilizes in Iris Moon in *Dreams of Sleep* and Lucille Odom in *Rich in Love*. Humphreys herself calls these characters "bearers of hope." Why is Billie so engaging to the characters within *The Fireman's Fair*? Why do the other characters want to help her, and what kinds of help do they think she needs? Rob initially believes he is helping her, but of course, it turns out that Billie is doing the helping. How does Billie help Rob commit himself to living?

4. *The Fireman's Fair* presents women written from the perspective of a male character. Rob spends much of his time thinking about Billie, but also about Louise, who has been the love of his life. We also see his mother, Maude, exclusively through Rob's perspective. How accurate is Rob as an observer of women? What perplexes or mystifies him about women? Why might Josephine Humphreys have been interested in writing about women through the eyes of a man? Do you think she has created a believable male character in Rob? Does she write convincingly from a male perspective? We frequently hear the adage, "Write what you know." Why might an author want to move beyond this?

5. The main characters in *The Fireman's Fair* are white, but Albert Swan, Rob's best friend, is black, and two supporting characters, Huong and Anna, are Vietnamese. Part of the "storm damage"

concerns Rob's friendship with Albert. What has Rob done or not done? What do we learn about Albert's past? Why hasn't Rob been a better friend to Albert? What do we learn about Huong and Anna? Why are they living in Charleston?

Other books by Josephine Humphreys

Humphreys's other novels are: *Dreams of Sleep* (1984), *Rich in Love* (1987), and *Nowhere Else on Earth* (2000). Read an autobiographical essay by her in Alex Harris's *A World Unsuspected: Portraits of Southern Childhood*.

If you like *The Fireman's Fair,* you will like...

The Salt Eaters by Toni Cade Bambara. A novel about faith-healers set in a small southern town.

Charms for the Easy Life by Kaye Gibbons. A historical novel weaving the stories of three generations of women, this is based in part on Gibbons's own grandmother.

The Hard Blue Sky by Shirley Ann Grau. The story of a Louisiana community torn apart by a hurricane.

Ferris Beach and *July 7th* by Jill McCorkle. Wonderful novels about growing up in the South.

Mama Day by Gloria Naylor. A hurricane features in the plot of this mesmerizing tale of an island community off the coast of Georgia.

The Salt Line by Elizabeth Spencer. A novel set in a Gulf-of-Mexico community in the devastation of a hurricane's aftermath.

Video resources

Director Bruce Beresford adapted Humphreys's second novel, *Rich in Love*, for the screen in 1992. Beresford's earlier film, *Crimes of the Heart* (1986), is an unforgettable look at a family of southern sisters (and a hurricane features in the sisters' past history). *Steel Magnolias* (Herbert Ross, 1989) is a drama about a southern community.

Internet resources

Read an interview with Humphreys about her most recent novel, *Nowhere Else on Earth*, at www.bookpage.com/0009bp/josephine_ humphreys.html. Learn more about Charleston, South Carolina, at www.charlestoncvb.com. View images of Hurricane Hugo at rsd.gsfc.nasa.gov/rsd/images/HugoRed.html. Hooked on hurricanes? You'll love hurricanes.noaa.gov.

August/Catastrophic Reading
Classic
A Night to Remember by Walter Lord, 1955, available in paperback from Bantam Books for $6.50

What is this book about?

The sinking of the supposedly unsinkable *Titanic* has aroused keen interest since it occurred in 1912. *A Night to Remember*, first published in 1955, was the first history of the *Titanic* disaster. Using oral testimony, Lord was able to trace the *Titanic's* last hours almost minute by minute, crafting a popular history that recreated all the suspense and drama of the events of April 14, 1912. All of the details that linger in the imagination are here: the iceberg that was spotted too late, the deadly proportion of lifeboats to passengers, the other ships which hovered nearby ignoring or misunderstanding the *Titanic's* SOS calls, the band playing on as the lights went out. Lord spotlights the individuals at the center of the drama and takes us all over the ship, from the crow's nest to the boiler room to the first-class saloon, pursuing acts of weakness and bravery.

As its title suggests, *A Night to Remember* closely follows the events of just one night. The book opens seconds before the sighting of the iceberg, about 11:40 P.M., and ends with an image of the rescue ship *Carpathia* steaming ahead to New York on April 15. This is history at its most focused and readable. The clarity and neutrality of Lord's writing style only emphasize the bad luck, poor planning, and hubris at the root of this tragedy.

Extra credit

Book groups rarely include works of history in their reading repertoire, but after reading *A Night to Remember*, your group may elect to read more history. We recommend the following authors: Barbara Tuchman, Dava Sobel, David McCullough.

What should I know about the author?

Born in Baltimore, Maryland, in 1917, just five years after the sinking of the *Titanic*, Lord became interested in the disaster when he was nine years old and crossed the Atlantic on the *Titanic*'s sister ship, the *Olympic*. Lord was educated at Princeton and Yale and served in the Office of Strategic Services during World War II. *A Night to Remember* was his second book. He has lived much of his life in New York and has written twelve books and numerous articles and essays.

Questions for reflection and discussion

1. Lord wrote, "I am interested in the people who are caught in great events more than the events themselves." How accurate a description is this of *A Night to Remember*? Which characters are especially memorable? Who emerges as the hero of the night? Whose behavior most surprised or disappointed you? Some readers have complained that there are simply too many characters, and we don't get to know any of them well enough. Is this a fair assessment?

2. One problem Lord faced when crafting his story was that the ending was already known. How could he write a gripping page-turner when everyone knows that the ship hits an iceberg and sinks? Nonetheless, *A Night to Remember* is a suspenseful story. As you're reading, look closely at the chapter breaks and think about how

this book is organized. How does it begin? How chronological is it? When do we find out important facts? How is the book structured? How does Lord create suspense when the reader already knows that the *Titanic* is going to sink?

3. Part of the suspense may come from the discrepancies in eyewitness accounts and the difficulty of discovering precisely what happened on April 14, 1912. After sifting through conflicting accounts, Lord chooses to present all sides of each controversy, all versions of each event. Is *A Night to Remember* a better book because of this? Why is memory fallible in a crisis? How can an author find the true story? Is there a true story? Which eyewitnesses seem most credible?

4. Lord claims that the *Titanic* disaster marked the end of innocence, the beginning of disillusionment: "People have never been sure of anything since." Why would this particular disaster at sea lead to such widespread disillusionment? What other disasters can you think of that have had such an effect? What kind of faith or innocence is eroded and destroyed by them?

5. *A Night to Remember* initiated a small industry of *Titanic* studies: eyewitness accounts, histories, documentaries, films, children's books, plays. Even before the phenomenal success of the movie starring Leonardo DiCaprio and Kate Winslet, most of us knew at least the broad outlines of the sinking of the *Titanic*. Why does the story of the *Titanic* inspire such worldwide interest? Why do you think so many readers become enthralled by this event—to the point of becoming experts in *Titanic* studies? In a sequel to *A Night to Remember*, Walter Lord suggests that the *Titanic* plays into a "nostalgia binge." But what are we nostalgic for?

Other books by Walter Lord

Lord's twelve books tackle a wide range of historical events, but with an emphasis on war and battle. *Day of Infamy* (1957) is a gripping history of the Pearl Harbor attack. *The Good Years* (1960) covers the fourteen years preceding World War One. *A Time to Stand* (1961) dramatizes the Alamo. *Peary to the Pole* (1963) chronicles the journeys of Arctic explorer Robert Peary. Lord takes on civil rights and race riots in *The Past That Would Not Die* (1965). *Incredible Victory* (1967) recounts the Battle of Midway. *The Dawn's Early Light* (1972) is an informative and readable account of the War of 1812. *Lonely Vigil: Coastwatchers of the Solomons* (1977) tells the little-known story of courageous Australians who risked their lives to report on Japanese activities in the Solomon Islands during World War II. *The Miracle of Dunkirk* (1982) is a paean to the courage of those who organized and effected the rescue at Dunkirk. You will probably want to pick up *The Night Lives On* (1986), a sequel written after the discovery of the remains of the *Titanic*, the moment you finish *A Night to Remember*.

If you like *A Night to Remember*, you will like...

The Loss of the S.S. Titanic: Its Story and Its Lessons by Lawrence Beesley. This account by survivor Beesley was published just months after the disaster.

Down with the Old Canoe: A Cultural History of the Titanic Disaster by Steven Biel. Biel looks at the legends and myths that sprang up about the disaster.

Titanic: Triumph and Tragedy by and Charles A. Haas. A handsome volume released for the *Titanic*'s seventy-fifth anniversary, this book recounts the story and includes photographs from the wreckage.

The Titanic Reader edited by John Wilson Foster. This anthology collects and excerpts writings about the *Titanic*. A good place to begin further reading.

Dusk to Dawn: Survivor Accounts of the Last Night on the Titanic by Paul J. Quinn. Uses survivor accounts to create an hour-by-hour timeline of the ship's last hours.

Fiction about the *Titanic*

Every Man for Himself by Beryl Bainbridge. A historical novel about the sinking of the *Titanic*.

The Titanic Murders by Max Allan Collins. A mystery using the *Titanic* as backdrop.

Psalm at Journey's End by Erik Fosnes Hansen. This historical novel focuses on the stories of the members of the *Titanic*'s band, who famously played as the ship sank.

Operation Titanic by Carolyn Keene. All aboard the *Titanic* with Nancy Drew and the Hardy Boys!

Futility or the Wreck of the Titan by Morgan Robertson. This novel, mentioned by Lord and published fourteen years before the *Titanic* disaster, dramatizes the sinking of the supposedly unsinkable *Titan*.

Video resources

The *Titanic* story has been pop culture fodder since 1912. The very first film version of the disaster was released just one month after the ship sank. *Titanic: The Musical* was a recent Broadway success. James Cameron's *Titanic* is a must-see for readers of Lord's history. Luckily, there is a good adaptation of *A Night to Remember* (Roy Ward Baker, 1958), which many find superior to Cameron's film. There are several good documentaries about the *Titanic*. A&E's *Titanic* (1994) is long, but one of the best. National Geographic's *Secrets of the Titanic* is also excellent.

Internet resources

Learn more about the *Titanic* at the official archives site, www. titanic-online.com. An excellent general site, with much information and a wealth of links, is www.execpc.com/~reva/html3.htm. Finally, for fun, visit the official *Titanic* movie website at www.titanicmovie. com where you can read interviews with the stars.

August/Catastrophic Reading
Challenge
Matigari by Ngugi wa Thiong'o, 1986, available in paper-
back from African World Press for $20.00

What is this book about?

Matigari is set in the aftermath of an unnamed African country's successful bid for independence. The colonial settlers have been expelled,
but independence, we soon find out, is a disaster. The novel begins
when its hero, freedom fighter Matigari ma Njiruungi, emerges from
the forest and lays down his weapons to take up the belt of peace. On
one level, this is a simple story. Because Settler Williams, the master for
whom he built a house, has finally been killed, Matigari thinks nothing
should stand in the way of his peaceful homecoming. He wants to
gather his dispersed family around him once again and claim the house
that he built with his own hands. But, of course, things are not so simple. In search of his children, Matigari finds only cruel gangs of
orphans. In search of his women, Matigari finds Guthera, who propo-
sitions him and asserts that "the most important thing is money."
When he finally reaches his house, he finds it occupied by another man,
who has Matigari arrested. Upon his miraculous release from prison,
Matigari wanders through the countryside in search of truth and justice
and meets a cross section of society—men, women, and children, rich
and poor, managers and workers, politicians and prisoners, blacks and
whites, Africans and colonists. The conversations Matigari has with
these people illuminate the modern condition of Africa. The corrupt
government of the white colonizers has been overthrown thanks to the
efforts of patriots like Matigari, only to be replaced with an even more
corrupt government of black African dictators. This powerful novel
dramatizes the disasters of postcolonial Africa through means of oral
narrative structures, such as the quest. There is no truth and justice in
Matigari's country, but because Matigari confronts the corrupt and
speaks up on behalf of the oppressed, there is hope.

What should I know about the author?

Ngugi wa Thiong'o (pronounced un-googi wa t-onggo) was born in Kenya in 1938. He began writing in high school and first found success with short stories published while he was a student at Makere University College in Uganda. His family took part in the Mau Mau peasant/worker rebellion against the colonists (1952–1956). Ngugi traveled to England for postgraduate studies and wrote his first two novels there. From 1967 to 1969, he held a post as professor of literature at the University of Nairobi; after teaching for a time in the United States, he returned to Kenya. While his novels had always been critical of the government of independence, it was his popular play, *Ngaahika ndeenda*, which led to his arrest. He spent one year in prison; since 1982, he has lived in England and the United States, in exile from Kenya, where authorities threatened to arrest him if he returns.

Did you know...?

There are over six million native Gikuyu speakers in Kenya, about 20 percent of the population. While children may speak Gikuyu at home, they are educated in the official languages of Kenya: English and Kiswahili. As novelist Mwangi wa Mutahi notes, once children enter middle school, they are punished if caught speaking their native tongue. Gikuyu is one of about fifty languages spoken in Kenya.

Questions for reflection and discussion

1. In *Talking Indian: Reflections on Survival and Writing*, Anna Lee Walters writes that in oral cultures, "the spoken word is believed to be power which can create or destroy." How does speech create and destroy in *Matigari*? Think about the power of names. When Matigari tells his name to the policemen who are harassing Guthera, they stop. What power do words hold? Think also about the repetition Ngugi uses: Matigari repeats his story to each person he meets. Why?

2. When Matigari tells his story to the corrupt Minister for Truth and Justice, the minister orders him to, "Stop speaking in parables. If

you want to ask a question, then do so in plain language." Examine the note, "To the Reader/Listener," at the beginning of *Matigari*, in which Ngugi asserts that this is not a story bound by time or place. Why does Ngugi use the parable to tell this particular story? Why does the minister want Matigari to speak in plain language? Why would parable be more powerful than plain language?

3. Western nations are represented at the meeting among government leaders, factory managers, and striking workers. They witness the gross corruption of the government, yet they immediately offer to support it. Britain and the EEC offer a loan, while the United States is willing to supply Phantom jets, tanks, and attack helicopters. And, of course, the original corrupt government *was* European. What do we learn about European and Western involvement in Africa in *Matigari*? How does Ngugi depict Europeans? How responsible are other nations—particularly America and the European nations—for the catastrophic conditions of modern Africa?

4. Examine the speech John Boy Jr. makes about individual versus mass culture (in part one, chapter twelve). He is the enemy, and he is a proponent of individualism. It stands to reason, then, that Matigari must support a clan culture. What does Matigari say or do to express his allegiance to the masses, to family, to a clan? The argument about individualism divides along lines of race and class. Why? Does individualism always have to be corrupt? Has individualism worked for Western nations? A student in the novel defines democracy as meaning, "first, fending for oneself." Is this an accurate description? Is he describing an ideal or reality as he perceives it? Can democracy also be about caring for others?

5. Although the Christian democratic government is criticized in *Matigari*, Ngugi's use of the Christian tradition itself provides the novel with much of its power. The role of religion and Biblical stories is most obvious, perhaps, in the prison scene. What biblical stories are alluded to in this scene? Why might Ngugi make parallels between his novel and the Bible? What other connections do you notice between biblical stories and characters and the characters and situations in *Matigari*? How is Matigari a Christ figure?

Other books by Ngugi wa Thiong'o

The prolific Ngugi has written novels, plays, short stories, and essays. His first novel, *Weep Not, Child* (1964), focuses on the Mau Mau rebellion against the colonists in which his family took part. His third novel, *A Grain of Wheat* (1967), won critical acclaim for its story and technique, which skillfully utilizes extended flashback. *Petals of Blood* (1977) is an indictment of repressive postcolonial governments in independent Africa. Ngugi's memoir about being imprisoned was published as *Detained: A Writer's Prison Diary* (1981). An important collection of essays, *Decolonising the Mind* (1986), explains his decision to write in his native language, Gikuyu. His 1980 novel, *Caitaani Muthari-Ini* (*Devil on the Cross*), was the first modern novel originally written in Gikuyu; it focuses on the exploitation of Kenyan women.

Did you know...?

Ngugi wa Thiong'o is the best-known author writing his works in Gikuyu, but he is not the first. Gakaara wa Wanjau, born in 1921, is a writer of pamphlets on Kenyan history and Gikuyu culture, short fiction, and primers for schoolchildren, as well as an important publisher. His 1946 novel, *Uhoro wa Ugurani* (*Marriage Arrangements*), was the first novel published in Gikuyu. He spent the years 1952 to 1959 in prison; his prison diary was published in English as *Mau Mau Author in Detention*. Novelist Mwangi wa Mutahi, born in 1963, published *Ngoima* in his native language. Read his essay about the importance of writing in Gikuyu at www.unesco.org/courier/2000_04/uk/ doss12.htm.

If you like *Matigari*, you will like...

Trouble with Nigeria by Chinua Achebe. Written in 1983, this slim volume by acclaimed novelist Achebe tackles the problems of Nigeria, post-independence.

We Wish to Inform You That Tomorrow We Will Be Killed with Our Families by Philip Gourevitch. An account of genocide in Rwanda, where the Hutus slaughtered nearly one million members of their neighboring tribe, the Tutsis.

The Poisonwood Bible by Barbara Kingsolver. A well-researched, absorbing novel about an American missionary family who sets off for the Congo.

The Open Sore of a Continent: A Personal Narrative of the Nigerian Crisis by Wole Soyinka. Essays by Nigerian Nobel laureate.

In the Footsteps of Mr. Kurtz: Living on the Brink of Disaster in Mobutu's Congo by Michaela Wrong. British journalist spent six years living in Congo; this account looks at the catastrophic thirty years of Mobutu's rule.

Video resources

Check your local independent video store or university/museum film series for *Afrique, Je Te Plumerai* (Jean-Marie Teno, 1992), which looks at cultural genocide in Cameroon, whose history closely parallels the situation in *Matigari*. The French title translates in English as *Africa, I Will Fleece You*. The African-made *The Kitchen Toto* (Harry Hook, 1987) is set in Kenya under British rule in the 1950s. *Chocolat* (Claire Denis, 1988) is also set in colonial Africa in the 1950s; it begins with its adult protagonist returning to Africa, where she grew up. African writer Chinua Achebe is featured in a PBS interview special with Bill Moyers titled, *Chinua Achebe: A World of Ideas*.

Internet resources

Emory University's incredible postcolonial studies website provides much useful information, including definitions of important terms, a history of postcolonial literatures, and links to significant authors and theorists, including Ngugi wa Thiong'o: www.emory.edu/ENGLISH/Bahri/Intro.html. Find a brief biography of Ngugi at www.africana.com/Articles/tt_379.htm. Learn about Kenya at www.kenyaweb.com.

August/Catastrophic Reading
Memoir
The Last Voyage of the Karluk: A Survivor's Memoir of Disaster by William Laird McKinlay, 1976, available in paperback from St. Martin's Griffin for $12.95

What is this book about?

During the first decades of the twentieth century, Arctic and Antarctic explorers elicited the sort of admiration from the public that we associate with sports stars and pop singers. They were brave, strong, and willing to put their lives on the line in the pursuit of scientific knowledge. They were active agents in the cause of progress. Small wonder then that when twenty-four-year-old Glasgow schoolteacher William Laird McKinlay received an invitation to be magnetician and meteorologist in an expedition planned by the famous Vilhjalmur Stefansson, he jumped at the chance. The crew put their lives on the line, but glory and advances in science were not the result. *The Last Voyage of the Karluk* tells the story of an expedition where everything that could go wrong did—from the incompatibility of the crew to the irresponsibility of the expedition leader. The ship became trapped by ice and crushed, leaving its crew and scientific staff to fend for themselves on ice floes and an island for nearly a year until help arrived. How they kept themselves clothed, fed, and occupied during the long, dark Arctic winter is a harrowing and amazing tale.

What should I know about the author?

William Laird McKinlay published his memoir of the disaster in 1976 when he was eighty-eight years old. He did not publish earlier because the memories were too painful, and he was unwilling to get involved in a public battle of accusations and counter-accusations. McKinlay, like too many others on the voyage, had neither training nor experience in Arctic exploration. Immediately upon his return from the Arctic, McKinlay became an officer in the British Army and served on the western front. After the war, he returned to Scotland to teach, eventually became a headmaster, and devoted much of his time to researching accounts of the *Karluk* and other expeditions.

Questions for reflection and discussion

1. What are McKinlay's aims in writing this book? Why does it bother him that Vilhjalmur Stefansson continued to have a reputation as a heroic explorer even after the *Karluk* disaster? What does McKinlay think Stefansson should have done differently? Why does McKinlay admire Captain Bartlett? How does the captain behave toward the ship and crew?

2. McKinlay quotes Stefansson as saying that gains in scientific knowledge are worth the loss of a few lives. Do you agree? What about the analogy Stefansson draws between lives sacrificed for political causes and lives sacrificed for scientific gain? Do you think the analogy is a valid one? Is the loss of lives in a war any more or less worthy than the loss of lives in the pursuit of knowledge?

3. What activities does McKinlay engage in to avoid despair and physical illness? Describe the celebrations aboard ship. How do the men and women keep busy? Why is keeping busy important to them? McKinlay remarks that the lack of camaraderie among staff and crew is the hardest burden to bear. Even his time later spent in the battlefields of the First World War does not compare to the bad feeling of the year in the Arctic. How does this lack of friendship or even kindness make the experience worse for him?

4. Discuss the Eskimo family in *The Last Voyage of the Karluk*. Why are they there? How do they help the crew and scientific staff? What do you think of McKinlay's account of them? What does he learn from them? What opinion does he have of them?

5. Do you think that a commitment to spirituality helps people overcome adversity? Do you think McKinlay's spirituality has anything to do with his ability to weather the year spent with the *Karluk* and its crew? How does McKinlay's spirituality reveal itself? What is his experience of the aurora borealis? Why does he attribute an almost

mystical character to that phenomenon? In *Arctic Dreams*, Barry
Holstun Lopez (see our January Potluck selection) says that it is
impossible to feel the emotion of self-pity when confronted with
the aurora borealis. Do you think McKinlay would agree?

DISCUSSION/REFLECTION STRATEGY

Almost all of us have read at least one book that qualifies as catastrophe literature. You may remember staying up late into the night to
find out what happens next, only to find it impossible to fall asleep
due to your vicarious adrenaline rush. Why do we actively seek out
stories of devastating natural or human-made disasters and survival
tales of horrific physical suffering and endurance? Examples of this
genre include such titles as *Into Thin Air*, *The Perfect Storm*, and
Endurance: Shackleton's Legendary Antarctic Expedition, all of which
stayed on bestseller lists for months. Your group may want to discuss
our fascination with reading about other people's incredible feats of
daring.

Books about the Karluk disaster

Jennifer Niven fleshes out McKinlay's memoir into a full-fledged
account of the disaster in *The Ice Master: The Doomed 1913 Voyage of
the Karluk and the Miraculous Rescue of Her Survivors*. Captain Bartlett
of the *Karluk* wrote a memoir that has been edited, added to, and published by Ralph T. Hale as *The Karluk's Last Voyage*.

If you like *The Last Voyage of the Karluk*, you will like...

*In the Land of White Death: An Epic Story of Survival in the Siberian Arc-
tic* by Valerian Ivanovich Albanov. A first person account of Arctic
exploration written in 1914, but not translated into English from
Russian until 1997.

Ice Blink: The Tragic Fate of Sir John Franklin's Lost Polar Expedition by
Scott Cookman. Recounts Franklin's disastrous 1845 search for the
Northwest Passage. Andrea Barrett's excellent novel, *Voyage of the Nar-*

whal, tells the story of a fictional rescue mission sent out ten years after the Franklin expedition went missing.

Barrow's Boys: A Stirring Story of Daring, Fortitude, and Outright Lunacy by Fergus Fleming. Details thirty years of British exploration in the Arctic, Antarctic, and Africa.

Ghosts of Cape Sabine: The Harrowing True Story of the Greely Expedition by Leonard F. Guttridge. Yet another disastrous Arctic expedition, this one in Greenland.

Farthest North by Fridtjof Nansen. Classic chronicle by one of the original European explorers of the North Pole.

Video resources

Sea Tales: The Deadly Arctic Expedition is a documentary about the *Karluk* available from A&E Home Video.

Internet resources

Check out the incredible photographs of Arctic phenomena at the page maintained by the National Oceanic and Atmospheric Administration at www.arctic.noaa.gov/exploration.html. Arctic Exploration Online, sponsored by NASA and the Coast Guard, is also worth a visit: quest.arc.nasa.gov/arctic/. If you are interested in outfitting your own Arctic Expedition (or just looking for more pictures), visit www.explorenorth.com and www.arcticphoto.co.uk.

August/Catastrophic Reading
Potluck
Fire on the Mountain: The True Story of the South Canyon Fire by John N. Maclean, 1999, available in paperback from Washington Square Press for $13.95

What is this book about?

During the summer of 1994, the news that fourteen firefighters died while battling a blaze on Colorado's Storm King Mountain shocked the nation. Initial reports misidentified the place as South Canyon, and the fire is still known as the South Canyon fire, a mistake Maclean finds typical of the events surrounding the blaze. The dead were part of a firefighting elite of smoke jumpers and hot shots—people rigorously trained to contain and control wildfires. An official investigation began immediately to discover how and why the deaths occurred.

This fire was disturbingly reminiscent of another great blaze—that of Mann Gulch, Montana, in 1949, when thirteen smoke jumpers died. After that fire, changes were made in wildfire fighting practice, and until 1994, no smoke jumpers had died as a result of fire. (The classic text on the Mann Gulch fire is *Young Men and Fire* by Norman Maclean, who is John N. Maclean's father.) *Fire on the Mountain* is a reconstruction of the South Canyon disaster, the efforts made to contain and extinguish the blaze, as well as the infighting among the various agencies assigned to fight the fire. But it is also a tribute to the spirit and courage of the dedicated men and women who perished.

What should I know about the author?

John N. Maclean spent thirty years as writer, reporter, and editor for the *Chicago Tribune*. He was the newspaper's correspondent in Washington, D.C., and its diplomatic correspondent, mostly covering Henry Kissinger, for several years. He retired from the *Tribune* in 1995 to write *Fire on the Mountain*. Maclean lives with his wife, Frances, in both Washington D.C. and Montana.

Questions for reflection and discussion

1. *Fire on the Mountain* is a detailed piece of investigative journalism. Keeping the sequence of actions and the roles of individuals and agencies straight in one's mind is important for appreciating what happened. What is a "smoke-jumper" and a "hot shot"? Which agencies shared responsibility for fighting fires at Storm King Mountain, and how did politics play a role in this disaster? What was the role of the meteorologists in fighting the fire? What

happens when a fire "blows up"? What conditions must be in place for a blow-up to happen?

2. Though it is impossible to lay blame for what happened on a single person or agency, it is possible to see that different people and different procedures contributed to the catastrophe. What went wrong? Summarize and discuss the mistakes made on and off the mountain. What sorts of things kept happening?

3. *Fire on the Mountain* delivers a strong emotional impact. Which part of the story did you find most affecting? Which of the people came alive for you on the page? How does the author create an emotional response in the reader? Evaluate the various components of the book: profiles of key players, analysis of bureaucracy, detailed explanations of fires and firefighting. In your opinion, did Maclean balance these components successfully?

4. Are situations relying on human judgment, communication, and technology ever entirely foolproof? Can catastrophes like the South Canyon fire be prevented or only made more unusual? In his excellent book, *Why Things Bite Back: Technology and the Revenge of Unintended Consequences*, science journalist Edward Tenner amasses reams of data regarding the effects of efforts to make life safer, e.g., the use of antibiotics leading to resistant bacteria. Are we in control of the technology we use to make life safer?

5. What changes have been made in wildfire fighting policy and practice as a result of the South Canyon fire? Do you think these are reasonable changes? What about the role of women fighting wildfires that Maclean raises? Do you think that the presence of women hot shots made a difference in what happened on the mountain? Do you think the male firefighters were inclined to treat the female firefighters differently? If so, how?

If you like *Fire on the Mountain,* you will like...

The Great Peshtigo Fire: An Eyewitness Account by Peter Pernin. In 1871, on the same day the Chicago fire broke out, the Peshtigo fire in rural

Wisconsin began. By the time the fire died out, twenty-four hundred square miles had been destroyed and several hundred people had lost their lives.

Fire on the Rim: A Firefighter's Season at the Grand Canyon by Stephen J. Pyne. Engrossing memoir about fighting fires in Arizona.

Jumping Fire: A Smokejumper's Memoir of Fighting Wildfire in the West by Murry A. Taylor. A first-person account of smokejumping.

Fire Line: The Summer Battles of the West by Michael Thoele. Investigative report on the subculture of wildfire-fighting.

DISCUSSION/REFLECTION STRATEGY

Young Men and Fire by Norman Maclean is about the Mann Gulch fire. John Maclean refers to his father's book frequently throughout his own. The South Canyon fire and the fire at Mann Gulch were similar with respect to the circumstances surrounding the blaze and, tragically, with respect to the deaths of firefighters. John Maclean's writing style is quite different from that of his father. A paired reading of the two will lead to some interesting discussions. An essay comparing both can be found on the Web at www.crescentblues.com/3_1issue/fire.shtml.

Video resources

Plans are in the works for both a feature film version of *Fire on the Mountain* and a documentary version made for A&E. The History Channel offers such documentaries as *Fire in Mann Gulch* and *Wildfires: Fighting Fires with Fires*.

Internet resources

The *New York Times*'s review of *Fire on the Mountain* is at www.nytimes.com/books/99/10/31/reviews/991031.31flookt.html. www.talkcity.com carries a transcript of a chat with John N. Maclean. On its site, there is a photo of the monument erected in memory of the firefighters at www.azstarnet.com/~dschlos/glenpost/explore/stormking.html. Maclean is also a contributor to the "Writers on the Range" portion of *High Country News,* described as "A Paper for People who Care about the West." Their address is www.hcn.org.

CHAPTER 9

September
Back to School

CROWD-PLEASER
Bee Season by Myla Goldberg

CLASSIC
Jane Eyre by Charlotte Brontë

CHALLENGE
Moo by Jane Smiley

MEMOIR
Dangerous Minds by LouAnne Johnson

POTLUCK
The Power of Their Ideas by Deborah Meier

Caring and compassion are not soft, mushy goals. They are part of the hard core of subjects we are responsible for teaching. Informed and skillful care is learned. Caring is as much cognitive as affective. The capacity to see the world as others might is central to unsentimental compassion and at the root of both intellectual skepticism and empathy.

—Deborah Meier, *The Power of Their Ideas*

Even if we have been out of school for a long time or don't have school-age children, September always brings with it memories of new pencil cases, new clothes, and fresh boxes of crayons. Our schooling stays with us forever. If we agree with Deborah Meier that respect, compassion, education, and democracy are all deeply intertwined, then serious examination of our own education and the education of the children in our community ought to be one of the chief concerns of everyone.

This month's selections portray a variety of educational experiences. Myla Goldberg's *Bee Season* examines a gifted child's relationship to her family. It is safe to say that the hellish Lowood school described by Charlotte Brontë in this month's Classic selection, *Jane Eyre*, wouldn't meet the criteria for fairness and respect put forward by Deborah Meier. Jane Smiley's academic satire, *Moo*, also charts the many ways in which schools can veer off course. *Dangerous Minds* is a fine addition to the genre of teacher memoirs, while Meier lays out an ambitious and inspiring manifesto for American schools in *The Power of Their Ideas*.

September/Back to School
Crowd-Pleaser
Bee Season by Myla Goldberg, 2000, available in paperback from Knopf for $13.00

What is this book about?

School has failed nine-year-old Eliza Naumann, and she has failed at school. Eliza is an unimpressive C student in a family of overachievers; academic success has never interested her. But Eliza cannot escape the structures and expectations of school because school, study, and academic pursuits permeate her family life. In fact, more intense learning takes place at home than at school. Her father, Saul, and her older brother, Aaron, closet themselves for hours at a time in Saul's study, examining the tenets of Judaism (Saul is grooming his son to be a rabbi) and practicing music. Her mother, Miriam, a high-powered lawyer with a secret life which is slowly revealed to the reader over the course of the novel, spends her evenings composing hyperarticulate letters to the editors of her favorite academic journals. The Naumanns attack everything with the habits of study they learned in school. Moreover, parental praise is earned through perfectionism in scholarly pursuits. What role can an nonintellectual child play in such a family? Only a small one, until Eliza reveals herself to be a spelling prodigy.

Bee Season opens on the day of Eliza's momentous discovery that she can spell. The family cohesion fostered by her success at the school spelling bee, however, is all too transitory; the Naumanns are on a downward spiral. The siblings, Eliza and Aaron, embark on parallel trajectories as Saul transfers his attention from his diligent son to his prodigy daughter; as Eliza goes deeper into word study, Aaron researches religion. Connected to his father only through their study of Judaism and music, Aaron rebels by joining a Hare Krishna temple. But Aaron is not the only one undergoing religious conversion; in a dazzling move by Goldberg, spelling becomes religion, quite literally.

Bee Season offers readers a chance to reflect on the importance of school in forming our personalities and perspectives, but it also features parenting choices that will inspire lively discussion.

What should I know about the author?

Myla Goldberg was born in Maryland in 1972. She traveled in Prague after graduating from college and, after returning to the U.S., soon settled into a series of part-time jobs that gave her time to write. She published a few short stories in small magazines before hitting the bestseller lists with *Bee Season*. To research the novel, she attended the National Spelling Bee in Washington, D.C., and posed as a potential recruit at a Hare Krishna temple. Goldberg lives with her husband in New York, where she is currently at work on a new novel.

Questions for reflection and discussion

1. The pain of family relationships is at the heart of *Bee Season*. What do you think causes the tragedy of miscommunication in the Naumann family? Does it have one cause, or has it built slowly over time? What could family members do differently? One problem seems to be that each parent has been assigned his or her child: Saul

has Aaron, while Miriam has Eliza. And yet neither parent really connects with "his" or "her" child. How alike are Saul and Aaron? Miriam and Eliza? Saul believes he discovers that Eliza is truly "his" child, but do they really have more in common than he and Aaron?

2. Perfectionism plays out both in the spelling bees that punctuate the novel and in the study of Jewish religion and mysticism to which Saul devotes his life. These are characters who desire perfection. Why? What do they hope to find in the perfect world? When does the search for perfection become dysfunction? Why does the kaleidoscope symbolize perfection for Miriam? While some readers have criticized Goldberg's handling of Miriam, she is certainly a fascinating character. What do you think of the way Miriam replicates her kaleidoscope as an adult?

3. Each member of the Naumann family has his or her role. Over the course of the novel, these roles begin to change and disintegrate. What do the parents expect from their children? What do the children expect from their parents? Think about the ways we get trapped into certain roles in our families. What role do you play in yours? Have you ever tried to break free? What happened? Saul and Miriam have the best intentions; how and why do they fail?

4. Reviewers and readers comment frequently on *Bee Season*'s ending. Did you find it satisfying or abrupt? Goldberg has commented in interviews that she likes books that drop you into the characters' lives and pull you out at the end without wrapping things up and telling you what's going to happen. Did she achieve that kind of ending in *Bee Season*? What's appealing about an ending that resolves all the crises set in motion by the plot? Why might an author want to write an ending that leaves certain threads of the story unresolved?

5. Goldberg has been praised by reviewers for her ability to evoke the atmosphere of elementary school. What resonated for you in her descriptions of Eliza's classroom? School memories tend to be clear and sharp. What memories does *Bee Season* evoke for you? Reviewers and readers alike have been fascinated by the spelling bee plot and motif. What is compelling about this theme?

DISCUSSION/REFLECTION STRATEGY

What can you learn about an author's choice of subject, style, and techniques from reading her favorite books? Myla Goldberg's favorites include *Pale Fire* by Vladimir Nabokov, *CivilWarLand in Bad Decline* by George Saunders, *The Life of Insects* by Victor Pelevin, and *Infinite Jest* by David Foster Wallace. Assign these books to book group members who can then report on what Goldberg's reading taste says about her and her work.

If you like *Bee Season,* you will like...

The Romance Reader by Pearl Abraham. Heroine secretly rebels against her family's Hasidic beliefs by checking out romance novels from her library and taking lifesaving lessons.

Skirts by Mimi Albert. This novel about three young women negotiating the 1960s turns up on many recommended reading lists.

The Family Markowitz by Allegra Goodman. Critically acclaimed interconnected short stories about a Jewish family.

Allegra Maud Goldman by Edith Konecky. Coming-of-age novel with family conflict and humor.

Schooling by Heather McGowan. A challenging novel about an American girl attending an English boarding school.

Video resources

Goldberg notes that *Welcome to the Dollhouse* (Todd Solondz, 1996) shares themes with *Bee Season*. *Searching for Bobby Fischer* (Steve Zaillian, 1993) is about a child chess prodigy. In *Little Man Tate* (Jodie Foster, 1991), Foster plays a working-class single mom trying to do the right thing for her prodigy son. *Matilda* (Danny DeVito, 1996) stars the adorable Mara Wilson as a precocious child.

Internet resources

Read an excellent interview with Goldberg and listen to her read from *Bee Season* at www.randomhouse.com/boldtype/0500/goldberg. An interview with BookSense, on the independent booksellers' website, is archived at www.booksense.com/people/archive/goldbergmyla.jsp. Find a reading group guide with lots of discussion questions at www.randomhouse.com/vintage/read/beeseason/.

Did you know...?

The word *kabbalah* is Hebrew for "tradition." Kabbalah refers to a body of written texts and oral teachings constituting Jewish mysticism. The chief document of kabbalism is the *Zohar*, a thirteenth-century document which purports to reveal—to those trained to understand it—the deepest mysteries of the universe such as the nature of the divine, the course of human destiny, and the true meaning of the commandments. Kabbalistic studies flourished in Europe from the thirteenth century through the eighteenth. Like its counterparts in Christianity and Islam, Jewish mysticism occupies an uneasy relationship to Jewish orthodoxy. To find out more, read *Kabbalah* by Gershom Scholem and *The Essential Kabbalah: The Heart of Jewish Mysticism* by Daniel Chanan Matt.

September/Back to School
Classic
Jane Eyre by Charlotte Brontë, 1847, several paperback editions available, including one from Penguin Classics for $7.95

What is this book about?

Jane Eyre is a coming-of-age story about a poor orphan despised and exiled by her only living relative to the Lowood School for girls to become a governess. Her school years are a nightmare of deprivation and abuse, but Jane survives and takes a position as governess at the gloomy and isolated Thornfield, home of Mr. Rochester. Thus the first half of the novel finds Jane grown into an intelligent, independent woman, seeking to sustain herself through the ill-paid position of governess. Readers are not surprised to find Jane inevitably falling in love with the moody Mr. Rochester, but Brontë denies us the happy ever after when revelations of Rochester's dark, secret past force Jane to run away from him just before their wedding. The rest of the novel sees Jane nearly dying of starvation and exposure before finding refuge and more with the Rivers family. Brontë keeps her readers in suspense as to when and where Jane will again meet Rochester, perhaps adding to the intense satisfaction felt when circumstances contrive a reunion of the two.

What should I know about the author?

Charlotte Brontë was born in 1816, the third child of an Anglican clergyman and his wife. She spent most of her life living with her father (her mother died when Charlotte was a child), except for brief periods at school in England and Belgium and later when she left home to teach and work as a governess. Her first published work was a volume of poetry coauthored with her sisters, Emily and Anne, published under the pseudonyms Currer, Ellis, and Acton Bell. Brontë also published *Jane Eyre* as Currer Bell to avoid criticism and celebrity, but her identity eventually become known. She corresponded with several leading literary figures of her day and wrote four novels altogether. She married her father's vicar in 1855 and died nine months later from what is thought to be complications from pregnancy.

Questions for reflection and discussion

1. Think about Jane Eyre as a small child and as the adult she becomes. In what ways does she live up to the promise seen in the feisty little girl who defies her aunt and then thinks, "[M]y soul began to expand, to exult with the strangest sense of freedom, of triumph, I ever felt. It seemed as if an invisible bond had burst, and that I had struggled out into unhoped-for liberty." How would you describe Jane Eyre's character? What specific events and circumstances shaped her personality?

2. Charlotte Brontë acknowledged basing the Lowood School on her own childhood boarding school where her two oldest sisters became ill and afterward died. Scholar Juliet Barker claims that as difficult as Lowood and the real school upon which it is modeled are, they are not outside the norm for schools of that time. Based on your understanding of Lowood, your group may want to discuss why parents and guardians continued sending young girls to such schools. Are there any justifications for the privations to which the girls were exposed? For what are the girls in Lowood being prepared?

3. Victorian critics of *Jane Eyre* criticized the depiction of passion in the novel—they thought it too intense and that Jane and Rochester's relationship was an inappropriate model of relationships for young women. There is no question about the sexual energy between Jane and Rochester, but what else about Rochester might Jane find compelling? Is Rochester a standard romantic hero? If you have read Jane Austen's *Pride and Prejudice*, compare Rochester to Darcy. How does Austen's idea of the romantic hero differ from Brontë's? Did your opinion of Rochester change when you found out about Bertha? Do you think he was cruel or a victim of circumstance (or both)? Did you want Jane to be with him?

4. Moral decision-making is an important component of *Jane Eyre*. What role does it play in Jane's decision to leave Rochester? What does Jane find wrong in Rochester's arguments for her to stay? Within the context of the novel's setting, could it be argued that she is being overly scrupulous? How is her decision to leave consistent with her behavior in the rest of the novel? Were you disappointed in her, or did you support her decision? What about her return to Rochester in the end? Why was it okay for her to be with him at that point?

5. Brontë presents us with three different models of Christianity in Reverend Brocklehurst, Helen Burns, and St. John Rivers. How does each of these characters model Christianity, and how do they think people ought to live? Though Brocklehurst and Rivers are both clergymen, what differences between them are evident in the ways they think about God and duty? How does Jane talk about responsibility, duty, sacrifice, and God? Based on your group's discussion

of these questions, what personal ideas about Christianity, the clergy, and duty might Brontë be revealing to her readers?

Did you know...?

In *Jane Eyre* there are several instances where characters attempt to figure out what other individuals are like by studying their physical appearances—most usually the size and shape of the skull. The study of character from appearance is called **physiognomy** and has been around for centuries. The early nineteenth century saw the attempt to standardize and codify physiognomic practices into a science called **phrenology**. For more information about phrenology, visit the Web at www.jmvanwyhe.freeserve.co.uk/what_is_phren.htm.

Other books by Charlotte Brontë

The Professor, the first novel Charlotte Brontë wrote, was not published until after her death in 1855. *Shirley*, written in the months after her sisters' deaths, is historically interesting for its account of disputes between workers and factory owners in the early nineteenth century. The Brontë family lived during a violent period as mechanization replaced manual labor in the north of England, and much of what Brontë relates in *Shirley* is based on actual events. *Villette*, Brontë's last novel, expands and improves upon themes from *The Professor*, but rivals *Jane Eyre* in its passion and power.

Books about Charlotte Brontë

The Life of Charlotte Brontë by Elizabeth Gaskell was written at the request of Charlotte's father and published just a few years after her death. It is fascinating to read, but Mrs. Gaskell is guilty of almost dehumanizing Brontë through her idolization of her.

Excellent biographies of the Brontës include *The Brontës: Charlotte Brontë and Her Family* by Rebecca Fraser; *Charlotte Brontë: A Passionate Life* by Lyndall Gordon; and *Charlotte Brontë: The Evolution of Genius* by Winifred Gerin. Juliet Barker's *The Brontës* is a detailed, scholarly work studying the entire family. Barker has also edited *The Brontës: A Life in Letters*.

If you are now hooked on the Brontës, you may wish to read *The Brontë Myth* by Lucasta Miller. Miller writes not so much about the Brontës themselves, but about what has been said about them in the 150 years since they died. Miller undertakes a review of biographies and critical studies of the Brontës in order to demonstrate how shifting social and literary concerns have influenced interpretations of their lives and works.

If you like *Jane Eyre,* you will like...

Wuthering Heights by Emily Brontë. A strange and powerful story of passion and romance that haunts readers with its dual portrayal of love between two generations of Catherines and their Heathcliffs.

Agnes Grey and *The Tenant of Wildfell Hall* by Anne Brontë. The first features a governess, while the latter portrays a disturbing view of an abusive, alcoholic husband, perhaps based on her brother Branwell.

North and South, Mary Barton: A Tale of Manchester Life, and *Wives and Daughters* by Elizabeth Gaskell. Charlotte Brontë's friend, first biographer, and an excellent novelist in her own right, writes of love and family among English villagers.

Deerbrook by Harriet Martineau. A delightful novel by a novelist, essayist, and historian and a contemporary of Charlotte Brontë. Martineau also wrote a biographical sketch of Brontë which was part of a larger work, *Biographical Sketches*.

Wide Sargasso Sea by Jean Rhys. In this novel published in 1966, Bertha Rochester finally tells her story.

Video resources

Filmmakers are drawn to the dramatic intensity of *Jane Eyre* and *Wuthering Heights*. From the sinister halls of Thornfield to the wild landscape of the Yorkshire moors, the Brontës created a cinematographer's dream. The many film versions of these novels include classic Hollywood versions: the 1944 *Jane Eyre* (Robert Stevenson) starring

Joan Fontaine and Orson Welles with a young Elizabeth Taylor as Helen Burns, and the 1939 *Wuthering Heights* with Merle Oberon and Laurence Olivier (William Wyler). Most recently, *Wuthering Heights,* starring Ralph Fiennes and Juliette Binoche, was released in 1992 (Peter Kosminsky). Also available is the much-praised 1983 BBC dramatization with Zelah Clarke as Jane Eyre and Timothy Dalton as Rochester (Julian Amyes). Charlotte Gainsbourg and William Hurt took over the lead roles in Franco Zeffirelli's lush 1996 adaptation. Just one year later, Samantha Morton and Ciaran Hinds (who makes a memorable Captain Wentworth in Roger Michell's adaptation of Jane Austen's *Persuasion*) starred in another made-for-television movie. *Wide Sargasso Sea,* Jean Rhys's novel about Bertha Rochester, was made into a movie starring Karina Lombard (John Duigan, 1993).

Extra credit

"You examine me, Miss Eyre," said he; "do you think me handsome?" I should, if I had deliberated, have replied to this question by something conventionally vague and polite; but the answer somehow slipped from my tongue before I was aware: "No, sir."

Since he burst onto the literary scene in 1847, Mr. Rochester has been one of English literature's most compelling romantic heroes. He is neither conventionally handsome nor charming. He's moody, tempestuous, and, at times, arrogant. Why is he so popular? Who plays him best on film? Rent or borrow from libraries as many different versions of *Jane Eyre* as you can find. Have them all cued to the same scene (for example, when Rochester falls off his horse and meets Jane, the wedding, the final scene). Who is your favorite Rochester and why? Be prepared— sparks may fly in the ensuing argument!

Internet resources

Visit www.bronte.org.uk for information about the Brontë family, the Brontë Society, the Haworth Parsonage (the Brontë family home, now a museum), and the history of Yorkshire. For an extensive site on Charlotte Brontë, her life and place within the history of Victorian literature, go to landow.stg.brown.edu and click on The Victorians. Stop by the Internet Movie Data Base, www.imdb.com, to read viewer comments and reviews about the films adapted from *Jane Eyre*, including lots of arguments about which actor makes the best Rochester.

September/Back to School
Challenge
Moo by Jane Smiley, 1996, available in paperback from Ivy Books for $7.99

What is this book about?

Jane Smiley's tour-de-force academic satire, *Moo*, is set at the fictional Moo U., a large midwestern agricultural university. The cast of characters is enormous, ranging from Mary, one of the few minority students at Moo U., to Cecilia Sanchez, the beautiful Spanish professor whose South American parents immigrated to L.A., to "the Albino Nordic twins"—administrators Niles and Ivar Harstad, to Loraine Walker, the provost's powerful secretary, to Earl Butz, a special experimental pig who's bred to eat. In seventy short chapters, Smiley inhabits each character in turn, including Earl Butz, masterfully juggling dozens of plot strands that ultimately converge. Smiley uses the university as microcosm and plays its petty power struggles for farce. Unlike much academic satire, *Moo* goes behind the scenes at the university, moving out of the classroom to the business behind education, exposing the cutthroat financial machinations of departments and university offices, the territorial battles of building maintenance staff and groundskeepers, and the infiltration of big business—in the form of McDonald's and the dairy industry—into the university. But the university is not Smiley's only target; in fact, it could be argued that she uses the university setting to land the bigger fish of agribusiness and technology. *Moo* is an incredibly satisfying read, building tension through a suspenseful plot and, in true comic fashion, portioning out just desserts in the final chapters.

Readers who find *Moo* a departure from Smiley's previous works, especially *A Thousand Acres*, will be interested to learn about her master plan: "I always wanted to write both a tragedy and a comedy on the same theme. *A Thousand Acres* was the tragedy, the theme was American agriculture and technology, and *Moo* was the comedy."

What should I know about the author?

Jane Smiley was born in California in 1949 and grew up in Missouri. She obtained her masters and doctorate degrees from the University of Iowa, and taught at Iowa State University for fifteen years. She has published ten novels since 1981; in 1992, she won the Pulitzer Prize and the National Book Critics Circle Award for *A Thousand Acres*. She currently lives in California. Readers of her novel *Horse Heaven* should note that she owns over a dozen horses.

Extra credit

Attend a college sporting event, lecture, author reading, play, or concert at a local college or university. Most colleges also offer continuing education classes. Why not take a literature class?

Questions for reflection and discussion

1. Smiley chronicles the life of Moo U. through the characters who live and work there. The novel is divided into seventy chapters that cycle through the large cast of characters. Because Smiley must juggle so many plot lines, the organization of *Moo* takes on great importance. How is this book organized? How does Smiley enable the reader to keep track of the characters? What role do the chapter titles play? What about the unusual information she sometimes presents in chapters, like memos, letters, even a Spanish-language newspaper article? What plot elements or devices recur throughout and help keep the reader focused and the plot moving forward?

2. Alison Lurie argues that Earl Butz is the central character in *Moo*. What does Earl represent? Why is Smiley's characterization of this pig so effective? What is comic about him? How do you read Earl's ultimate fate? Ironically? Poignantly?

3. Issues like technology, the environment, and the uses and abuses of power are obviously important to Smiley. She herself observes that, "I feel that my novels have an underlying political purpose." Does *Moo* have a moral purpose or deliver a moral or ethical message? Smiley is very conscious of writing a comedy. Think about the comedies you have read. Do comedies need to deliver moral lessons? What about satire? Is the purpose of writing satire to expose an evil and prescribe a cure, or merely to relish the irony and wit that emerges from exposé?

4. *Moo*'s ending satisfies the demands of comic resolution: good characters are rewarded, bad characters are punished, and there's even a wedding. Is this a satisfying ending, or do you find it too pat? What happens to the different characters in the end? How are the crises of the plot resolved?

5. One criticism of this novel is that there are simply too many characters, requiring too much concentration on the part of the reader to keep them straight. Do you agree with this characterization of *Moo*? Did you have trouble following the story? One potential drawback to creating such a large cast is that the story can never focus too long on any individual character. Were there some characters you wanted to know better or spend more time with? How does Smiley manage to convey the history of an individual succinctly? Which characters strike you as the most well-rounded? The most effective?

Other books by Jane Smiley

With the publication of *The All-True Adventures of Lidie Newton* in 1998, Jane Smiley reached the goal she set for herself as a writer: to produce works in the four fundamental genres of epic, tragedy, comedy, and romance. Her epic is *The Greenlanders*, a lengthy saga of Iceland (1988); her tragedy is *A Thousand Acres*, a retelling of the *King Lear* story set on a farm in Iowa (1991). The comedy, of course, is *Moo* (1995). And *The*

All-True Adventures of Lidie Newton counts as her romance. Both her first and her most recent novels center around horses: *Barn Blind* (1980) is a family tragedy, while *Horse Heaven* (1999) satirizes the world of horse racing. *At Paradise Gate* (1981) is another family drama, while *Duplicate Keys* (1984), which Smiley has called an exercise in craft, is a compelling mystery. Her novellas and shorter fiction are collected in *The Age of Grief* (1987) and *Ordinary Love and Good Will* (1989). Smiley also contributes frequent—and good—essays to a variety of publications; be on the lookout for her writing.

If you like *Moo*, you will like...

Lucky Jim by Kingsley Amis. *The* classic academic satire, set in postwar Britain.

The Handmaid of Desire by John L'Heureux. Clever academic satire set in an English department at a California university.

Small World, Changing Places: A Tale of Two Campuses, and *Nice Work* by David Lodge. Fantastic trilogy of academic satires set in America and Britain.

The Groves of Academe by Mary McCarthy. Biting look at the pettiness and absurdities of academic life, set on the campus of a small college.

Blue Angel by Francine Prose. Disturbing novel about a creative writing professor who is accused of sexual harassment by a student.

Straight Man by Richard Russo. Perhaps the funniest academic satire ever written, this novel focuses on a creative writing teacher.

Video resources

Smiley's *A Thousand Acres* (Jocelyn Moorhouse, 1997) stars Michelle Pfeiffer and Jessica Lange. *Lucky Jim* was adapted by John Boulting in 1957. *In Custody*, a comedy set on a college campus in India and starring the great Indian actor Om Puri, was a Merchant-Ivory adaptation in 1994.

Internet resources

Read a brief interview with Smiley, focusing on *The All-True Travels and Adventures of Lidie Newton*, at www.bookpage.com/9804bp/jane_smiley.html. www.powells.com has a detailed interview concentrating on *Horse Heaven*: www.powells.com/authors/smiley.html. The *New York Times* archive contains a page devoted to Smiley, including reviews and interviews, at www.nytimes.com/books/98/04/05/specials/smiley.html.

September/Back to School
Memoir
Dangerous Minds by LouAnne Johnson, 1992, originally published as *My Posse Don't Do Homework*, available in paperback from St. Martin's Paperbacks for $6.50

What is this book about?

Dangerous Minds is a quick, easy read of inspirational stories about tough high school students encountering an even tougher English teacher. If September finds members of your book group pressed for time, this would make a good selection.

LouAnne Johnson is a former member of the U.S. Navy and the U.S. Marine Corps who teaches English in an inner-city high school. She is horrified by the apathy and ignorance of her students. Students play cards in class, paint their fingernails, sleep, and in general, do everything but pay attention. The students, who are used to being able to intimidate new teachers, do not expect Johnson to last long, but they are in for a surprise. She is determined to reach these kids and show them how to work to their full potential. Johnson's commitment and hard work are truly impressive, and her story is affecting and inspiring. For many of these teenagers, Johnson is the first person ever to extend her hand, her mind, and her heart to them. She listens, advises, cajoles, teaches, and even screams when necessary. She is there for her students, and they know it. The reader cheers when Johnson succeeds and worries when she fails.

What should I know about the author?

LouAnne Johnson was born in 1953 in Pennsylvania. She received a B.S. from the University of LaVerne and an M.A. and teaching certification from the College of Notre Dame in Belmont, California. She has worked in a plastics factory on the assembly line and on a newspaper as staff writer and editor. From 1971 to 1980, she was in the United States Navy. In addition, she spent time in the Marine Corps.

Extra credit

Share your personal favorites or recently-reads with members of your book group by organizing an annual book swap. Each member should bring three or four books to swap. This is a great way to discover new books and authors and a fun way to recycle your own books. You might want to schedule your book swap around the holidays and add a cookie-swap component!

Questions for reflection and discussion

1. What does Johnson reveal about herself in this memoir? Or could the reader argue that she hides more than she reveals? What leads Johnson to become a teacher? In spite of her success with many of her students, Johnson does not have long-range plans to continue teaching in the inner-city school in this story. What qualities does she evidence that would suggest that teaching there could have been a "calling" for her? Reading about a powerful teacher can bring back memories of our own favorite and best teachers. Your group may want to pool the qualities that you think are needed in order to be a successful teacher, and then discuss how Johnson compares with your list.

2. Discuss the students Johnson works with. Which ones made the greatest impression on you? What characteristics, attitudes, and behaviors do the students share? What do they believe in, and how do they feel about themselves? How do the students relate to Johnson? What does she do that reaches them?

3. In addition to focusing on the problems of her students, Johnson has provided insight into our educational system. In what ways does Johnson think we are failing our young people? The Academy, which is the last hope for these students, is riddled with internal problems. What are some of Johnson's greatest concerns? How does the school in this story compare to the schools with which you are familiar?

4. This book is marketed as a memoir, but has the author really shared much about her own life? What, in general, do you expect from a memoir? Have those expectations been met in *Dangerous Minds*? Your group may want to discuss how Johnson's students and fellow teachers might describe the same events that Johnson relates. In comparison with the picture Johnson provides of herself, how might the views of her students and colleagues differ?

5. High school is, for better or worse, an important formative experience in our lives. Your group may want to spend some time discussing your individual high school experiences. In *Dangerous Minds*, these students and their school reflect the problems of the inner-city community: violence, intimidation, racial tensions, teen pregnancy and fatherhood, but also the positive traits of loyalty, importance of family and friends, determination, and hope. In what ways did your high schools and classmates reflect your own communities' problems and values? What might Johnson's students have termed the best part of high school? What parts of your high school experiences would you claim as the best? Is there any correlation between what you found memorable in a positive sense and what you think might have been positive for Johnson's posse?

Other books by LouAnne Johnson

The Girls in the Back of the Class is the sequel to *Dangerous Minds*. Johnson has also written a memoir about her time in the military called *Making Waves*.

If you like *Dangerous Minds*, you will like...

Small Victories: The Real World of a Teacher, Her Students, and Their High School by Samuel G. Freedman. True story of a teacher and her students in an inner-city school.

Goodbye, Mr. Chips by James Hilton. The heartwarming (and heart breaking) story of an English schoolteacher in the nineteenth century.

The Blackboard Jungle by Evan Hunter. Bestselling novel of 1954 about student violence.

My First Year as a Teacher edited by Pearl Rock Kane. Twenty-five true stories from first-year teachers about their trials and triumphs.

Educating Esme: Diary of a Teacher's First Year by Esme Raji Codell. A new teacher describes how her first year of teaching was equally about her own learning experiences.

Video resources

My Posse Don't Do Homework became the mediocre *Dangerous Minds* when it was adapted for film (John N. Smith, 1995). For a look at America's high schools in films with better critic and viewer response, you might want to try *Stand and Deliver* (Ramon Menendez, 1988).

Extra credit

September is a great time to revisit all the terrific movies made about schools and teachers. Don't miss *The Blackboard Jungle* (Richard Brooks, 1955) with Glenn Ford and Sidney Poitier and *Rebel without a Cause* (Nicholas Ray, 1955) starring James Dean. *Lean on Me* (John Avildsen, 1989) stars Morgan Freeman as a high school principal who turns the institution around, while Robin Williams shows in *Dead Poets Society* (Peter Weir, 1989)

---

that inner-city youth aren't the only ones who can be disaffected. The classic 1939 version of *Goodbye, Mr. Chips* (Sam Wood) is a wonderful film. *To Sir, with Love* (James Clavell, 1967) stars Sidney Poitier as an inspirational teacher and features that great theme song by Lulu, who also appears in the movie. Maggie Smith won an Oscar for her portrayal of the teacher in *The Prime of Miss Jean Brodie* (Ronald Neame, 1969). *Educating Rita* (Lewis Gilbert, 1983) is a wonderful movie with Michael Caine as a burnt-out college professor and Julie Walter as a tough working-class woman eager for an education. And, of course, there are the comedies. John Hughes contributed several good movies to the genre, including *The Breakfast Club* (1985) and *Ferris Bueller's Day Off* (1986), as has Amy Heckerling with *Fast Times at Ridgemont High* (1982) and the delightful *Clueless* (1995). And don't forget the crude (but still funny) *High School High* (Hart Bochner, 1996).

Internet resources

Visit the Department of Education's website at www.ed.gov/gearup/, and read about the GEAR UP Program whose mission is "to significantly increase the number of low-income students who are prepared to enter and succeed in postsecondary education." For a site with links to articles on educational reform, try vocserve.berkeley.edu/CW63/notes.html. Be sure to check out the link at this site to NCRVE, the National Center for Research in Vocational Education at the University of Berkeley. This eleven-year project was designed to develop a new program for improving America's future workforce through school reform.

September/Back to School
Potluck
The Power of Their Ideas: Lessons for America from a Small School in Harlem by Deborah Meier, 1995, available in paperback from Beacon Press for $13.00

What is this book about?

The Power of Their Ideas is a collection of essays on school reform. Meier's work is informed by a single, core belief that public education is essential to a democracy, and democracy is essential for good public education. She favors small classes, lots of interaction between teachers and students (and teachers with other teachers) and parents, a commitment to teaching to different learning styles, and portfolio-based assessments. Somewhat surprisingly, she also favors school-choice initiatives since, she argues, choice gives communities the opportunity to operate the schools that work best for them.

Meier's book is grounded in her practical experience as an educator and activist and sharpened by her sense of history. Readers who think that public education has never been as bad as it is now will find her chapter "Myths, Lies, and Other Dangers" illusion-shattering. Anyone who has ever taught or has ever been taught will appreciate her thoughts on the five characteristics of a good teacher. If you are concerned about the behavior of young people, read the chapter "Respect." At the heart of *The Power of Their Ideas* is the belief that our schools hold the key to a brighter democratic future.

What should I know about the author?

Deborah Meier has been a teacher and advocate for school reform for over thirty years. She was the founder and teacher-director of the Central Park East Schools. She is an advisor to the Coalition for Essential Schools and a 1987 winner of a MacArthur Fellowship. Meier is currently the principal of the Mission Hill Elementary School in Boston.

Extra credit

Write a letter to the author of a book you've read. If you have been puzzled or intrigued by a book, or if you just love it, you can let the author know. Sometimes they even write back! (However, we don't recommend sending hate mail.) You can send letters to authors in care of their publishers; check publishers' websites for addresses.

Questions for reflection and discussion

1. What are the five "habits of mind" Central Park East Schools encourage students to acquire? What are the values of these habits and through what means does the school instill them in students? Why does the school rephrase the habits in different contexts? Meier claims that the five habits of mind are useful for almost any work that people do. Do you agree? Do you use these habits in your work?

2. What connections does Meier draw between public education and democracy? Why does she consider public education to be essential for democracy? Do you agree with her argument? Meier lists four reasons against the privatization of public schools. What are they, and do you find her arguments valid?

3. What are some of the myths and lies about education that Meier thinks distort our understanding of high school in the present? What was your own high school experience like? Did you experience or witness racism, bullying, poor standards, or violence? If you are a high school teacher or have children in high school, how does their experience differ from yours? How is it the same?

4. Deborah Meier lists six advantages that small schools have over big schools. What are they? Is she right? Are her plans for school reform feasible? Do her thoughts about small schools accord with your own experience?

5. What makes for a good teacher according to Meier? What qualities, characteristics, attitudes, and behaviors should they possess? Think of some of the teachers you have had in school. Were there any you really liked or who inspired you to work hard? How did they do it? Were there any who inspired your interest in a particular field or in a future career? How did they accomplish this?

Did you know...?

Reading discussion groups may seem like a new phenomenon, but they have a long and varied history. When books were difficult to come by, colonial Americans used to get together to purchase books and then read them aloud to one another. When African slaves were prohibited by law from learning to read and write, those that knew how would surreptitiously teach those that didn't. Later, African-American study groups continued to meet for learning and support. Community-based study groups have always been popular among groups of people barred from higher education. Women's study groups were plentiful during the latter half of the nineteenth century and well into the twentieth. Women frequently combined sewing groups with reading groups. Working men and women's associations held study groups for factory and mill workers. For more information, read *The Sound of Our Own Voices: Women's Study Clubs 1860–1910* by Theodora Penny Martin and *Intimate Practices: Literacy and Cultural Work in U.S. Women's Clubs, 1880–1920* by Anne Ruggles Gere. If you haven't already read *…And Ladies of the Club* by Helen Hooven Santmyer, a fictional account of a women's group, then do so. You will love it.

Other books by Deborah Meier

Will Standards Save Public Education? is edited by Meier with contributions from other educators. *The Passionate Teacher: A Practical Guide* is coauthored by Meier and Robert L. Fried. Deborah Meier and David Bensman wrote *Central Park East and Its Graduates: Learning by Heart*.

If you like *The Power of Their Ideas*, you will like...

Habits of the Heart: Individualism and Commitment in American Life by Robert N. Bellah et al. A landmark sociological study of American attitudes toward citizenship and community addressing many of the issues Meier raises.

The Right to Learn: A Blueprint for Creating Schools that Work by Linda Darling-Hammond. Darling-Hammond emphasizes collaboration and learning as a process and de-emphasizes testing and bureaucratization.

Experience and Education by John Dewey. A classic account of the short-comings of our education system and the ideals we should aspire to.

Savage Inequalities: Children in America's Schools by Jonathan Kozol. Exposes the problems in America's public schools, but also presents solutions.

Lives on the Boundary by Mike Rose. A look at how the underprivileged get labeled and educated.

Video resources

Check your local PBS station to see when they will be rebroadcasting *American High*, a documentary series that follows fourteen Chicago-area high school students. Also available from PBS is an episode of *Frontline* called, "The Battle Over School Choice."

Did you know...?

Central Park East Secondary School was fortunate to attract the attention of one of the world's best documentary filmmakers, Frederick Wiseman. In 1995, he released *High School II* a 220-minute documentary of life at CPESS. Like all of Wiseman's films, including the much-praised *High School* (1969) filmed at Philadelphia's Northeast High School, *High School II* is done in the style of *cinema verité* or direct cinema. There is no voice-over narration; the editing of the film provides the narrative structure. It is Wiseman's method to practically live with his subjects so that they will trust him and become more comfortable in front of the camera. He shoots lots of footage and spends a great deal of time on each film. To find out more, visit his website at www.zipporah.com.

Internet resources

Find the Coalition of Essential Schools at www.essentialschools.org. An interview with Deborah Meier in *Technos Quarterly* is at www.technos.net/journal/volume5/2meier.htm and an article by Meier, *Educating a Democracy*, can be found at bostonreview.mit.edu/BR24.6/meier.html.

CHAPTER 10

October
Scary Stories

CROWD-PLEASER
The Haunting of Hill House by Shirley Jackson

CLASSIC
Frankenstein by Mary Shelley

CHALLENGE
Lives of the Monster Dogs by Kirsten Bakis

MEMOIR
On Writing by Stephen King

POTLUCK
Neverwhere by Neil Gaiman

No live organism can continue for long to exist sanely under conditions of absolute reality; even larks and katydids are supposed, by some, to dream. Hill House, not sane, stood by itself against its hills, holding darkness within; it had stood so for eighty years and might stand for eighty more. Within, walls continued upright, bricks met neatly, floors were firm, and doors were sensibly shut; silence lay steadily against the wood and stone of Hill House, and whatever walked there, walked alone.

—Shirley Jackson, *The Haunting of Hill House*

What's so scary about the opening to Shirley Jackson's psychological thriller, *The Haunting of Hill House*? Well, nothing—until you've read the novel and come across the same passage in the concluding chapter. The same words resonate altogether differently after we've watched the house torment one of the main characters and ultimately cause her to break down. What reads as straightforward narrative description on the first page changes to creepy terror by the last. Horror is, as Jackson's novel proves, a state of mind.

October is the month traditionally set aside for thrills and chills. We scare ourselves with haunted houses, midnight hayrides, and talk of ghosts and goblins. Our choices for October reflect the seasonal emphasis on fear. Shirley Jackson reworks the classic plot of the haunted house, while Neil Gaiman imagines a dark underworld of assassins, rats, and beasts living in London Below. *Frankenstein* and *Lives of the Monster Dogs* provide a different kind of terror—the disturbing vision of technology run amok. These two tales of mad scientists and the monsters they create should appeal to any group wishing to think more deeply about the issues of technology and genetic manipulation that confront us daily on the news. For readers who don't want to be scared even in October, we suggest Stephen King's charming memoir, *On Writing*, which mixes autobiography with insight and practical advice about the writing life.

October/Scary Stories
Crowd-Pleaser
The Haunting of Hill House by Shirley Jackson, 1959, available in paperback from Viking Press for $13.00

What is this book about?

No less a master of suspense than Stephen King himself called *The Haunting of Hill House* one of the greatest horror novels of all time. The plot is set into motion by Dr. Montague, a scientist. He decides to gather a group of people who have a previous history of paranormal contact at Hill House, already believed to be haunted, and to record what takes place. But very few people respond to his inquiry, and he's left with a group of three: Theodora, Eleanor, and Luke, who will one day inherit the house from his aunt. Added to this cast of four are the Dudleys, the peculiar caretakers who will only enter Hill House during daylight hours. Hill House is oddly designed, and even odder things have happened there, including several deaths. Unsurprisingly, strange things begin to happen almost immediately; it soon becomes clear that the target of the house's ire is Eleanor. This psychological thriller investigates how the house and the tension caused by the claustrophobic atmosphere and manifestations that may or may not be supernatural bring out quirks and neuroses in the characters—especially in Eleanor. This is a good, old-fashioned ghost story, but also a thought-provoking study of the power of place to affect the mind.

What should I know about the author?

Shirley Jackson's family heritage includes an interest in architecture; her great-great-grandfather was an architect who designed some of San Francisco's oldest buildings and mansions. Born in 1916, she grew up in California and began writing as a child. She began publishing her fiction in well-known magazines like the New Republic and the New Yorker in 1941. Her first novel, The Road through the Wall, was published in 1948, but more importantly, this year also saw the publication of her most famous story, "The Lottery," which is still frequently anthologized. One of her biographers notes that she was at her most productive when her time was most limited; she wrote and published most during the 1950s, when her four children were small. Another biographer chronicles the health problems—both physical and mental—which increasingly plagued her as she aged. She died in 1965.

Did you know...?

In a 1949 interview, Shirley Jackson called Samuel Richardson and Frances Burney, both eighteenth-century novelists, her favorite writers, along with Katherine Anne Porter and Elizabeth Bowen.

Questions for reflection and discussion

1. Shirley Jackson did not write exclusively in the horror or thriller genre, but she did claim, "I've always loved to use fear" in her writing. Why would Jackson find fear so powerful? What fears does she play on? Why do we like to be scared? What makes *The Haunting of Hill House* a horror novel? Do you think this novel is as affecting today as it was in 1959 when it was first published, or have we become desensitized to creepiness and spookiness?

2. Hill House functions as a major character in this novel; both the opening and closing paragraphs focus exclusively on the house's sensations. What role does the house play? How does Jackson describe it? What is strange about Hill House? Jackson wrote two other "novels of setting," as literary scholar Lenemaja Friedman describes these house novels: *The Sundial* and *We Have Always Lived in the Castle*. What might a writer find attractive about the limited setting of a house?

3. Group dynamics play an important role in contributing to the suspense of *The Haunting of Hill House*, but the characters also seem somewhat generic, even stereotypical. How would you describe each of the characters, and what roles do they play in the story? How do they work together as a group? Does the ghost story in general depend on generic characters? Why or why not?

4. As Eleanor becomes the focus of the paranormal manifestations, she also becomes the novel's main character. The other characters accuse her of creating the manifestations. What is her role in the persecution? Is she responsible? What is Eleanor's history, and why is she here? Is she an effectively drawn, well-rounded character? Does her fate at the end of the novel provide closure satisfactorily?

5. Point of view refers to the vantage point from which the story is told. From whose point of view is *The Haunting of Hill House* told? Does it shift, change, or develop as the novel progresses? The reader is more than once left questioning the authenticity of Eleanor's interpretation of events. Who is our authority for what is happening? Whom do we believe? How does the point of view

contribute to the suspense of the story? Is the book chilling only because we often see events through Eleanor's eyes?

Other books by Shirley Jackson

Jackson is the author of five novels in addition to *The Haunting of Hill House*: *The Road through the Wall* (1948), *Hangsaman* (1951), *Bird's Nest* (1954), *The Sundial* (1958), and *We Have Always Lived in the Castle* (1962), which many critics consider her best work. She wrote two humorous memoirs about family life: *Life Among the Savages* (1953) and *Raising Demons* (1957). Her short fiction, which we highly recommend, is collected in *The Lottery and Other Stories; Come Along with Me: Part of a Novel, Sixteen Stories, and Three Lectures*; and *Just an Ordinary Day*. She also wrote children's books, essays, and reviews, some of which are still in print or collected in the above volumes.

Books about Shirley Jackson

Lenemaja Friedman's study of Jackson's fiction, *Shirley Jackson*, is useful and includes a brief biography. Judy Oppenheimer's full-length biography, *Private Demons: The Life of Shirley Jackson*, is well worth reading.

If you like *The Haunting of Hill House*, you will like...

Northanger Abbey by Jane Austen. In this early novel, Austen has great fun parodying eighteenth-century gothic novels.

The Amityville Horror: A True Story by Jay Anson. Supposedly true story of what happened to the Lutz family who lived in this home in Amityville, New York.

The Oxford Book of Gothic Tales edited by Chris Baldick. This collection takes a look at the development of the gothic genre from the early eighteenth century to its modern form.

The Turn of the Screw by Henry James. A classic ghost story, notorious for its sexual undertones.

Hell House by Richard Matheson. Another story of an investigation into a haunted mansion where horrible events have occurred.

Video resources

The Haunting of Hill House has been adapted twice, both times under the title *The Haunting*: in 1963, directed by Robert Wise and starring Julie Harris and Claire Bloom, and in 1999, directed by Jan de Bont and starring Catherine Zeta Jones and Lili Taylor. *The Turn of the Screw* has been adapted many times; Rusty Lemorande's 1992 version is especially memorable. *The Legend of Hell House* (John Hough, 1973) is a suspenseful adaptation of Matheson's novel. *Haunted* (Lewis Gilbert, 1995) features a great cast trapped at a haunted British estate. *The Others* (Alejandro Amenábar, 2001) is an excellent psychological thriller starring Nicole Kidman as a mother trapped in a haunted house with her two children.

Internet resources

The Shirley Jackson website organizes biographical, critical, and bibliographical information, as well as many helpful links at www.courses.vcu.edu/ENG-jkh/. Learn all there is to know about the Amityville murders and haunted house at www.amityvillehorror.com.

October/Scary Stories
Classic
Frankenstein: Or, the Modern Prometheus by Mary Shelley, 1818, several paperback editions available, including one from Signet Books for $3.95

What is this book about?

Victor Frankenstein is the brilliant, driven son of a wealthy, loving family. While studying the life sciences at university, Frankenstein becomes determined to master the secrets of nature. He collects body parts from hospitals, morgues, and cemeteries that, through his knowledge of science and technology, he brings to life. The creature resulting from this experiment is the hideous-looking monster familiar to us all. Frankenstein soon loses control of his creation and is forced to watch the destruction of all that he holds dear.

Mary Shelley wrote *Frankenstein* in the early days of the Industrial Revolution. The world was changing rapidly as discoveries altered the traditional rhythms of society. The labor of craftsmen was being replaced by the work of machinery, and the role of the scientist was beginning to usurp the authority of the clergy with respect to matters of ultimate importance. *Frankenstein's* popularity, both in its own day and in our own, is due to Shelley's ability to illustrate the excitement and the fear that constitutes our relationship with science and technology. Shelley asks us to consider whether the goals of advancing knowledge and making the world a better place are really worth the cost. How much do we pay for our reliance on technology? What responsibility do we bear for our creations?

Did you know...?

Mary Shelley was inspired to write *Frankenstein* after she and her husband, poet Percy Bysshe Shelley, spent an evening at Lord Byron's villa on Lake Geneva in Switzerland. Prevented by bad weather from returning to their own rented villa, the guests entertained their host by reading aloud German ghost stories. Inspired by these stories, Byron suggested the company compete to see who could write the best ghost story. Mary Shelley was not immediately inspired, but a few nights later, after discussing science's capacity to bring a corpse back to life, she had a "waking nightmare" in which she envisioned Dr. Frankenstein and his creation. She set to work on her tale immediately.

What should I know about the author?

Mary Shelley lived from 1797 to 1851. She was the only daughter of political theorist William Godwin and feminist writer Mary Wollstonecraft (author of *A Vindication of the Rights of Women*), who died giving birth to her. Shelley's father educated his daughter well, and the family knew many of the leading artists and thinkers of the day. When she was seventeen, Mary Shelley ran off with the poet Percy Bysshe

Shelley, only marrying him after his wife committed suicide two years later. After his death in a sailing accident in 1822, Mary Shelley edited, annotated, and published volumes of his poetry and supported herself and their only surviving child by writing novels.

Questions for reflection and discussion

1. In ancient Greek mythology, Prometheus is a Titan (not human, but not a god either) who steals fire from the gods and bestows it on humanity. Fire is both a great benefit to people, but also a terrible danger. For his action, Prometheus is severely punished by Zeus: he is chained to a rock and everyday an eagle swoops down upon him, tears open his belly, and rips out his liver. Every evening Prometheus's liver grows back so the torture can continue the next day. Why did Mary Shelley subtitle the book *Or, the Modern Prometheus*?

2. Consider the book as an allegory about our reliance on science and technology. Are people still afraid of changes in the way we live? We, like Mary Shelley, are living in a period of rapid technological change altering our lives in dramatic ways. Discuss some of the scientific changes happening in your lifetime. Do you ever find these changes threatening? Why or why not? Are these changes always "progress"?

3. There are many descriptions of natural scenery in the book. What effect might Shelley be seeking to create on her readers? What is Victor Frankenstein's relationship with nature? What is the significance of setting the beginning and end of the book upon the Arctic Sea? What does Shelley convey through her use of land and sea descriptions?

4. One of the major themes of the novel is the issue of moral responsibility. Does Victor Frankenstein behave responsibly toward his creation or toward other characters? Why does he not confide to someone what he has created? Why does Frankenstein hate the monster so much—even before the monster has done anything wrong? What is Shelley saying about the moral responsibility of scientists for their discoveries, inventions, and creations?

5. The story of Victor Frankenstein and his creation is told through the character of Walton, the Arctic explorer. What do the letters of Walton to his sister tell us about him? What habits of mind or character do Walton and Frankenstein share? Do they differ in significant ways? What, if anything, does Walton learn from his encounter with Frankenstein? Do his actions at the end of the book signal any changes he has made in his thinking? Do you think Shelley is challenging conventional wisdom by questioning the value of the "explorer mentality"?

Other books by Mary Shelley

None of her other works ever achieved the popularity of *Frankenstein*, but Mary Shelley also wrote *Lodore*; *The Fortunes of Perkin Warbeck*; *Falkner*; *The Last Man*; and *Valperga: Or, the Life and Adventures of Castruccio, Prince of Lucca*. Modern readers might find *The Last Man* especially interesting—it is set in the future, and the human race is battling a plague that threatens to annihilate it. Shelley also wrote *History of a Six Weeks' Tour 1817*, a travel piece covering time spent with Percy Bysshe Shelley and Lord Byron.

Books about Mary Shelley

Mary Shelley's extraordinary life has been treated in several biographies and studies. *Mary Shelley: Romance and Reality* by Emily Sunstein and *Mary Shelley: Her Life, Her Fiction, Her Monsters* by Anne K. Mellor are two of the best. Her letters and journals are also well worth reading.

If you like *Frankenstein*, you will like...

The Monk by Matthew "Monk" Lewis. Lewis's sensational Gothic novel, published when he was just nineteen, influenced Mary Shelley.

The Memoirs of Elizabeth Frankenstein by Theodore Roszak. Historian and social critic Roszak has Elizabeth Frankenstein provide an alternative vision for science that emphasizes holism and cooperation with nature in opposition to Victor Frankenstein's insistence on mastery over nature.

The Strange Case of Dr. Jekyll and Mr. Hyde by Robert Louis Stevenson. Another classic exploration of the themes of evil and personal responsibility.

Dracula by Bram Stoker. If you've never read it, we highly recommend this classic tale of vampires and evil.

The Picture of Dorian Gray by Oscar Wilde. Dorian Gray leads a life of dissipation and depravity, but he never ages and his face never shows his character. His portrait, however, shows every sin.

Video resources

Try the 1931 *Frankenstein* with Boris Karloff (James Whale) along with its sequel, the 1935 *Bride of Frankenstein* starring Karloff and Elsa Lanchester (James Whale). Also recommended is the 1994 *Mary Shelley's Frankenstein* directed by and starring Kenneth Branagh as Victor and Robert DeNiro as the monster. *Haunted Summer* (Ivan Passer, 1988) is an atmospheric story of the summer the Shelleys met Byron. Ken Russell's *Gothic* (1986) imagines what happened the night the Shelleys and Byron told each other ghost stories. *Frankenstein Unbound* (Roger Corman, 1990) imagines a scientist from 2031 traveling back in time and meeting Mary Shelley.

Extra credit

Schedule a book group Halloween film festival. Rent or borrow several Frankenstein adaptations. Invite your families, serve a potluck dinner, and discuss how the different films treat key scenes from the book, e.g., the awakening of the monster or the death of the child.

Internet resources

The National Library of Medicine has an online exhibition on Mary Shelley and *Frankenstein* providing the scientific and intellectual context for the novel and tracing the correlations between scientific discoveries and popular resurgences of the Frankenstein story. The website is www.nlm.nih.gov/hmd/frankenstein/frankhome.html. Also worth exploring is the Mary Shelley webpage at www.english.udel.edu/swilson/mws/mws.html,

---

October/Scary Stories
Challenge
Lives of the Monster Dogs by Kirsten Bakis, 1997, available in paperback from Warner Books for $12.99

What is this book about?

Winner of the Bram Stoker Award for Best First Novel in 1998, this haunting novel opens with an excerpt from the diary of Monster Dog historian Ludwig Von Sachar. Like any good historian, Ludwig has collected old documents, conducted interviews, read and digested countless volumes, and taken notes. He is now trying to come to terms with his subject, to put the pieces in order, to find the narrative structure that best fits his story. The only catch? Ludwig is a German Shepherd. Like the other Monster Dogs, a race of surgically altered superintelligent canines, Ludwig, dressed in the latest Prussian fashions from circa 1890, leaves the northern Canadian city of Rankstadt after participating in a bloody rebellion to free the Monster Dogs from their human masters and heads for New York City to begin a new life. His diary narrates his intellectual struggles as a historian investigating the brilliant but unstable Augustus Rank, a nineteenth-century Prussian scientist whose dream was to create a race of super-dogs, and his own physical struggles as a Monster Dog whose mental and physical health is fast deteriorating.

Interspersed with Ludwig's history of the Monster Dogs' past is the first-person narration of NYU senior Cleo Pira, who describes what happens to the Monster Dogs in New York. Like all New Yorkers, Cleo had been well aware of the comings and goings of the Dogs: their arrival in New York is greeted with a blitz of media activity that never lets up. But a chance meeting with Ludwig leads to a job as the Dogs' official journalist. With access to the Dogs' leaders and friendship with the sympathetic Lydia Petze, a Samoyed, Cleo is well placed to document the apocalyptic last days of the Monster Dogs. Mixing beast fable, science fiction, and fantasy genres, as well as narrative forms including diary entries, journalism, and even an opera libretto, *Lives of the Monster Dogs* is one of the most unusual novels you'll ever read.

What should I know about the author?

Lives of the Monster Dogs is Kirsten Bakis's first novel. After graduating from New York University, she pursued graduate studies in creative writing at the Iowa Writers' Workshop. She describes herself, not surprisingly, as a dog-lover.

Questions for reflection and discussion

1. *Lives of the Monster Dogs* offers Bakis a chance to inhabit the voices and explore the motivations of a wide variety of characters, including a nineteenth-century mad scientist, a twenty-first-century college student, and, of course, the dogs themselves: quiet but passionate historian Ludwig von Sachar, fanatic Mops Hacker, dignified Lydia Petze, eager librettist Burkhardt, forceful financier Klaue. Many of these characters narrate their stories in their own voices, in the form of excerpts from diaries or letters. How convincing are the different voices? Some critics have claimed that Bakis's minor characters are underdeveloped. Do you agree? Which characters need to be fleshed out? Alternately, which voices and experiences resonate and why?

2. *Lives of the Monster Dogs* is a melange of different narrative styles and genres. Why do you think Bakis uses this complex mix of diary entries, reporting, newspaper articles, letters, plays, and opera librettos to tell her story? Why filter the history of Augustus Rank through Ludwig? What does the first-person narration and outsider perspective of Cleo offer? Added to the use of different genres is the juxtaposition of different time frames. The preface begins with Cleo post-Monster Dogs, while Ludwig's diary is written during the New York years, but recounts over one hundred years of history. Bakis's

narrative oscillates from past to present throughout the novel. Why do you think she chose to vary the time frame? Which scenes are especially effective when juxtaposed?

3. Do you think there is a connection between the mix of narrative modes and time scale and the different literary genres Bakis draws upon: beast fable, parable, science fiction, fantasy? John Clute, in his *Science Fiction Weekly* review, notes that nothing about the cover and marketing of *Lives of the Monster Dogs* indicates that it is science fiction or fantasy. Why might Bakis's publishers have chosen to market the novel as literary rather than science fiction? What would appeal to science fiction or fantasy enthusiasts about this novel?

4. Bakis obviously draws on a tradition of mad scientists and scientific experiments to craft her novel. If you've read *Frankenstein*, what similarities do you see between Dr. Frankenstein and Augustus Rank and between the creatures they create? The ethical issues raised by experimentation are especially pointed today. Your group may want to discuss the ethical limitations of experiments on animals—or humans. When is experimentation justified? For cosmetics? For medical purposes? Never? Find out more about the animal experimentation debate at www.peta-online.org and at www.pcrm.org (the website for the Physicians Committee for Responsible Medicine).

5. *Lives of the Monster Dogs* comes to a tragic conclusion as the dogs begin to deteriorate mentally and physically and the castle they build for New York catches fire during a party. How does the party work as a structuring device? (You might also think about the function of the party in novels like Virginia Woolf's *Mrs. Dalloway* or Margaret Drabble's *The Radiant Way*). What happens at the Monster Dogs' party? Why would Bakis choose to have the action of her novel culminate in a party? Does it work as an ending?

Did you know...?

In the simplest terms, **theme** refers to "the dominant idea of a work of literature," according to Merriam-Webster's *Encyclopedia of Literature* (1995). You will find that occasionally our discussion questions ask that you think about a certain theme within a book or genre. It is not necessary to search obsessively for the themes that may be in the books that your group reads, but often these themes that we discover as we read offer a rich field for discussion. For example, many of our Classics for December have as a theme a child's struggle for emotional survival; in our food-inspired selections for November, the books often concentrate on themes of family, women's friendships, secrets, and betrayal; our selections of travel narratives for July share a theme of self-discovery and spiritual enlightenment through a physical journey.

If you like *Lives of the Monster Dogs*, you will like...

The Plague Dogs by Richard Adams. Recounts an escape from an animal experimentation laboratory by the heroes, two dogs.

The Dogs: A Modern Bestiary by Rebecca Brown. A surreal fable about a young woman held captive in her apartment by a pack of imaginary Dobermans. Kirsten Bakis interviewed Brown for a short *Village Voice* piece, accessible online at http://www.villagevoice.com/vls/159/bakis.shtml.

Watchers by Dean Koontz. Suspenseful tale of a genetically manipulated super-intelligent dog on the run from a genetics lab.

Doctor Rat by William Kotzwinkle. An inventive, disturbing novel told from the point of view of the lab rat.

The Island of Dr. Moreau by H. G. Wells. In this 1896 classic, mad scientist Dr. Moreau tries to create a race of beast people.

DISCUSSION/REFLECTION STRATEGY

A quick read, *Lives of the Monster Dogs* lends itself to a **paired reading** with another novel. We suggest that you pair it with one of the classic tales of science gone wrong, such as *Frankenstein* or *The Island of Dr. Moreau*. What are the ethical implications of the plot of the mad scientist? Why do novelists continue to be drawn to this archetype?

Reading a contemporary novel alongside a classic in the same genre enables you to investigate how literary genres develop and evolve. What themes emerge in both works? Does the plot follow a similar trajectory? How does the later author's work build on the earlier work? How is it a revision? It could be just as instructive to choose a similarly themed bestseller to compare and contrast: *Lives of the Monster Dogs* and *Watchers*, for example. What's the difference between "popular" and "literary" fiction? What makes one book a bestseller and another a critics' favorite?

Video resources

Tim Burton explores some of the themes that interest Kirsten Bakis in *Edward Scissorhands* (1990), starring Johnny Depp as a young man whose creator, memorably played by Vincent Price, has died, leaving him alone and unfinished. Disturbing confrontations with civilization ensure. Burton's *Planet of the Apes* (2001) is about a pilot who crash-lands on another planet where animals, not humans, rule.

Internet resources

Bakis talks about writing, reading, and science fiction in an online interview at www.omnimag.com/archives/chats/ov071097.html. Find a Reader's Guide to *Lives of the Monster Dogs* at www.hha.com. au/reading_monsterdogs.htm.

October/Scary Stories
Memoir
On Writing: A Memoir of the Craft by Stephen King, 2000, available in paperback from Pocket Books for $14.95

What is this book about?

This engaging, slim volume combines King's autobiographical account of becoming a reader and writer with a practical guide for the aspiring writer. "C.V.," the first section, is a streamlined memoir of coming to the writing life and achieving success. We learn about King's early attempts to write stories, a short-lived but successful venture selling his fiction to high-school classmates, and the horror films and stories that inspired him. We are introduced to his wife, Tabitha, also a novelist, and learn that she had to fish the manuscript of *Carrie*, his first published novel and a major success, out of the trash and urge him to finish it. We follow King as he descends into drug addiction and alcoholism and later gets clean. And we learn much about the discipline and dedication King brings to his work. An opinionated interlude on grammar and style precedes the second section, "On Writing," which provides a functional overview of the writing process. King defines important vocabulary, like story and pace, and guides the beginning writer through establishing a writing routine, revising her work, and finding an agent. But you don't need to be an aspiring writer to appreciate *On Writing*. King's discussion of story, situation, character, and theme can be applied to any novel you or your group reads.

King returns to the autobiographical in his postscript, "On Living," which recounts with stark simplicity the aftermath of a car accident that almost killed him. In June, 1999, King was struck by a van while out for his daily walk; he endured several operations and months of painful physical therapy, only gradually returning to writing.

On Writing is idiosyncratic and opinionated, an intriguing glimpse into the mind and working habits of one of America's most prolific, bestselling, and beloved authors.

What should I know about the author?

King was born in Maine in 1947; the state serves as a setting for many of his novels and stories, and he still lives with his family in Bangor. He began writing when he was seven and amassed an impressive collection of rejection letters before he sold the paperback rights to *Carrie* for $400,000 in 1974. He has been married to novelist Tabitha King since 1971; they have three children. King's productivity is renowned; he writes ten pages a day, seven days a week, and had to use a pseudonym when his publishers refused to publish more than one of his books at the same time.

DISCUSSION/REFLECTION STRATEGY

Stephen King suggests that all aspiring writers should **mark examples of good writing** in the books they read—good advice for the book group member, too. Make a habit of marking favorite passages as you read, and spend a few minutes in your group reading aloud to each other.

Questions for reflection and discussion

1. One of the questions most often asked King is: where do you get your ideas? He protests that no idea bank exists where writers can withdraw good ideas. Instead, he believes the good ideas are out there all around us, waiting to be discovered. Although King does not answer this question directly, what kind of indirect answers can you find in his memoir? What significant moments from his past—what themes and situations, to use his own language—inspire his writing? If any members of your group write, discuss where their ideas come from. What themes and situations seem worth writing about?

2. King has been praised and reviled for his great gift of storytelling. Why do you think the ability to tell a cracking good story is sometimes denigrated by reviewers and critics? King theorizes that stories are relics, fossils, part of a pre-existing world that must be discovered and painstakingly excavated by the writer. In fact, he argues that writing is excavation. What do you think of this theory? Why might King believe this? Does thinking about writing as excavation help the reader? What kinds of metaphors can we use to describe the reading process?

3. It may come as a surprise to readers who find King's novels heavily plotted that he doesn't plot at all and, in fact, scorns it. He doesn't use outlines, and he doesn't know how a story will end when he begins writing it. Instead, he places a group of characters in a predicament and keeps writing to see what happens, how they behave, how they resolve the problem. Can you think of other books you've read where situation, rather than character or plot, seems to be the driving force? Your group may want to discuss whether an emphasis on situation, rather than character or theme, is the mark of a certain kind of fiction. How is writing based on situation different from writing

based on the plot wheel King describes, where the stuck writer spins the wheel for a solution to the story's problems?

4. All of the reviews of *On Writing* comment on its double structure of memoir and how-to. What connections does King make between "C.V." and "Toolbox," "On Writing" and "On Living"? How does each section lead to the next? What is the effect of this segmented narrative? Does *On Writing* feel like a coherent and cohesive whole? What kind of relationship does King establish with the reader in each section? Which section did you enjoy reading the most and why?

5. King offers lots of practical advice on the craft of writing. Spend some time discussing that advice. What's the best? What do you disagree with? What would be most helpful to a beginning writer? Based on the advice he gives to writers, how would you character-ize King as a reader? What are his prejudices? What does he love? Loathe? The only way to learn to write, he says, is to read a lot and to write a lot. What five books would you recommend to an aspir-ing writer? What could they learn from these books? Toni Morrison once said that she became a writer because she couldn't find the kind of story she wanted to read. Based on the books that you love to read, what kind of books would you write? What story would you like to read that's never been written?

Extra credit

On Writing doesn't offer many writing exercises, but King does throw in one writing prompt. After recounting a somewhat stereotypical situation of spousal abuse, he shakes things up by changing the genders of his characters and asking his readers to write the next five pages of the story. Why shouldn't the group that reads together write together as well? Set aside some time during your meeting—or use email—to write a group story based on King's writing exercise. Enthusiastic response to this exercise led King to sponsor a writing contest at his official website. Read the winning submission at www.stephenking.com.

Other books by Stephen King

If you haven't read any of King's fiction, you should. As his memoir illustrates, he is a careful and conscientious crafter of language and stories. You may want to begin with some of the books he writes about in *On Writing*—*Carrie, Misery, The Stand, Bag of Bones*. Or try the book version of films you may have seen—*The Shining, Cujo, The Green Mile*. Some of his most recent books delve more into psychology than horror—try *The Girl Who Loved Tom Gordon* or the linked story cycle *Hearts in Atlantis*. Readers who are interested in learning more about King's attraction to the supernatural should read *Danse Macabre*, an early work of nonfiction about the horror genre.

If you like *On Writing*, you will like...

Escaping into the Open: The Art of Writing True by Elizabeth Berg. User-friendly how-to-write book by a successful author who believes in her readers' abilities. Her many writing exercises are a bonus.

A Dangerous Profession: A Book About the Writing Life by Frederick Busch and *Letters to a Fiction Writer* edited by Busch. Both offer a hard dose of reality to all would-be writers, while emphasizing the writer's love of and dedication to her/his craft.

The Writing Life by Annie Dillard. A slim volume recounting her own writing life and making suggestions for aspiring writers.

Bird by Bird: Some Instructions on Writing and Life by Anne Lamott. Mixture of practical advice to fledgling writers and memoir of her own writing life.

How Reading Changed My Life by Anna Quindlen. Celebration of the author's lifelong love of reading.

Video resources

Many of King's novels and stories have been adapted on screen. We recommend *Carrie* (Brian DePalma, 1976), *The Shining* (Stanley

Kubrick, 1980), *The Stand* (Mick Garris, 1994), *Misery* (Rob Reiner, 1990), *The Shawshank Redemption* (Frank Darabont, 1994), and *Stand by Me* (Rob Reiner, 1986).

Internet Resources

King's presence online is, not surprisingly, overwhelming. But we've narrowed the essential sites to three. Find the official news at the official site: www.stephenking.com. Your most obscure King inquiry has already been anticipated at the informative and entertaining www.horrorking.com, where you'll find interviews and links galore, among much else.

October/Scary Stories
Potluck
Neverwhere by Neil Gaiman, 1996, available in paperback
from Avon Books for $7.99

What is this book about?

Richard Mayhew works in a securities firm in London. He has a nice apartment, a beautiful fiancée, good prospects—everything a young man could want. Or does he? While on their way to an important dinner engagement, Richard and his fiancée stumble over an injured young woman on the sidewalk. When Richard insists on helping her, an argument ensues and his fiancée, now his ex-fiancée, storms off. Richard produces first aid and shelter for Door, the mysterious injured woman, but the consequences of his gallantry prove the truth of the saying, "No good deed goes unpunished," for Richard is swept into a maelstrom of violence and horror which manages, through the deft touch of the author, also to be very funny.

The city that Richard has known as "London" turns out to be "London Above"—the city of cars, parks, buildings, and relative stability. Beneath this city in the sewers and in the underground transportation systems lies "London Below"—a dark, dirty, dangerous place of rats, hired assassins, sewer folk, the Beast of London, and even an angel. Richard finds that before he can leave London Below, he must first traverse it, encountering all manner of evil along the way. Can Richard survive his encounters with the assassins, the rat-speakers, and the Beast of London? Can he help the Lady Door complete her quest to find out what happened to her family? Will he get his regular life back?

What should I know about the author?

Neil Gaiman was born in 1960 in the United Kingdom. He worked as a journalist in England before turning to writing novels. In addition to novels, Gaiman writes poetry, essays, and even children's books. He is best known for the multi-award winning series of graphic-please-don't-call-them-comic-books novels, *Sandman*. He is married with three children and divides his time between the United Kingdom and the United States.

Did you know...?

Both fantasy and science fiction are examples of what is called **speculative literature.** The terms are not interchangeable, though it is not always easy to tell if a book is a work of fantasy or of science fiction because the genres often overlap. The term **fantasy** generally refers to works of literature that employ imaginary worlds peopled by supernatural or mythical beings. In these works, impossible things may happen (impossible in our world anyway), but no explanation is given. For example, in *Neverwhere*, the possibility that an entire city of strange beings could exist under London without anyone in London being aware of it is just never addressed. In **science fiction**, stories are usually set in the future and plots tend to rely on particular aspects of science and/or technology. For example, an author may create an entire culture living on another planet, but may explain features of that culture as resulting from characteristics of the planet's atmosphere or geography.

Questions for reflection and discussion

1. Readers who like fantasy literature tend to like it passionately. What do you think is the appeal of this genre? Is it mere escapism or

something more? For example, much fantasy literature is a vehicle for social criticism. What is it about the genre that lends itself to allegorical readings? If you do not like reading fantasy, discuss what precisely you do not like. Is your distaste an intellectual one (e.g., outlandish worlds, wooden characters) or an emotional response (e.g., a sense of dread or anxiety accompanying your reading)?

2. Were the characters in *Neverwhere* beings you could care about? Were they three dimensional, or did they seem like cartoon figures? Were there some characters that were more fully realized than others? For example, was Richard more developed than Mr. Vandemar? What about Door? Hunter?

3. There are many violent episodes in *Neverwhere*. Certainly if we read such scenes of violence in a realistic novel, we might be horrified or revolted. But the fantasy framework allows us to read the violent scenes with a certain detachment. Do you agree? If so, what is it about fantasy that makes this detachment possible? Does Gaiman's use of humor increase our detachment? Your group may want to discuss the desensitization to violence in America and its causes.

4. Gaiman employs different fables, elements of folklore and myth, and numerous references to other texts in *Neverwhere*. How many of these "borrowings" can you find? Can you find references or similarities to *Alice in Wonderland* by Lewis Carroll? *The Wizard of Oz* by L. Frank Baum? *The Inferno* by Dante? Why do you think he "quotes" earlier texts?

5. Why does Richard make the decision he does at the end? What has he gained from his time in London Below? What has he lost? Has he grown as a human being? Discuss what we know of his character before he went under. How has he changed by the end of the book? What has he come to value? Is there some social criticism at work in the novel's end? What could Gaiman be saying about modern, ordinary life?

Other books by Neil Gaiman

American Gods dramatizes a battle between ancient pagan gods and our modern gods (the gods of credit cards, the Internet, television, etc.) in America. *Stardust* tells of young Tristan, who leaves the safety of his village to travel into the land of Faerie to catch a falling star for his beloved. *Good Omens*, cowritten with Terry Pratchett, is a comic romp through the apocalypse. Gaiman's graphic novels include: *Sandman*, *Death*, *The Books of Magic*, *Miracleman: The Golden Age*, and *Black Orchid*.

If you like *Neverwhere*, you will like...

The Hitchhiker's Guide to the Galaxy by Douglas Adams. Neil Gaiman's sense of humor is comparable to that of Douglas Adams. In fact, Gaiman wrote *Don't Panic: The Official Hitchhiker's Guide to the Galaxy Companion*.

Discworld by Terry Pratchett. A multivolume series by a prolific, humorous fantasy writer who collaborated with Gaiman on *Good Omens*.

The Gormenghast Trilogy: Titus Groan, Gormenghast, Titus Alone by Mervyn Peake. An excellent trilogy set in a complex fantasy world, which, though it can be funny, presents a much more disturbing world than *Neverwhere*.

The Golden Compass by Phillip Pullman. First in a riveting and literary trilogy of young adult fantasy/sci-fi inspired by John Milton's *Paradise Lost*.

Harry Potter and the Sorcerer's Stone by J.K. Rowling. Rowling may write this series for children, but she counts many adults among Harry's fans. Like Richard Mayhew, Harry discovers there is more to London than meets the eye.

Video resources

Neverwhere is a six-part series produced by the BBC. Its availability in the United States is limited. Plans for a feature film version for

Neverwhere: The Movie are in the works. *The Hitchhiker's Guide to the Galaxy* (Alan Bell, 1981) is available on video, as is a stunning miniseries dramatization of *Gormenghast* (Andy Wilson, 2000). *Wyrd Sisters*, based on Terry Pratchett's *Discworld* series, is also available in a well-received animated miniseries.

Internet resources

The best place to start is www.neilgaiman.com, the author's own website. But also go to www.sfsite.com for information and an interview with Neil Gaiman. If you are looking for a comprehensive site about folklore and myth, try The Big Myth at www.bigmyth.com.

CHAPTER 11

November
Comfort Food, Comfort Reading

CROWD-PLEASER
She Flew the Coop by Michael Lee West

CLASSIC
The Gastronomical Me by M.F.K. Fisher

CHALLENGING
The Passion by Jeanette Winterson

MEMOIR
*Tender at the Bone: Growing Up
at the Table* by Ruth Reichl

POTLUCK
Stand Facing the Stove by Anne Mendelson

When asked why she always wrote about food, M.F.K. Fisher replied:

> It seems to me that our three basic needs, for food and security and love, are so mixed and mingled and entwined that we cannot straightly think of one without the others. So it happens that when I write of hunger, I am really writing about love and the hunger for it, and warmth and the love of it and the hunger for it...and then the warmth and richness and fine reality of hunger satisfied...and it is all one.
>
> —Foreword to *The Gastronomical Me*

The interconnections among love, security, and food are present all year, but perhaps never so apparent as in November, when winter truly begins and the holiday season beckons. The weather keeps us inside, the summer's harvest is celebrated, we settle in for the long winter ahead, making plans to see—and most certainly to eat with—family and friends.

This month's selections could have been written with Fisher's remarks in mind, for each book demonstrates that the most important relationships of our lives are mediated or shaped by our relationships with food. And how we understand and treat food reveals a lot about our needs for security and love. Michael Lee West's humorous account of the lives and loves of a fictional southern town is garnished with relevant recipes. M.F.K. Fisher expands on the theme of the interconnection of needs in her demanding and classic memoir. *The Passion*, this month's Challenge, explores human obsession in all its guises. Ruth Reichl's memoir is a poignant account of her introduction to fine food, and we end with Anne Mendelson's multigenerational family saga chronicling the life of a book—the *Joy of Cooking*.

November/Comfort Food, Comfort Reading
Crowd-Pleaser
She Flew the Coop: A Novel Concerning Life, Death, Sex, and Recipes in Limoges, Louisiana by Michael Lee West, 1994, available in paperback from HarperPerennial for $14.00

What is this book about?

She Flew the Coop chronicles life in small-town Limoges, Louisiana, in the year 1952. The novel's long subtitle, *A Novel Concerning Life, Death, Sex, and Recipes in Limoges, Louisiana*, announces its plot and major metaphor. Southerners and transplanted Yankees will not be surprised by the focus on food as an important part of southern culture. *She Flew the Coop* uses food as a metaphor for the important issues in life, but West goes further: she considers food itself as one of the big subjects, on par with death and sex. Food unites family and community. West is particularly interested in how southern women use food to nurture and to comfort, but also as art, as a form of self-expression. The plot of

She Flew the Coop is set in motion by the suicide attempt that opens the novel: sixteen-year-old Olive Nepper drinks a potion of orange Nehi and rose poison after she discovers she's pregnant by the local Baptist minister. The aftermath of Olive's suicide attempt reveals that the town of Limoges, quiet and sleepy on the surface, seethes with turmoil underneath. West weaves the voices of an omniscient narrator with first-person accounts by eight of Limoges's 905 eccentric inhabitants to construct a novel that is by turns tragic and comic.

What should I know about the author?
Michael Lee West was raised in Louisiana and now lives with her family outside Nashville, Tennessee, in a renovated funeral home. She has published fiction in a number of magazines and written two novels. Her most recent project is a set of sequels to *Crazy Ladies*. Her memoir, *Consuming Passions: A Food-Obsessed Life*, makes a fine companion piece to *She Flew the Coop*.

Questions for reflection and discussion
1. In this novel, religion, preachers, and church groups wield a great deal of power in the lives of the characters. In the end, Reverend Kirby is punished in a way that seems most appropriate to this backwater village. West may be poking fun at what she perceives as the falsely grounded sense of comfort we derive from church attendance, Bible reading, and ministering preachers. In what ways do West's women characters, such as Vangie, Sophie, and Aunt Butter, find strength and comfort, if not through religion? In what ways do they find empowerment? Do their forms of power undermine the patriarchal power of the community?

2. West weaves recipes into her narrative, including them in the body of the novel and listing them as chapter codas or introductions. Clearly, the recipes are meant to do more than expand the reader's cooking repertoire. Discuss how the recipes enlarge our understanding of the characters and how they affect the development of the story. Two recipes in particular may be worth noting: Sophie's recipe for beaten biscuits and Billie's recipe for peach swirl.

3. This novel has been alternately praised and criticized for its moral message. Is it simply a retelling of the biblical warning about "an eye for an eye"? If *She Flew the Coop* is not about "'vengeance is mine,' sayeth the Lord," then is it about "what comes around goes around"? Is there a reward for the righteous and deserving implied in Vangie's and Sophie's being widowed by the end of the story? To continue with the food metaphor, do the characters get their "just desserts"?

4. Setting is an important element of southern fiction. Limoges is presented as a typical southern town. What features make it typical? Why is setting important in this novel? Can you imagine these characters existing and interacting in another region? The novel also takes place in 1952. What details does West include to give the flavor of the 1950s? Why does she choose to set the story in this decade? What elements of the plot require this setting?

5. West examines notions of home and family throughout the novel. What does home mean for her characters? Why do the efforts of some characters to escape from home and family lead only to more tragedy? What is the moral of the novel? Do you agree with West's message?

Other books by the author

West has written two other novels, *Crazy Ladies* and *American Pie*. Her memoir about growing up southern is titled, *Consuming Passions: A Food-Obsessed Life*.

If you like *She Flew the Coop,* you will like...

Crazy in Alabama by Mark Childress. Childress continues the legacy of southern literary icons Flannery O'Connor and William Faulkner in his dark, coming-of-age story.

Home Cooking and *More Home Cooking* by Laurie Colwin. Combination memoir and cookbook by former food columnist for *Gourmet*.

Like Water for Chocolate by Laura Esquivel. Number one bestseller in Mexico in 1990. Filled with romance, recipes, and remedies.

Fried Green Tomatoes at the Whistle Stop Café by Fannie Flagg. If you've only seen the movie adaptation (*Fried Green Tomatoes*), you've missed many of the delights and secrets of this southern novel.

My Mother's Southern Kitchen: Recipes and Reminiscences by James Villas. More than 150 succulent recipes to enjoy along with mother-son chitchat and stories.

Video resources

Michael Lee West's novels have not been made into movies—yet. Your group might enjoy viewing film versions of some of our further reading suggestions: *Fried Green Tomatoes* (Jon Avnet, 1991), *Like Water for Chocolate* (Alfonso Arau, 1992) and *Crazy in Alabama* (Antonio Banderas, 1999). Though it's not set in the South, *Soul Food* (George Tillman Jr., 1997) depicts a large family bonding over Sunday dinners.

Internet resources

For suggestions on creating your own reading group cookbook, see West's publisher's website: www.harpercollins.com/hc/readers/0061056391fea.asp; this address features a short memoir by West and her recipe for banana pudding. The site www.gritlit.com offers southern cookbooks and groceries for sale, as well as a recipe swap. For a collection of recipes for southern dishes, see www.cbt.net/dedwards.

Extra credit

She Flew the Coop includes several recipes. Have members choose a recipe from the book, prepare it, and share during the meeting.

November/Comfort Food, Comfort Reading
Classic
The Gastronomical Me by M.F.K. Fisher, 1943, available in
paperback from North Point Press for $13.00

What is this book about?

The Gastronomical Me is a memoir of M.F.K. Fisher's life from about
age four to her early thirties. She was thirty-five when it was published
in 1943. Fisher covers her childhood in California, her sojourns in
France and Switzerland, her return visits to the United States, time
spent on trans-Atlantic cruises, and a visit to Mexico. She presents a
series of vivid recollections of people, landscapes, and above all, the
food that mediates all these relationships. For Fisher, food is the primary lens through which she views and understands her family, her
friends, herself. Some of the more memorable characters include a
murderous cook from Fisher's childhood, a bilious and fundamental-
ist grandmother, widowed French landladies, French train conductors
trying to maintain dignity and civility during the Nazi occupation, a
love-obsessed *mariachi* singer, and the last female virgin truffle-hunter
in France.

What should I know about the author?

Mary Frances Kennedy Fisher was born in 1908 and died in 1992. She
grew up in Whittier, California, the eldest child of a privileged family.
Her father owned and published the local newspaper, and her education at an exclusive private school was greatly supplemented by her
own prodigious reading. She moved to France in the late 1920s with
her first husband (there would be three altogether) and began writing
her memorable tales of French people and French cuisine. M.F.K.
Fisher, whose publisher insisted she use her initials because, "Women
don't write this way," published dozens of books and essays over the
next sixty years and is considered one of the finest American writers
of the twentieth century.

Questions for reflection and discussion

1. Pick one or two memorable scenes or characters from *The Gastronomical Me*. What makes them memorable? Chances are what makes the scene or character stand out is not pleasantness or likeability. What, then, accounts for the clarity with which scenes are rendered? Your reading group may wish to read favorite passages aloud.

2. Many people are surprised and put off by the way Fisher presents herself in the book. How does she come across? Since this is a story of her life, why might she choose to present herself in a way that does not invite sympathy? Why do we expect that a memoirist would want her readers to like her?

3. *The Gastronomical Me* raises more questions about Fisher's life than it answers: what happened to Al? Who is Chexbres? What is his illness? What kind of a name is 'Chexbres'? Once again, Fisher seems intent on confounding our expectations of memoirs. Consider an analogy with photography or painting. A good photograph can pack a powerful or devastating emotional punch. Think of photographs from important news events. The photos are powerful despite the fact that they may be blurry in parts, the participants are not named, or it is not clear exactly what is happening in the picture. The picture is powerful despite—or perhaps even because—of what is left out. Do you think Fisher's work also derives its power from the absence of expected detail or does it suffer from it?

Extra credit

Check your local community's adult education program for classes and demonstrations on food and wine during November. Most of these programs last only one or two evenings and are inexpensive, fun ways for book group members to enjoy culinary adventures and to develop wine expertise.

4. One can read *The Gastronomical Me* as an historical document chronicling California before sprawl—dining clubs in the French countryside, meals that last for hours, and travel by ocean liner. One can certainly see differences in transportation, living arrangements, and, of course food selection and preparation between Fisher's time and our own. What has been lost and what has been gained in the sixty years since this book was published? Are we living better? Or simply more quickly?

5. In the quotation that opens this chapter, Fisher makes reference to "our three basic needs...food and security and love." She says that it is impossible to separate these three, that to speak of one is to speak of the others as well. Do you agree? Does she demonstrate the intertwining of the three in this book? If our need for food were simply biological, would we be drawn to writing and reading about it so much?

Other books by M.F.K. Fisher

M.F.K. Fisher was a prolific food writer and autobiographer. Her books on food include: *An Alphabet for Gourmets*; *Consider the Oyster*; *Dubious Honors*; *How to Cook a Wolf*; *Serve It Forth*. Her autobiographical writings are collected in: *To Begin Again: Stories and Memoirs, 1908–1929*; *Stay Me, Oh Comfort Me: Journals and Stories, 1933–1941*; *Last House: Reflections, Dreams, and Observations, 1943–1991*; and *As They Were*. *The Measure of Her Powers: An M.F.K. Fisher Reader* is an anthology of selections from Fisher's works with an introduction by Ruth Reichl, author of *Tender at the Bone: Growing Up at the Table*. In addition to writing about food, Fisher wrote travel narratives. *Long Ago in France: The Years in Dijon* is a memoir of Dijon in the 1930s, while *Two Towns in Provence: Map of Another Town and A Considerable Town* describes life in Aix-en-Provence and Marseilles.

Did you know...?

M.F.K. Fisher would have loved the **Slow Food Movement**. Founded in 1986 in Italy, the Slow Food Movement dedicates itself to preserving and reviving regional cuisines and eating habits. The movement argues that "fast food" is more than just bad food cheaply priced. It is gastronomically and nutritionally poor, it forces local food purveyors out of business, thereby hurting local economies, and it contributes to the breakdown of the family and society by undermining the practice of preparing food and eating together. The Slow Food Movement consists of *convivia*, or clubs, sharing meals and cooking techniques, educating one another about local farming practices, and organizing against the incursion of fast food outlets in historic regions. Find out more at www.slowfood.com.

Books about M.F.K. Fisher

Joan Reardon's *M.F.K. Fisher, Julia Child, and Alice Waters: Celebrating the Pleasures of the Table* contains profiles of three important food writers and chefs. (Reardon is also at work on a biography of Fisher.) *Conversations with M.F.K. Fisher*, edited by David Lazar, contains interviews with Fisher. Jeannette Ferrary became friends with Fisher in her last years and wrote a memoir about their friendship entitled *M.F.K. Fisher and Me: A Memoir of Food and Friendship*. Though out of print, Dominique Gioia's *A Welcoming Life: The M.F.K. Fisher Scrapbook* is a must-read for those interested in learning more about Fisher's life; the many excellent photographs enable readers to put faces with the names that turn up throughout her autobiographical works.

If you like *The Gastronomical Me,* you will like...

An Omelette and a Glass of Wine by Elizabeth David. Classic food writing by important British food writer.

The Olive Farm: A Memoir of Life, Love, and Olive Oil in Southern France by Carol Drinkwater. In the tradition of Peter Mayle and Frances Mayes, Drinkwater and her husband buy a decrepit villa on an olive farm in southern France and begin restoration.

Honey from a Weed: Fasting and Feasting in Tuscany, Catalonia, the Cyclades, and Apulia by Patience Gray. Gray travels to Greece and Italy and writes lyrically about the places she visits, the cooks she meets, and the food she eats.

Between Meals: An Appetite for Paris by A.J. Liebling. The classic memoir of memorable meals in Paris.

Reflexions by Richard Olney. A memoir by the celebrated food writer.

Video resources

Bill Moyers interviewed M.F.K. Fisher for his series, *The World of Ideas*. The result is *Food for Thought with M.F.K. Fisher*. Only die-hard Fisher fans will be interested in this twenty-eight-minute conversation. Fisher was in failing health (and in fact would die only a year later), making conversation difficult.

Internet resources

Check out www.mfkfisher.net. Need we say more?

November/Comfort Food, Comfort Reading
Challenge
The Passion by Jeanette Winterson, 1987, available in paperback from Grove Press for $12.00

What is this book about?

In *The Passion*, a young French soldier who serves as a kitchen attendant to Napoleon meets a beautiful Venetian woman sold by her husband as a prostitute for French generals during Napoleon's catastrophic Russian campaign. Henri is a simple farm boy whose job is to kill chickens for Napoleon to eat. Napoleon's obsessive, single-minded preference for devouring hordes of chickens provides the key to his character and is an ominous foreshadowing of his treatment of his armies. Henri's passionate devotion to the service of Napoleon is ultimately undermined by his love for Villanelle and the freedom from servitude she offers. Villanelle is the daughter of a Venetian gondolier and has inherited the webbed feet of the gondoliers. She is the first woman to have that characteristic, and her physical oddity is exceeded only by her behavioral transgressions: crossdressing, thieving, working in a casino, loving both men and women as the mood strikes her. Like Henri's love for Napoleon, Villanelle's love for another woman is at war with her desire for freedom. Henri and Villanelle's stories, their destinies, their loves are intertwined in realistic and fantastic ways. This is a story that imbues historical circumstances with a fairy tale atmosphere.

Did you know…?

The word myth comes from the ancient Greek word *mythos*, which means word or story. In its historical sense, it rarely means untrue stories. Myths explain fundamental questions such as the nature of the universe, human experience, and the meaning of life. They are usually said to have happened in an unspecified, long-ago time. **Fairy tales** tell of strange creatures (gnomes, elves, etc.) interfering in human affairs—these stories don't explain the nature of the universe, but sometimes are meant to explain misfortune and extraordinary luck.

What should I know about the author?

Jeanette Winterson was born in 1959 in Manchester, England, and currently resides on a small farm. As an infant, she was adopted by a Pentecostal family and raised in an evangelical environment; in her youth, she was a sermon writer and preacher. She received her B.A. in 1981 from St. Catherine's College, Oxford. Winterson is the author of several novels that have garnered prestigious awards, including the Whitbread Prize for best first novel in 1985 and the John Llewellyn Rhys Prize for *The Passion* in 1987. Her first novel, *Oranges Are Not the Only Fruit*, is a semiautobiographical account of those years, but Winterson has cautioned readers against reading the book as a memoir.

Questions for reflection and discussion

1. *The Passion* explores the relationship among passions, among people, and between passion and obsession. What are the different types of passions present in the novel? Which characters are associated with which passions? Does anyone in the novel find any joy or

sustenance from his/her passion? What is said to be the difference between passion and obsession?

2. In the introduction to this chapter, we quote M.F.K. Fisher on the connections people build around food, security, and love. How are these three needs interdependent for the characters in *The Passion*? Find examples in the text that address the interconnections.

3. "I'm telling you stories. Trust me." These two sentences are repeated several times throughout the novel. Why do you think Winterson employs this device? What does it add to the story? Is the statement, "Trust me," likely to inspire trust, or does it make us lack confidence in our narrators? Does it make any sense to believe or not to believe the words of fictional narrators?

4. Winterson explores the connection between place and character in this novel. How does the physical environment echo or accentuate the passions of the characters? What is it about Venice (as described in the book) that embodies the obsessions of its inhabitants and tourists? What role did Henri's village play in forming his character and passions?

5. In a 1997 interview, Winterson said, "I don't believe in happy endings. All of my books end on an ambiguous note because nothing ever is that neatly tied up, there is always another beginning, there is always the blank page after the one that has writing on it. And that is the page I want to leave to the reader." Is this an accurate description of the ending of *The Passion*? Does the novel end ambiguously? If so, how? Isn't Henri happy? Why would an author writing stories that blend fantasy and reality care to emulate real life when ending a novel? What do you think will happen to the characters in *The Passion*?

Other books by Jeanette Winterson

In addition to *Oranges Are Not the Only Fruit*, Winterson's novels include *Written on the Body*, whose narrator is nameless and genderless. In *Gut Symmetries*, physics serves as a metaphor for love in an account of a romantic triangle among a married physicist, his wife, and their physicist lover. Like *The Passion*, *Sexing the Cherry*, set in Restoration England, is a fusion of history, myth, and fairy tale. *Art & Lies: A Piece for Three Voices and a Bawd* also mixes history and myth. Winterson's most recent novel, *The Powerbook*, though rich with historical allegory and allusion, takes place in cyberspace. Her essays are collected in *Art Objects: Essays on Ecstasy and Effrontery* and her stories in *The World and Other Places: Stories*.

DISCUSSION/REFLECTION STRATEGY

You may wish to consider the different types of narrators when reading this book and others. A **first-person narrator** is a character telling the story; she is a **naïve narrator** if she does not understand the entire story or an **unreliable narrator** if we suspect that the narration is not truthful. An **omniscient narrator** knows everything that is happening. An omniscient narrator who interjects personal opinion or explanations is called an **intrusive narrator**.

If you like *The Passion*, you will like...

Master Georgie by Beryl Bainbridge. Follows the title character, a surgeon and amateur photographer, through the Crimean War.

Nightwood by Djuna Barnes. An atmospheric modernist classic of women falling in love.

The Emperor's Last Island: A Journey to St. Helena by Julia Blackburn. A wonderfully written combination memoir, biography, and travel memoir to St. Helena where Blackburn visits the last home of Napoleon.

The Pillow Book of the Lady Onogoro by Alison Fell. Mixes the historical novel (set in eleventh-century Japan) with erotica.

The Blue Flower by Penelope Fitzgerald. A historical novel about the eighteenth-century German poet, Novalis, and the fourteen-year-old girl with whom he fell in love.

Video resources

Directed by Beeban Kidron, *Oranges Are Not the Only Fruit* was released in 1990. In 1993, Kidron released *Shades of Fear* with a screenplay written by Jeanette Winterson. A film adaptation of *The Passion* with Gwyneth Paltrow as Villanelle is in the planning stages. Sally Potter's *Orlando* (1993) is a stunning adaptation of Virginia Woolf's novel about a woman who lives for hundreds of years and even changes gender.

Internet resources

Both the official Jeanette Winterson site, www.jeanettewinterson.com, and the Jeanette Winterson reader's site, www.winterson.net, offer lots of good information on the writer's life and activities. A 1997 interview with Winterson is on www.salon.com.

November/Comfort Food, Comfort Reading
Memoirs
Tender at the Bone: Growing Up at the Table by Ruth Reichl, 1998, available in paperback from Broadway Books for $14.00

What is this book about?

Ruth Reichl's memoir chronicles the author's childhood, adolescence, and early adulthood—from learning to eat, to learning to eat well, to learning to write about food. *Tender at the Bone* charts Reichl's culinary adventures across two continents and thirty years. Like M.F.K. Fisher, she believes that "how we eat has a huge impact on the quality of our lives." Her memories revolve around food; the table—and the kitchen—become ways of structuring a life story and of making sense of the world. She is at her best memorializing the people who were instrumental in shaping her attitudes to and understanding of food: her mother, who regularly sent guests home with food poisoning; her Aunt Birdie, whose housekeeper, Alice, fried the best oysters; Monsieur du Croix, the father of a school friend, who introduced her to soufflés and fine French cuisine; the high school friends who praised her devil's food cake; her colleagues at L'Escargot who taught her to cook fine French cuisine; her husband, Doug, whose mother specialized in cottage-cheese-filled canned peaches; Nick, the roommate who taught her to scrounge in dumpsters; and, finally, Marion Cunningham, her mentor and author of *The Fannie Farmer Cookbook*. By the end of the book, Reichl has embarked on the career that will engage her for the rest of her life: food writing.

What should I know about the author?

Reichl grew up in New York City. In college, she studied social work, but she began her career as a food writer at the age of twenty-one with a cookbook, *Mmmmmmm: A Feastiary*. She worked in restaurants and as a caterer throughout her twenties, eventually cofounding a cooperative restaurant in Berkeley, California. She wrote restaurant reviews and feature articles on food for *New West Magazine* before spending nine years as restaurant critic for the *Los Angeles Times*. In 1993, she transferred to the *New York Times*, where she won renown and notoriety for the disguises she would wear while eating out and her insistence on dining not only at the finest restaurants, but at eateries where real people eat. In 1999, she accepted the position of editor-in-chief at *Gourmet*.

Questions for reflection and discussion

1. Reichl claims that food nourishes more than our bodies. In what ways do you see food nourishing Reichl and her family and friends in *Tender at the Bone*? How are relationships structured and defined by food? Think especially about Reichl's relationship with her mother, her Aunt Birdie, and her husband. Obviously, Reichl would never have become a food writer had food not been significant to her, so it makes sense that her relationships would be mediated by food. Is this a pattern you see in your own life? What foods or meals do you associate with your family and friends? Why?

2. In an interview, Reichl notes that she began writing *Tender at the Bone* because she wanted to write stories about the characters she

knew growing up. She wanted to memorialize her mother, Aunt Birdie, Mrs. Peavey, and others. Originally, she conceived of the memoir as a collection of short stories, but she ultimately decided to add herself as the thread uniting the stories. To what extent is *Tender at the Bone* a series of portraits of memorable characters? Because Reichl was consciously using herself only as a thread, do we learn too little about her? Where do you want to know more? Or did the memoir evolve as she was writing it into a more autobiographical document than she had expected?

3. Reichl's relationship with her mother is especially interesting. At what point do you realize that her mother is not merely eccentric, but seriously ill? What do you think of Reichl's honesty in portraying her own reluctance, as a teenager and adult, to spend time with her mother? Review the section called "Another Party." How does this chapter provide closure to Reichl's vexed relationship with her mother?

4. Reichl has been criticized by some reviewers for not writing lovingly enough of food: she does not make us hungry enough, they claim, in her descriptions of memorable meals. Is this a fair criticism? Should writing about food make us want to eat? How do the recipes function in the memoir in terms of making us want to eat? Which descriptions of meals stood out for you? Your group may want to try one of her recipes.

5. Food is not only comfort in *Tender at the Bone*, but also a form of power, a way of taking control and making meaning. How does Reichl use food, specifically the preparation of food, to wield power?

Did you know...?

Some psychologists argue that food and eating mediate important aspects of relationships between mothers and daughters. Sometimes this is positive—as when mothers teach daughters food preparation skills and pass on family traditions. But food and eating can also become the destructive battleground on which displays of power are exercised or resisted. For insight into these issues, we recommend Kim Chernin's *The Hungry Self: Women, Eating, and Identity* and *The Obsession*.

Other books by the author

Reichl's sequel to *Tender at the Bone* is *Comfort Me with Apples: More Adventures at the Table.*

If you like *Tender at the Bone,* you will like...

Through the Kitchen Window: Women Writers Explore the Intimate Meanings of Food and Cooking edited by Arlene Voski Avakian. A highly recommended collection of essays about family and food by writers including Dorothy Allison, Maya Angelou, and Marge Piercy.

Kitchen Confidential: Adventures in the Culinary Underbelly by Anthony Bourdain. The unvarnished truth about what goes on in restaurant kitchens. Not for the squeamish!

Pig Tails 'n Breadfruit: A Culinary Memoir by Austin Clarke. Clarke reflects on food and culture in Barbados.

Miriam's Kitchen: A Memoir by Elizabeth Ehrlich. Ehrlich connects her family's sometimes tragic Jewish history with delicious recipes and her own spiritual journey.

Pass the Polenta and Other Writings from the Kitchen by Teresa Lust. Special recipes plus revelations of the author's passion for food and her family traditions connected with eating it.

Video resources

Your group might enjoy the following films about family and food: *Babette's Feast* (Gabriel Axel, 1987), *The Wedding Banquet* (Ang Lee, 1993), *Eat Drink Man Woman* (Ang Lee, 1994), *Home for the Holidays* (Jodie Foster, 1995), and *The Myth of Fingerprints* (Bart Freundlich, 1997).

Internet resources

See www.randomhouse.com/atrandom/ruthreichl/ for an interview where Reichl discusses what being a restaurant critic entails. An interview with www.salon.com also highlights Reichl's approach to restaurant reviewing. Finally, read an interview with her about *Comfort Me with Apples*, the sequel to *Tender at the Bone*, at www.ontherail.com/site/news/reichl.asp. You may also want to check out *Gourmet's* website at www.gourmet.com.

DISCUSSION/REFLECTION STRATEGY

Find a guest speaker by calling your local newspaper and inviting the food editor to visit your book group. Ask her to speak about her job, how she became interested in food, why she writes about recipes and eating. You may even persuade her to read *Tender at the Bone* and participate in the discussion! Before she comes, photocopy her columns and circulate them in your group. Members can then formulate specific questions based on her work.

November/Comfort Food, Comfort Reading
Potluck
Stand Facing the Stove: The Story of the Women Who Gave America 'The Joy of Cooking' by Anne Mendelson, 1996, available in hardcover from Henry Holt Publishers for $29.95

What is this book about?

Stand Facing the Stove is a combination of genres. It is part biography, part cultural history, part culinary history, part publishing history, and it reads like a novel. It is the biography of a book, *The Joy of Cooking*, told mostly through the lives of its authors, Irma Rombauer and her daughter Marion Rombauer Becker. In telling their story, Mendelson tells the story of the German-American community of St. Louis where the Rombauers lived. Those readers interested in immigration and assimilation in American culture will find the history of St. Louis and the history of the Rombauers fascinating. Mendelson also recounts the story of cooking and eating in the United States from the mid-nineteenth century to the mid-twentieth, and this is where the book really shines. Mendelson takes us from a time when food preparation was the major work of women and children in a family (often including several generations and some domestic servants) and cooking was something learned by working with ingredients grown at home, to a time when a lone housewife in a tiny kitchen made dinner from various manufactured products. *Stand Facing the Stove* also devotes a considerable portion of its bulk to chronicling the acrimonious relationship between the Rombauers and their publisher. Readers may not find these sections as interesting as the others; if they choose to skim these chapters, they won't miss much.

What should I know about the author?

Anne Mendelson is a freelance writer and editor specializing in culinary subjects; she is also a columnist for *Gourmet*. She is currently writing a book on changes in cooking and eating in New York City from 1870 to 1920.

Extra credit

Add a community service component to your group for the month of November. Volunteer your book group's services at a local homeless shelter or nursing home for an evening. Before everybody gets too wrapped up in their own holiday celebrations, group members can prepare and/or serve meals to people in need, extending the respect and affection book group members have for one another to the wider community. Check your local chapter of the Red Cross or Habitat for Humanity for suggestions about where you are most needed.

Questions for reflection and discussion

1. Do you own a copy of *The Joy of Cooking*? Did your mother own one when you were growing up? How do you use it? There is a difference between consulting it and cooking from it. For some people, *The Joy of Cooking* is an indispensable reference book rather than an

actual cookbook. For others, it is the only cookbook they ever use. If you own *The Joy of Cooking,* do you use it more or less than other cookbooks? Why?

2. Mendelson claims that it is the Rombauers' authorial voice that makes *The Joy of Cooking* unique and greatly contributes to the book's success. Do you like the tone that permeates *The Joy of Cooking*? How would you describe it? How does it differ from other cookbooks you have known and loved?

3. One of the most interesting sections of Mendelson's book is the chapter called, Chronicles of Cookery I. In this section, Mendelson describes the changes taking place in American food choices and preparation from the late nineteenth century to the publication of *The Joy of Cooking* in 1931. The easy question here is: how did life become easier for cooks during this time period? What changes in technology and social arrangements contributed to the new ease of food preparation? A harder question is: how did life become more difficult for cooks during this time period? How did the same technological advances that seemed to make cooking easier also provide new difficulties for cooks?

4. *The Joy of Cooking* has always been a compilation of recipes collected and tested by the Rombauers from other sources, e.g., friends, relatives, manufacturer's test kitchens, and in time, readers of earlier editions of the book. One of the book's strengths, however, has been the sections on desserts that emphasize Irma Rombauer's own recipes drawn from the German and German-American communities in which she grew up. Today we eat and prepare food from places all around the world. Do you think we lose something by expanding our reach? Has anyone in your group grown up with a particular cuisine not learned through cookbooks, but through working with different generations in the kitchen?

5. *Stand Facing the Stove* does a nice job of reviewing changes in food fashions for most of the twentieth century. Are there any foods you grew up eating that you continue to eat and prepare for your family? Are there any foods that you grew up with that you would never

dream of eating again or making for family and friends? Why do you think these foods were once popular and no longer are?

DISCUSSION/REFLECTION STRATEGY

Ask everyone in your reading group to bring treasured family recipes to share. Members can make copies of the recipes for other members, but be sure also to examine the original document of the recipe. Is it a cookbook with your grandmother's handwriting in the margins or an obviously well-used index card in which the recipe has been typed with a manual typewriter? Is the document itself as precious to you as the recipe? Why?

Other books by the author

Stand Facing the Stove is Anne Mendelson's first book.

If you like *Stand Facing the Stove*, you will like...

American Appetite: The Coming of Age of a Cuisine by Leslie Brenner. A study of the struggle to create an American cuisine with an emphasis on Julia Child's and James Beard's influences.

The Solace of Food: A Life of James Beard by Robert Clark. A biography of the famous food writer.

More Work for Mother: The Ironies of Household Technology from the Open Hearth to the Microwave by Ruth Schwartz Cowan. A social history about technological change in the home.

Revolution at the Table: The Transformation of the American Diet by Harvey A. Levenstein. Describes the revolution in eating habits during the years 1880 to 1930.

Fashionable Food: Seven Decades of Food Fads by Sylvia Lovegren. This history of twentieth-century food fads includes recipes for those who want to revisit the joys of Tang and cheese balls.

Video resources

The A&E network offers videos of interest, such as *America Eats: History on a Bun* and *American Drinks: History in a Glass*, which look at the origins of America's most popular food. The program *Biography* has a documentary on the one person who has done at least as much to change American food habits as Irma Rombauer—see *Julia Child: An Appetite for Life*.

Internet resources

Many of Anne Mendelson's columns and cookbook reviews can be found online at www.epicurious.com. This site is a treasure trove of everything relating to food, including recipes, cookbook reviews, interviews with chefs, restaurant reviews, etc. There is even a section devoted to the buying and selling of antique cookbooks.

CHAPTER 12

December
Heartwarming Classics

CROWD-PLEASER
A Tree Grows in Brooklyn by Betty Smith

CLASSIC
Little Women by Louisa May Alcott

CHALLENGE
The Diary of a Young Girl by Anne Frank

MEMOIR
The Story of My Life by Helen Keller

POTLUCK
Watership Down by Richard Adams

Literature is my Utopia. Here I am not disenfranchised. No barrier of the senses shuts me out from the sweet, gracious discourse of my book-friends. They talk to me without embarrassment or awkwardness.

—Helen Keller, *The Story of My Life*

Jo spent the morning on the river with Laurie and the afternoon reading and crying over *The Wide, Wide World*, up in the apple tree...Jo had burned the skin off her nose boating, and got a raging headache by reading too long...Jo read till her eyes gave out and she was sick of books, got so fidgety that even good-natured Laurie had a quarrel with her...

—Louisa May Alcott, *Little Women*

How many of us experienced Helen Keller's awe and relief when the world opened up to us after we learned how to read? How many have shirked our work to read until we got a blinding headache like Jo March? How many formed the goal to read through every book in the library from A to Z like Francie in *A Tree Grows in Brooklyn*? Surely it's no coincidence that many of the books we loved to read or have read to us when we were young are about children who loved to read. Our favorite heroines were book-mad budding authors. Part of our excitement over their story was the excitement of seeing "story" take on the significance and centrality we had long sensed it had. It seems fitting, therefore, that our December selections dramatize the importance of reading and storytelling.

Most of these books you have already read. Some of them you may have read repeatedly, even obsessively. Perhaps you *were* Jo March. Perhaps you sobbed over Anne Frank's diary. Perhaps you closed your eyes and tried to enter imaginatively for just a moment into the mysterious world of Helen Keller.

We hope you will take time at this hectic holiday season to remind yourself of the gift of reading and rediscover the joy it has brought you by renewing your acquaintance with this month's classic stories. We leave the last word to Richard Adams, whose rabbits frequently halt their journey to listen to their storyteller, Dandelion, spin his tales: "Underground, the story continued."

December/Heartwarming Classics
Crowd-Pleaser
A Tree Grows in Brooklyn by Betty Smith, 1943, available in paperback from HarperPerennial Library for $13.00

What is this book about?

Francie Nolan lives in Brooklyn during the early years of the twentieth century. We are introduced to Francie when she is eleven years old, and we say good-bye to her as she leaves for college. Through Francie we meet her father, the charming but alcoholic Johnny Nolan, and her mother, Katie Nolan, still young and beautiful but burdened with trying to keep the family fed and housed. Francie's younger brother, Neeley, shares Francie's adventures and her dreams of a more stable life. Many critics and readers note that the real protagonist of the novel is not Francie, but Brooklyn itself. Francie is our guide to the borough, showing us its vitality, its energy, the joys and sorrows that afflict its residents. Early twentieth-century Brooklyn was home to an astonishing mixture of recent immigrants living in close proximity: we meet Chinese tea merchants, Jewish peddlers, Irish bartenders, and German laborers. Smith's gaze never flinches from the hard reality of these people's lives. She chronicles domestic violence, alcoholism, unemployment, and the grinding degradation of poverty, but she also reveals to us the strength of these people and demands that we acknowledge the dignity inherent in their lives.

What should I know about the author?

Betty Smith was born in 1896, the daughter of German immigrants. Her father died when she was small, and her mother remarried Michael Keogh, an Irish immigrant. The family lived in Brooklyn, and like Francie Nolan, Betty Smith left school after eighth grade to help support her family through retail, office, and factory work. In 1924, she married George H.E. Smith. Betty was able to continue her education, eventually attending Yale Drama School. In addition to writing *A Tree Grows in Brooklyn* and several other novels, she was a playwright who was deeply involved in the community theater movement from the 1930s through the 1950s. She died in 1972.

Questions for reflection and discussion

1. What do you make of all the ethnic slurs in the novel? Nasty terms for different people are part of the everyday language of the characters. Does this affect how you understand them and their lives? Does it affect your ability to empathize with the characters? How are the terms being used? Deliberately? Thoughtlessly? With hatred? With affection (is that possible?)? What circumstances of the characters' lives encourage ethnic divisiveness and name-calling? Consider the fact that within Brooklyn, the different ethnic enclaves are close to

one another and interdependent: for example, the Irish shop at Jewish groceries and go to Chinese launderers.

2. Consider the relationships between men and women in the novel. Do the Nolans have a good marriage? What is a good marriage according to this community? What do people seem to expect from their marriages? What do they get? How is sex treated in the novel—positively? negatively? openly? secretly?

3. The sights, the smells, the sounds of Brooklyn seem as real to readers as any of the characters do. Smith's descriptions of everything from candy stores to milk-wagon horses to tenement hallways are riveting. Share some of your favorite images from the book with your reading group. Could Smith have written an equally compelling description of any place, or is there something special about Brooklyn that lends itself to rich description? Compare the way she talks about Brooklyn with how she describes Manhattan. Do you think the different portrayals of the boroughs reflect or reinforce what is happening in the story?

4. What is the significance of the conversation between Miss Gardiner and Francie regarding the essays Francie wrote about her neighborhood? Is Miss Gardiner's advice good, or is Francie right to reject it? Francie argues that beauty can be found even in the sordid. Does *A Tree Grows in Brooklyn* demonstrate the truth of that? If Miss Gardiner could read *A Tree Grows in Brooklyn*, she would probably want all the issues raised in questions one and two above removed. Can they be removed without damaging the beauty of the book?

5. Finally, why is the book called *A Tree Grows in Brooklyn*? What does the tree symbolize? Why is it important? And how does the metaphor relate to the conversation between Francie and Miss Gardiner?

Other books by Betty Smith

Joy in the Morning is Smith's second most popular novel. *Maggie-Now* and *Tomorrow Will Be Better* are currently out of print, but check your local library.

If you like *A Tree Grows in Brooklyn,* you will like...

The Basketball Diaries by Jim Carroll. Growing up miserable in the New York of the 1960s.

Tea That Burns: A Family Memoir of Chinatown by Bruce Edward Hall. An account of the author's family from their arrival in New York's Chinatown in the mid-nineteenth century until today.

Brown Girl, Brownstones by Paule Marshall. Originally published in 1959, this novel tells of a young girl from Barbados living in New York.

When I Was Puerto Rican by Esmeralda Santiago is a memoir of growing up in Brooklyn.

The Chosen by Chaim Potok. This popular novel tells the story of two Jewish boys in Brooklyn in the 1940s.

DISCUSSION/REFLECTION STRATEGY

For an excellent paired reading, try *Daddy Was a Number Runner* by Louise Meriwether along with *A Tree Grows in Brooklyn*. Published in 1970, this novel about a young girl (also named Francie) growing up in Harlem in the thirties is a searing account of love and loss in the face of poverty and racism.

Video resources

In 1945, Elia Kazan directed *A Tree Grows in Brooklyn*, and in 1974, a television version was produced. Both are available on video. Leonardo DiCaprio starred in the adaptation of Jim Carroll's *Basketball Diaries* (Scott Calvert, 1995). A musical version of Smith's novel was produced on Broadway in 1950—revivals still pop up occasionally.

Internet resources

To find out more about Brooklyn go to www.brooklyn.com. Robert Cornfield has written a lovely appreciation of Smith's novel that can be found at www.nytimes.com/books/99/01/03/bookend/bookend.html.

December/Heartwarming Classics
Classic
Little Women by Louisa May Alcott, 1868, several paperback editions available, including one from Puffin Classics for $6.99

What is this book about?

Louisa May Alcott's classic tale of the poor but happy March family made her a celebrity upon its publication in 1868 and has been adored by generations of young—and not so young—readers ever since. Part I follows the March sisters and their mother through the privations of the Civil War when their father is away fighting. Loosely modeled after *Pilgrim's Progress*, *Little Women*'s first part is a moral tale of the trials that build character and discipline in Christians. But it is also a funny and vividly rendered "domestic drama" of four sisters struggling to grow up. Part II, originally published separately as *Good Wives*, opens three years later and follows the March sisters as they marry and establish families of their own. For most of us, reading *Little Women* as adults is rereading, a chance to revisit ourselves as young readers, a chance to remember and interrogate the understanding and expectations we brought to an earlier reading life.

What should I know about the author?

Louisa May Alcott lived her life in the long shadows cast by two fascinating parents: her father, Bronson Alcott, eccentric Transcendentalist and perennial dreamer, and her mother, Abigail Alcott, self-sacrificing, ambitious, unhappy. Both inspired and constrained her. Ralph Waldo Emerson and Henry David Thoreau were family friends. She spent a year of her youth at Fruitlands, a utopian commune established by her father and six like-minded reformers. The experiment was a dismal failure, as Alcott later chronicled in *Transcendental Wild Oats* (1872). Like her alter ego, Jo March, Alcott grew up in a family of four girls. Also like Jo, she worked in a variety of occupations: sewing, cleaning, teaching, as a governess, a ladies' companion, a magazine editor, and finally as an author. When she was thirty, she enlisted as an army nurse; shortly thereafter, she contracted typhoid fever and would suffer for the rest of her life from the poisoning effects of mercury, the only treatment then available. This experience, however, inspired her first successful longer work, *Hospital Sketches*, which was published in 1863. She wrote her way out of her family's debts, earning enough to support her entire family. Her ardent fans liked her best in domestic mode, and she churned out domestic tales to please them. But she wrote widely in many genres, publishing thrillers and sensation tales anonymously or pseudonymously. Born on her father's birthday in 1832, she died just two days after he did, in 1888.

Did you know…?

Because Louisa May Alcott published many of her works anonymously or pseudonymously, her manuscripts continue to be discovered. She made news in the 1990s when a collector sold the lost manuscript of *A Long Fatal Love Chase*, rejected by publishers during her lifetime, to Random House for over one million dollars, and a manuscript of *The Inheritance*, a story written when she was seventeen, was discovered in the Harvard Library. Alcott scholar Madeleine Stern talks about these discoveries in an interview with the Hartford *Courant* at www.alcottweb.com/reference/news/hartford2.html.

Questions for reflection and discussion

1. If you read *Little Women* as a child, do you remember what you found so powerful? Novelist Isabelle Holland claims, "I read and reread it—to the point where I read nothing else for about two years and could tell you in exactly what context any line quoted

from the book came." Columnist and novelist Anna Quindlen asserts that "*Little Women* changed my life." What accounts for *Little Women*'s enduring appeal? Why is this book such a centrally defining reading experience for so many girls and young women? What other books came alive for you as *Little Women* did for Isabelle Holland?

2. Scholar Ann Douglas claims, "What plot there is in *Little Women* runs contrary to Jo's wishes." What are Jo's wishes, and why do her desires resonate so strongly with the reader? Many readers who fall in love with this novel as young women exclaim that they *were* Jo March. What is so appealing about her character? Jo's ambition is to do something splendid. Does she meet this goal? Is there anything splendid about her fate? Is Jo the heroine of *Little Women*, or does she share that role with her sisters? Does anyone in your group identify more with another character?

3. How does the Civil War figure in the novel? What changes does it introduce into the March family's life? Can we read a novel like *Little Women* as providing an alternate history of the Civil War period, as filling in the gaps in "official" history? What kind of historical value do novels have?

4. Alcott has been criticized by literary scholars for writing didactic novels. Her publisher urged her to provide, in a sense, a conduct manual for young girls. What model for conduct does *Little Women* inculcate in its readers? What is the role of *Pilgrim's Progress* in the novel? What message do the March sisters learn from it? Do you think the moral of the novel contributes to its enduring appeal? If so, in what ways? How might its morality have played out differently for nineteenth-century readers than for readers today? Why is this novel still so popular when standards for behavior, gender roles, and morality are different today?

5. Consider the two endings found in *Little Women* (the first part concludes with the return of Mr. March from the war). In what ways does the ending provide closure for the trajectories of the March sisters, and in what ways does it open new beginnings? What do

you think of Meg's marriage to Mr. Brooke, Amy's marriage to Laurie, and Jo's marriage to Professor Bhaer? Why are some of these couplings more satisfying or more understandable than others? Some readers have criticized Jo's marriage. If you find yourself a resisting reader, why do you have this response? What other paths would realistically be open for Jo? What model of married life do Mr. and Mrs. March provide?

Other books by Louisa May Alcott

Alcott was enormously prolific: her works number more than 270, and cover a wide range of genres. Until recently, she was known as a children's author, whose works include three sequels to *Little Women*: *An Old-Fashioned Girl* (1870), *Little Men* (1871), and *Jo's Boys* (1886). But throughout the 1970s, 80s, and 90s, a feminist re-evaluation of her work has transformed our understanding of Alcott. Gain a sense of the adult, feminist Alcott in *Alternative Alcott*, a collection of stories, novellas, and sketches edited by Elaine Showalter. Experience her darker side in the sensational thrillers collected in *Behind a Mask: The Unknown Thrillers of Louisa May Alcott*, edited by Madeleine Stern.

Did you know...?

Little Women is a **bildungsroman**, a German term meaning a novel of formation. The *bildungsroman* typically traces the development—emotional, intellectual, social—of its protagonist as he or she grows up and tries to find a place in society. The quest plot often provides the structure for the *bildungsroman*. What are the objects of the March sisters' quests in *Little Women*? A **kunstlerroman** is a special kind of *bildungsroman*: a novel focusing on the growth of an artist. James Joyce's *Portrait of the Artist as a Young Man* is a classic example. To what extent does *Little Women* offer a female version of the *kunstlerroman*?

Books about Louisa May Alcott

Little Women and the Feminist Imagination, edited by Janice M. Alberghene and Beverly Lyon Clark, contains essays by scholars about

Little Women, as well as a useful introduction tracing popular response to the novel since its publication. Alcott has been the subject of many biographies; we recommend Madeleine B. Stern's *Louisa May Alcott: A Biography*. Learn more about her unusual family in Madelon Bedell's *The Alcotts: Biography of a Family*.

If you like *Little Women*, you will like...

Anne of Green Gables and *Emily of New Moon* by L.M. Montgomery. The beloved first novels in two series by Montgomery about orphan girls and their lives.

Pollyanna by Eleanor Porter. Popular novel from the turn of the century about a young orphan who is so unhappy with her new home that she invents a game of being "glad" about everything.

Five Little Peppers by Margaret Sidney. Funny, touching story of how five childrens' lives change after their father dies.

Rebecca of Sunnybrook Farm by Kate Douglas Wiggen. Another story of an orphaned girl that continues to win a loyal following among readers of all ages.

Little House on the Prairie by Laura Ingalls Wilder. Second in the delightful and much-loved series of nine autobiographical novels about the Ingalls family.

DISCUSSION/REFLECTION STRATEGY

What do four of these books have in common? *The children in the stories are orphaned by one or both of their parents.* The themes of childhood resilience and struggle for physical and emotional survival are played out again and again in classic children's novels. Your book group may want to discuss why the story of a child having to confront and overcome loneliness and the loss or absence of love in order to become an adult is such a popular theme for coming-of-age stories. Why do we love these books when we are children, and why do they continue to exert such a powerful hold on us when we become adults?

Video resources

There are three major adaptations of *Little Women*: in 1933, Katharine Hepburn starred as Jo (George Cukor); the 1949 version features June Allyson as Jo (Mervyn LeRoy); and the well-received 1994 remake stars Winona Ryder as Jo and Susan Sarandon as Marmee (Gillian Armstrong). Why not meet with your group for a double— or triple!— feature?

Internet resources

www.alcottweb.com, where you will find photographs and online texts of the novels, is a good place to begin your online reading. Take a virtual tour of Orchards House, the Alcott family home, at www.louisamayalcott.org.

Extra credit

Take a tour of a local author's home. Concord, Massachusetts, is a treasure trove of literary landmarks. Visit the houses and sites associated with Louisa May Alcott, Margaret Sidney (author of the *Five Little Pepper* series), Ralph Waldo Emerson, and Henry David Thoreau. Consult Shirley Hoover Biggers's *American Author Houses, Museums, Memorials, and Libraries: A State-By-State Guide* to find a literary landmark near you. Armchair travelers will want to dip into *Literary Trips: Following in the Footsteps of Fame*, edited by Victoria Brooks.

December/Heartwarming Classics
Challenge
The Diary of a Young Girl: The Definitive Edition by Anne Frank, 1947, available from Prentice Hall for $4.99

What is this book about?

Anne Frank's tragic story is a testament to the horrors of the Holocaust and a memorial to a young life interrupted long before its promise could be realized.

Anne Frank was the younger of two daughters of a German-Jewish family living in Holland during the Nazi occupation. Shortly after her thirteenth birthday, the family went into hiding in Amsterdam to avoid capture. The four members of the Frank family lived with four other people in small hidden rooms in a factory for just over two years, receiving food and supplies from friends and never going outside. Anne began keeping a diary when she received a blank notebook for her birthday. *The Diary of a Young Girl* is the edited collection of her writings. Anne at thirteen is precocious, voluble, and moody. Her interests in the beginning of her diary are boys, clothes, girlfriends, and school activities. But when her family goes into hiding, Anne's passionate and inquiring intellect is drawn to chronicling the day-to-day life of hiding from the Nazis.

What should I know about the author?

Anne Frank was born on June 12, 1929, second daughter to Otto Frank and Elizabeth Holländer. The Franks, originally from Germany, had moved to the Netherlands in 1933 to escape Nazi persecution, but the German occupation of Holland forced the family into hiding. After their capture, they were sent to Auschwitz, where Mrs. Frank died shortly before the camp's liberation. Anne and her sister, Margot, were transferred to Bergen-Belsen, where they died of typhus a few weeks before liberation of the camp in early 1945. Her father was the only member of the family to survive the war.

Questions for reflection and discussion

1. Reviews of *The Diary of a Young Girl* frequently say that when we first meet Anne she is a "typical teenager." Your group might first discuss what makes any young person a "typical" teen. How does Anne, as well as Margot and Peter, compare to teens you know? Teen years are often difficult for the best of parents and the most

well-intentioned of childless adults to tolerate. How do the adults in the annex respond to the three teens in their midst? Are they fair? Do you think they expect too much (or too little) from the adolescents?

2. Consider the inhabitants of the annex. Is Anne a reliable witness for us of what is taking place within the isolation of their quarters? For example, why does she dislike the dentist so much? What are your thoughts about him? The friends and coworkers helping those in hiding put their own lives and families at terrible risk. Safe on the other side of this terrible time in history, we all have probably wondered if we could have been as brave. Putting yourself in their position, do you think you could have done this?

3. How does Anne change over the two years in hiding? Select passages that illustrate her growing maturity. How does she explain the changes in her interests and temper? More specifically, how do her attitudes toward those in the secret annex change? It is impossible to read her diary and not speculate on her relationship with Peter. Was Anne in love?

4. Most people read *The Diary of a Young Girl* knowing that Anne does not survive the war. What does this knowledge bring to the reading of the text? How would your reading of the book differ if you did not know what happened to Anne? Do you think the book has merit on its own regardless of the fate of its author? If Anne had lived, would we be reading *The Diary of a Young Girl*?

5. Have you ever kept a journal? If so, who is your intended audience? Have you ever written in the form of letters to someone else? Do you think this would make it easier or harder for you to write? Anne personifies her diary as a friend named "Kitty." According to Rachel Feldhay Brenner in *Writing as Resistance: Four Women Confronting the Holocaust*, using the literary device of "Kitty" enables Frank to address herself to posterity more effectively. How does this choice of imaginary audience shape Frank's writing? How does writing to "Kitty" make it easier for Anne to write?

The published works of Anne Frank

There are several editions of *The Diary of a Young Girl*. We recommend *The Diary of a Young Girl: The Definitive Edition* published in 1995. Anne Frank had two different versions of her own diary. The first, which scholars refer to as Version A, is the diary she began to keep shortly before going into hiding. After hearing on the radio that diaries of war survivors would be published after the war, Anne began revising her diary for publication; scholars refer to the revised writing as Version B. After the war, her father edited her diary using material from both Versions A and B. This is referred to as Version C and is the edition of the book that was popular until the publication of *The Definitive Version*. This version includes material from Versions A and B that Otto Frank originally did not want published, most notably Anne's writings on sexuality and her dislike of her mother. In 1989, *The Diary of a Young Girl: The Critical Edition* was prepared by the Netherlands State Institute for War Documentation in an attempt to preserve this important historical record, but also in order to put to rest all controversy resulting from the number of different texts then in publication and the problems surrounding the plays written from Version C of the *Diary*.

Books about Anne Frank

Melissa Muller's biography, *Anne Frank: The Biography*, is a good place to start. Find out more about Anne Frank's legacy in *Anne Frank: Reflections on Her Life and Legacy* edited by Hyman Aaron Enzer and Sandra Solotaroff-Enzer. Miep Gies's *Anne Frank Remembered: The Story of the Woman Who Helped to Hide the Frank Family* (with Alison Leslie Gold) is the haunting story of Gies's commitment to saving the Franks.

If you like *Diary of a Young Girl,* you will like...

Etty Hillesum: An Interrupted Life and Letters from Westerbork by Etty Hillesum. A chilling account of the war years based on Hillesum's diaries and letters.

Witness: Voices from the Holocaust edited by Joshua M. Greene and Shiva Kumar. Riveting narratives transcribed from videotaped testimonies of Holocaust survivors and witnesses.

I Will Bear Witness: A Diary of the Nazi Years Volume I 1933–1941 and *Volume II 1941–1945* by Victor Klemperer. Former professor at University of Dresden avoided deportation to the camps because he was married to an Aryan.

Edith's Story: Courage, Love and Survival During WWII by Edith Velmans. A memoir written by a Dutch Jew about the Nazi occupation of Holland.

The Night Trilogy: Night, Dawn, The Accidental Night by Elie Wiesel. Chronicles of his wartime experiences by the winner of the 1986 Nobel Peace Prize.

Video resources

Anne Frank Remembered (Jon Blair, 1995) is an excellent documentary. In 1955, French film director Alain Resnais produced the documentary *Night and Fog* about the Holocaust. Steven Spielberg's *Schindler's List* (1993) is based on the true story of Schindler's efforts to save thousands of Polish Jews from the Nazis. *Judgment at Nuremberg* (Stanley Kramer, 1961), with an all-star cast including Spencer Tracy, is the story of the postwar effort to judge responsibility for Nazi war crimes.

Internet resources

Visit www.annefrank.com for a comprehensive account of Frank's life, death, and legacy. The building in Amsterdam that hid the Frank family is open as a museum. Check out www.annefrank.nl for a virtual tour of the Anne Frank house. You may also wish to spend time at the website of the United States Holocaust Memorial Museum at www.ushmm.org. Steven Spielberg has founded Survivors of the Shoah Visual History Foundation, which is a multimedia archive of information related to the Holocaust. Visit the website at www.vhf.org.

Extra credit

Your group might want to consider inviting their children to one of your meetings. It's a good opportunity for parents and children to interact in a new way and to inspire in your children a love of reading and talking about books. The group could also learn from the child's perspective. Prepare child-friendly snacks, and choose a book both children and adults will love. We like *Harry Potter and the Sorcerer's Stone* by J.K. Rowling, *Ramona Quimby, Age 8* by Beverly Cleary, *The Phantom Tollbooth* by Nortan Juster, *Catherine, Called Birdy* by Karen Cushman, *Tuck Everlasting* by Natalie Babbitt, and *Charlie and the Chocolate Factory* by Roald Dahl.

December/Heartwarming Classics
Memoir
The Story of My Life by Helen Keller, 1902, several paperback editions available, including one from Bantam for $4.95

What is this book about?

Named one of the most important books of the twentieth century by the New York Public Library, *The Story of My Life* recounts an extraordinary life. Blind and deaf since the age of eighteen months, Helen Keller was trapped in her own world for six years, unable to communicate even with her parents until teacher Anne Sullivan arrived at the Keller home. *The Story of My Life* describes Helen's awakening under the tutelage of Sullivan, who began spelling words into Helen's hands the day she arrived. One month later, exasperated by Helen's incapacity to understand hand spelling and to assign the word symbols to objects, Sullivan conducted her to the water pump, pumped cold water over her hands, and repeatedly signed w-a-t-e-r into her palm. As Helen later described it, "Suddenly I felt a misty consciousness as of something forgotten—a thrill of returning thought; and somehow the mystery of language was revealed to me." News of the "miracle" spread, and Helen Keller became a worldwide celebrity before she turned ten. Keller writes movingly of her early years, but much of her passion is devoted to her desire to get an education. The reading public of her day was enthralled by Keller's intellectual accomplishments: it seemed miraculous enough for her to have learned English, but Keller would go on to become proficient in French, German, Italian, Greek, and Latin, smashing the long-held suspicion that the deaf and blind must be dull-witted as well. Published in 1902 when the author was just twenty-two and in the middle of her college career at Radcliffe, *The Story of My Life* sketches a birth and a rebirth, a fierce determination not just to survive, but to excel.

What should I know about the author?

Keller called the day in 1887 when Anne Sullivan arrived to be her teacher her "soul's birthday." Using methods she had learned from the Perkins Institution for the Blind, but also experimenting and developing new methods, Sullivan taught her pupil how to communicate through hand language, how to read, and even how to speak. Though Sullivan later married, she and Helen were inseparable until Sullivan's death in 1936. Keller supported herself and Sullivan by working the lecture circuit and writing. She published fourteen books and hundreds of articles and essays. She was active in politics, joining the socialist party in 1909 and campaigning for Roosevelt in 1944; she also spoke out against racism and sexism. She was a tireless advocate for the blind and the deaf, using her celebrity to raise awareness and money. Keller remained single at her mother's insistence. She died in 1968.

Extra credit

Plan an outing to a writers' festival. The Helen Keller Festival, started in 1979, takes place each summer in her hometown, Tuscumbia, Alabama. There are arts and crafts exhibits, concerts, parades, and performances of William Gibson's play, *The Miracle Worker*. Visit the festival's website at www.wraygraphics.com /hkfest/ for more information. If you can't travel to Alabama, find a festival near you by searching online for your city's name and the phrase "writers festival," or by phoning your local library, university, or chamber of commerce.

Questions for reflection and discussion

1. *The Story of My Life* is by far the most frequently taught of Keller's books. Why is this particular book singled out as the most important one? Should this book be taught in schools today? What can children learn from it? Which of its qualities would have led the New York Public Library to dub it one of the most important books of the century? Helen Keller has been famous worldwide for over a century. What accounts for the widespread appeal of her story?

2. Anne Sullivan's methods rightly earned her the nickname "miracle worker," but she wasn't the first to try to teach Helen. Why do you think her methods were so successful? How much do we learn about her methods in *The Story of My Life*? Helen frequently battled the criticism that she was merely the product or the creation of Anne Sullivan. Is this true? Reviewers of this early memoir suspected that Sullivan had done the writing herself. Why do you think people had such a hard time accepting that Keller could think and write for herself?

3. Keller is so eager to go to college. Why? What does she hope to experience there? *The Story of My Life* recounts in detail the hardships both she and Anne Sullivan had to endure for Keller to get to Radcliffe. Why do you think she persisted? How typical was it for young women during this time period to go to college? Unfortunately, Keller discovers that college isn't exactly what she had hoped or expected it to be. What are her criticisms? Think back to your own college experience: was it everything you'd hoped it would be? Keller also writes in surprising detail about her study

habits and the subjects she takes in college. Why would a reading audience in 1902 be interested in these details?

4. Keller writes movingly about her happiness when surrounded by books or when reading, "Books have meant so much more in my education than in that of others," she claims. What books are most significant to her? Why? What are your childhood memories of reading some of the classics she mentions? What can she experience through books that she can't find in the world around her?

5. Rather than produce a dense, detailed chronicle of her life year by year, Keller writes "sketches." What themes emerge to tie the different chapters together? What would be the themes of your own life?

Other books by Helen Keller

Keller pays tribute to Anne Sullivan in *Teacher: Anne Sullivan Macy* (1955). A modern edition of *My Religion* (1927), published under the title *Light in My Darkness*, contains autobiographical writings on Keller's spiritual development. Her other works include volumes of poetry, journals, and essays. Readers of *The Story of My Life* will be most interested in *The World I Live In* (1908), which provides the details of daily life sometimes missing from her earlier memoir, and *Midstream: My Later Life* (1929), which picks up where *The Story of My Life* leaves off, following Keller on her journey after she graduates from Radcliffe.

Books about Helen Keller

Dorothy Herrmann's recent biography, *Helen Keller: A Life*, is not without its problems, but it provides much useful background to the stories in Keller's autobiography. Keller's relationship with her teacher, Anne Sullivan, was the central defining relationship of her life; Joseph P. Lash's monumental *Helen and Teacher: The Story of Helen Keller and Anne Sullivan Macy*, explores this important partnership. Most readers were introduced to the story of Helen Keller through William Gibson's popular play, *The Miracle Worker*, well worth a reread.

If you like *The Story of My Life,* you will like...

I Was #87: A Deaf Woman's Ordeal of Misdiagnosis, Institutionalization, and Abuse by Anne Bolander and Adair Renning. A harrowing look at the deaf author's childhood: misdiagnosed as retarded, institutionalized, and abused by her parents.

My Sense of Silence: Memoirs of a Childhood with Deafness by Lennard J. Davis. A moving look at growing up with deaf parents, written by a well-known literary scholar.

Sight Unseen by Georgina Kleege. Like Keller, Kleege is interested in using memoir to educate her sighted readers and to lobby for the rights of the disabled.

Exiting Nirvana: A Daughter's Life with Autism by Clara Claiborne Park. This fantastic sequel to Park's earlier memoir, *The Siege*, describes the adulthood of her autistic daughter.

Sounds Like Home: Growing Up Black and Deaf in the South by Mary Herring Wright. Deaf from age ten, the author describes growing up in a hearing world and attending school for the deaf and blind.

Video resources

Deliverance (1919) was the first film to be made about Helen Keller; though fictionalized in part, it actually starred Keller herself. The documentary, *Helen Keller: In Her Story* (1955), presents newsreels and photographs of the author before filming her (aged seventy-five) at her home. The documentary series, *Famous Americans of the 20th Century*, also has an entry on Keller titled *The Story of Helen Keller*. Anne Bancroft and Patty Duke both won Oscars for their roles as Anne Sullivan and Helen Keller in the 1962 adaptation of Gibson's play, *The Miracle Worker* (Arthur Penn). The most recent adaptation of *The Miracle Worker* is Disney's 2000 release directed by Nadia Tess.

Internet resources

Find photos of Helen Keller's birthplace in Tuscumbia, Alabama, along with information on planning a visit at www.bham.net/keller/home.html. The Information Center at the American Foundation for the Blind's website offers an overview of Keller's life and activism, photos, and information about her surviving letters and papers at www.afb.org/htm_asp/information.htm. Learn more about Anne Sullivan at www.graceproducts.com/keller/anne.html.

Extra credit

Several organizations continue Helen Keller's work for the blind and the deaf. Find out how you can volunteer at the Helen Keller National Center for Deaf-Blind Youth and Adults at www.helenkeller.org/national/ or at the American Foundation for the Blind at www.afb.org.

December/Heartwarming Classics
Potluck
Watership Down by Richard Adams, 1972, available in paperback from Avon Books for $7.50

What should I know about this book?

This epic tale of a group of rabbits who escape the destruction of their warren and set off across the downs on a dangerous adventure to find a new home is, without hyperbole, the greatest animal adventure ever told. The novel opens with a premonition: Fiver, the runt of his litter and a bit of a mystic, envisions the rabbits' field full of blood. His brother, Hazel, is skeptical, but, mindful that Fiver's earlier predictions have been accurate, he persuades several other rabbits, including officer Bigwig, to abandon their warren and seek a

new home—and just in time. A sign posted near the warren adver-
tises the construction of a housing development, which will destroy
the warren and most of the rabbits left in it. After numerous adventures and the introduction of many memorable characters, including
Kehaar, a seagull who befriends the rabbits after they nurse him back
to health, Hazel's band of adventurers must fight a pitched battle
with the well-trained rabbits from Efrafa before they can establish
their own warren.

Watership Down began life as a story Adams made up to keep his
two daughters quiet on a long car journey; they begged him to write
it down and finally, after reading one mediocre children's story too
many, he decided to follow their advice. Adams was conscious from
the beginning of using an overlay of mythology: he gave a line from
the story of Agamemnon to Fiver. But he believes that other connections with myth emerged organically through the writing process and
weren't intentional. Like The Aeneid, this is an epic tale of a people's
founding; the battle scenes are reminiscent of The Iliad, and the acts
of storytelling that punctuate the narrative recall The Odyssey. Adams,
though, downplays such classical comparisons, "A lot of people have
said this is a political fable or even a religious fable or social comment. I promise you it is not a fable or an allegory or a parable of any
kind. It is a story about rabbits, that is all."

What should I know about the author?

Richard Adams was born in England in 1920. He studied history at
Oxford, then became a civil servant. He was fifty-two years old and
assigned to the division on air pollution when Watership Down, his
first novel, was published. Earnings from Watership Down enabled
him to quit his job and turn to writing full time. Since 1972, he has
published seven novels and an autobiography.

Questions for reflection and discussion

1. Several of Adams's novels feature animals as protagonists. Do rabbits make especially good main characters for the story in Watership
   Down, or could another animal substitute? What is it about rabbits
   that might have triggered Adams's imagination for a quest novel?

What surprised you most about Adams's characterization of the individual rabbits? Which is your favorite character and why?

2. Storytelling occupies a central role in *Watership Down*. During moments of leisure—but also times of stress—the other rabbits call upon Dandelion to tell a story. How do his stories inspire or warn the rabbits? What mythological, religious, or folk tale traditions do you see Adams drawing upon for the rabbits' own traditions and beliefs? You may want to consult *Tales from Watership Down*, which includes more of Dandelion's stories.

3. Adams denies that *Watership Down* has significance beyond being "a story about rabbits." But the chapter headings, drawn from classical sources like the Bible, *The Epic of Gilgamesh*, the writings of Aeschylus, and canonical writers like Thomas Hardy, William Congreve, and Fyodor Dostoyevsky, suggest a larger purpose or at least a greater seriousness. Did you read the quotations at the beginning of each chapter as you were reading this novel? Choose a few chapters and discuss how the quotation relates to the content of the chapter it introduces. Why do you think Adams uses these kinds of quotations in his novel?

4. *Watership Down* has been a strong seller since its publication in 1972. Like J.K. Rowling's *Harry Potter* series, the novel has crossover appeal: both children and adults buy and read it. Why do you think this novel appeals to such a wide-ranging audience? Why has it been so successful for so long? How does it appeal to both adults and children? In other words, what makes it a classic?

5. Many readers have commented on the poignancy of *Watership Down*'s ending, and a number of critics have noticed Adams's sure hand with death scenes. Is this a proper ending for an epic, and is this a proper ending for *Watership Down*? Why do you think Adams chose to bring the story full circle in this way?

Other books by Richard Adams

Continue your journey with the rabbits in the sequel, *Tales from Watership Down* (1998). Adams considers his second novel, *Shardik*

(1974), an epic tale about a fantasy world that worships a giant bear, his best book; *Maia* (1985) is also set in the fantasy world he creates in *Shardik*. *The Plague Dogs* (1977) recounts the journey of two dogs escaping from an animal research center. *Traveler* (1988) depicts the Civil War through the eyes of General Lee's horse. *Girl in a Swing* (1980) is a supernatural ghost story. *The Outlandish Knight* (2000), set during the Tudor era in Britain, features human protagonists. Fans of *Watership Down* will want to read Adams's autobiography, *The Day Gone By* (1990).

If you like *Watership Down*, you will like...

Timbuktu by Paul Auster. A novel about homelessness told from the perspective of a dog.

The Cold Moons by Aeron Clement. The tale of a group of badgers threatened, like Adams's group of rabbits, by the destruction of their habitat. Considered by many to be the best of the post-*Watership Down* animal sagas.

The Princess Bride by William Goldman. A delightful fairy tale, this book is even better than the movie.

The White Bone by Barbara Gowdy. A novel about elephants told from the elephants' perspective.

The Lord of the Rings by J.R.R. Tolkien. A classic in the fantasy genre.

Video resources

Watership Down was filmed as an animated movie in 1978 (Martin Rosen). John Hurt and Denholm Elliot provide voices. You will also enjoy 1987's *The Princess Bride* (Rob Reiner) and the long-awaited *Lord of the Rings: The Fellowship of the Rings* directed by Peter Jackson and released in 2001.

Internet resources

There is a wealth of Web material on *Watership Down*. Begin your online search at www.watershipdown.org. Find photos and maps of the locale in England that inspired Adams at, www.mayfieldlow. freewire.co.uk/watershp/index.htm. Jamie Cohen recounts the afternoon he spent with Richard Adams and his wife, Elizabeth, at www.houserabbit.org/BaltWashDC/RichardAdams.htm.

FAQs for
Book Group Beginners

How do I find a book group to join?

Start by asking at your local library and independent bookstore. Librarians are often privy to what's happening in the community, while independent bookstores frequently advise local reading groups.

Many book group members participate in more than one reading circle, so try attending book groups that are open to the public. Independent bookstores and also superstore chains like Borders and Barnes & Noble sponsor reading groups for their customers; these can be a great place to network. Your state's Humanities Council may also have an active readers' program. Find out more about them at www.neh.gov.

Ask coworkers, friends, and acquaintances if they know of any groups.

Many book groups have active websites. You may discover the perfect group by entering "reading group" or "book group" and your city and state into a search engine like www.google.com.

How do I start my own book group?

In our experience, the best groups are composed of like-minded readers who share some—but not all—of the same interests. It's not necessary to know *all* members of the group before you start; book groups are a great way to broaden your circle of friends.

Think about people you already know who might be interested in joining a group. Surveying neighbors, coworkers, and friends is the best place to begin your search.

Network! Tell everyone you know that you want to start a book group and ask if they know someone who might be interested. Be sure to tell your librarian. He may be able to suggest likely members. You should also inform the manager at your local bookstore because she may have customers with similar reading interests.

Post notices. Look for bulletin boards at your library, college, church, community center or town hall, bookstores, women's resource centers, offices, apartment complexes, and gyms be sure to ask for permission before posting your sign. Your notice should give contact information—a first name and phone number or email address—and an idea of what kind of books you'll want to read in your group.

Place an ad in a local newspaper. Many events listings have a section for readers. Some local chapters of national organizations also publish newsletters that will accept notices.

Use an existing group as a springboard for a reading group. If you belong to a craft guild, see if some of the members would be interested in forming a book group. Women's groups, sports clubs, and church organizations also make good springboards.

If you have children, ask the parents you meet at sports events, recitals, or practices if they're interested. You could even combine a reading group with another activity—like waiting for the kids to finish soccer practice.

Make contact with members of already-established book groups. If they're full, they might have turned away people who would be great for your group.

Go where the readers are. Public readings and lectures, library programs, author events, adult education classes, and Humanities Council meetings are a great place to meet like-minded potential book group members.

How many people should be in our book group?

We recommend that your group limit membership to no more than twelve members at a time. If a few people miss a meeting, there will still be enough people to generate a good discussion. But when everyone comes, you will still have enough space—and place settings! Moreover, if you share duties like hosting, moderating discussions, or bringing snacks, each person will be responsible only once annually. Determine your cap on membership early on. This way, everyone in the group will know that once that number is reached, new members shouldn't be proposed until someone moves on.

Where should we hold our meetings?

Most book groups meet in members' homes, but for some people that is not feasible. Check with your local library to see if they have a community meeting room you can use. Your local bookstores and churches may also have similar facilities. In the summer months, you might want to take your meetings outdoors. Meet at a park or garden, gather 'round the pool, or picnic on a member's deck or porch. Be creative! We talked to one group of dog owners who meet each month at their local dog park—with their dogs.

How often should our book group meet?

Most of the groups we've talked to meet once a month at the same time. Meetings usually last for two hours. Meeting more frequently tends to lead to absenteeism or not being able to finish the book; less frequently makes it hard for the group to maintain continuity. It's important that schedules be set up in advance. Don't do it on a month-to-month basis—*How's Tuesday the sixth for everyone? No, well then what about Wednesday, the seventh?* That will just waste your discussion time. Set a schedule that extends for six or eight months and stick to it. This gives everyone plenty of time to organize and plan other events around book group meetings.

What should we do at the first meeting?

If your group is new, try an ice-breaker exercise. It's hokey, we know, but it can still be fun. Create a quiz with questions like: who has hiked the Appalachian Trail? Who has lived in a foreign country? Who speaks more than one language? Who has four or more brothers and sisters? Who owns more than three pets? To fill out the quiz, each member must walk around the room and find someone who has done the thing in question. Or ask each person to write down three books and three things they would take if stranded on a desert island, and then share.

Get down to business and discuss what types of books you'd like to read. Will your group have a theme (for example, women's literature, works of history, science fiction)? Have suggestions ready for the next meeting's selection.

Someone should volunteer to collect names and contact information and have this available for everyone at the next meeting.

Set a date and time for the next meeting and get volunteers to bring snacks.

How do we find books to suggest to our group?

You've come to the right place: with sixty fully annotated recommendations and hundreds of further reading selections, A Year of Reading could keep any group busy for a long time. If you do run out of books before we get around to writing the sequel, here are some other approaches to finding books that you might try.

Make a commitment to read book reviews, at least occasionally. The *New York Times Book Review*, published in the Sunday paper and for sale separately, is the most important, but we also like *Book* magazine and www.salon.com's Books page.

Subscribe to a newsletter about books. We like *Read Any Good Books Lately?* (call 800-475-3169 to subscribe).

Cultivate a reader whose opinion you trust at your local library or bookstore; he or she can let you know what other groups have been reading. Be sure to pick up a copy of *BookSense 76*, a newsletter highlighting book recommendations from independent booksellers across the country. You can also access *BookSense 76* at their website, www.booksense.com.

www.amazon.com is an invaluable resource for every reader; not only does Amazon generate personal recommendations for each customer, but you can also discover new authors through the helpful "Customers who bought this book also bought..." list.

A Common Reader is one of our favorite catalogs; its editors are opinionated and passionate about books and have an eye for the quirky title. You can request a catalog at their website, www.commonreader.com. *Bas Bleu* is another quirky catalog, strong on books by and about women; request a catalog at www.basbleu.com.

Each member should keep a personal reading journal. Since we often bring books by authors we love to our group, our personal reading generates many of the group's selections. We suggest a reading notebook where you can enter the titles of the books you've read—

perhaps with space for a few comments about what you thought—
and also space to enter titles you *want* to read.

How do we choose which books to read?

In our group, each member brings three books on selection night
(which happens twice a year). This gives us a pool of thirty titles to
choose from. We show off our choices, then each member votes for
the six books she'd most like for the group to read. The six books with
the most votes "win." This system isn't perfect, but it works for us
right now.

If your group is less structured but disciplined, you may want to
spend fifteen or twenty minutes at the beginning or ending of each
monthly meeting determining what to read for the next month. Don't
let the conversation get carried away: it's possible to spend hours talking over options. You can schedule the reading month to month, two
months in advance, four months, six months, one year. We don't recommend scheduling more than one year in advance, however,
because tastes and interests—and sometimes members!—change. If
your group is small, an open discussion may enable you to narrow the
selection and choose. You may want to assign one month per member and allow each member to select the book for that month. We
know other groups who debate their schedule over email or at the
group's website. Experiment with different styles until you discover
what works for you.

Am I going to have to cook for all these people?!

Many book groups meet at members' homes over dinner. But this
needn't be much trouble. The host provides a simple main course like
soup or pasta, and other members can bring salad or dessert. If you
keep the meal simple and split up the responsibility, no one person
will be overburdened. Of course, depending on when your group
meets and what you prefer, you may just wish to have snacks or
desserts during meetings. Just remember that food is secondary to the
conversation: don't get competitive with food preparation or feel that
you have to serve food that complements the book (though that can
be fun).

Should we serve alcohol at meetings?

Most of the groups we have talked to do not serve alcohol during meetings. This is mostly a matter of common sense. Many groups meet on weeknights and people have to drive to attend, so drinking is impractical. Sometimes groups do serve wine or beer and do just fine. Be prepared, though, for alcohol to change the dynamic of group discussion. We know of some groups who meet on Friday evenings, have wine with dinner, and linger over dinner and discussion. If you know your group well and enjoy socializing with them, this could be nice. But if you are just starting out and are meeting for once a month for two hours, you may wish to keep the meeting alcohol-free.

Does our group need guidelines or rules?

How do you resolve minor irritations, such as discussion monopolizers or chronic interrupters? How do you deal with those reluctant to take turns, to bring food, to do the author research, to be the host? With great tact and gentle remonstrance, of course—but who is responsible for speaking up? In an ideal book group, every member would feel equal to the task of helping the group dynamics work smoothly, but in the real world, this kind of task can require an "enforcer" stance, and most members of a group are not comfortable with that role. The best troubleshooting tip is to spend time with your group brainstorming potential problems along with solutions with which the whole group can agree. This can save much worry and stress, as well as hurt feelings. When emotions are high, it is difficult to be detached and objective. A book group is first and always a community of book lovers, and all members must feel valued and respected for the community to thrive. And remember to discuss your guidelines and resolutions with new members!

Twenty-Five Ways to Build a Better Book Group

---

1. **Keep in touch with your group between meetings by sending out a book group newsletter.** This could be as basic as a reminder for absent members (and the absent-minded!) about where you're meeting next month, what you're reading, and who has volunteered to bring snacks. Or recruit one or more members to put together a detailed newsletter to chronicle what happened at the meeting—who was there and what was said about the book. Add notable news from members, recommend books and movies, even list upcoming community events and activities. Your newsletter could be a page on your group's website (see next suggestion), or you can circulate it via email or snail mail.

2. **A website can make it easier for book group members to keep in touch between meetings.** It can provide easy access to useful information: what book is next? Whose house are we going to? Did I volunteer to bring dessert? And it's fun. Some book group sites provide links to online bookstores and popular reference sites. Others provide profiles of members and ratings of books. Building a website is easier than you think. Take a class at a local adult education center or teach yourself with one of the many instructional books available on the topic, like *HTML: A Beginner's Guide* by Wendy Willard or *Learning Web Design: A Beginner's Guide to HTML, Graphics, and Beyond* by Jennifer Niederst and Richard Koman. Get ideas for your own site by visiting the sites of other reading groups. Search www.yahoo.com for "reading groups" and enjoy.

3. **Keep a record of what your group reads—and what you think about what you read—by maintaining a book group logbook.**

Some groups enter this information on their website; you can also buy an inexpensive hardbound journal or blank book. Bring the book to each meeting, enter the title, author, and date of that month's meeting, and leave space for each member to write a few comments about the book.

4. **Establish a policy for adding new members early on.** It stands to reason that when you lose members, as you inevitably will—to moves, to other time commitments, to life circumstances—you may want to add new people. This can be one of the most difficult parts of the reading group experience, but also one of the most rewarding. The group dynamic you establish needs nurturing. We know of one group which ended up disbanding after adding a problematic—and tenacious!—new member. But new members more typically breathe life into a group through the different experiences, ideas, and reading interests they can offer. **Do** discuss how many members you would ideally like to have. **Do** think carefully before suggesting a new member. How well do you know this person? Does he have similar or complementary reading tastes? What can she offer the group? Will he get along with others? Will she be comfortable with the group's policies? You should discuss what qualities make for a good member, how you will add new people, and what you might do as a group if someone joins who turns out not to be a good match. An open discussion early on can prevent disgruntled members later!

5. **Your book group needs a guest policy.** Your book group is terrific. The selections are strong, the people are enthusiastic, the conversation flows. Now your nonbook-group friends want to get involved. They want to visit your book group. In fact, everyone in your group has a friend who wants to visit. Should friends be allowed to visit? How many can visit at any one time? What happens to the sense of trust your book group shares if strange people keep showing up? Here are some dos and don'ts for inviting guests. **Do** ask your group ahead of time if they would mind if you brought someone. **Don't** just show up with a surprise guest—it's rude. **Do** introduce your friend to everyone. **Do** have your friend read the book selection. **Do** encourage guests to par-

ticipate. **Don't** change your format too much to accommodate the guest or feel as if you must entertain the visitor. He or she is interested in how your group works normally. **Do** make it clear to guests that their inclusion in one meeting is not a trial visit or an invitation to join permanently. Your group may wish to consider setting aside one meeting when everyone can invite a guest. Designating one month as "guest month" ensures that no misunderstandings arise.

6. **Institute a policy to solve absenteeism.** It happens to all of us: a busy month when we don't have time to read the book or when other commitments intervene on our reading group night. But when this happens month after month with the same people or when so few members show up that discussion fails, absenteeism has become a problem in the group. The best way to solve it is to institute a policy early on. How strong a commitment can each member make to the group? Should members RSVP to the host before each monthly meeting? For groups where light snacks are served, this may be unnecessary, but when the host prepares a full meal, she must know how many to expect. Is it okay to come to the meeting if you haven't read the book? How will you deal, as a group, with members who are frequently absent? We know some groups that have instituted a policy of three-strikes-and-you're-out: if any member misses three meetings in a row, she is asked to leave the group. This may seem harsh, but it does make sense. Groups evolve a dynamic, and when the members who contribute to that dynamic don't show up, the group simply doesn't work as well. But there are also kinder, gentler ways of roping in absentees. When a member misses a meeting, why not call or send an email, bringing her up to date on what you've read and what's on the schedule for next month, and letting her know how much her contribution was missed?

7. **Be flexible about expectations of friendship.** Wouldn't it be wonderful if everyone in your book group adored one another and formed a tightly knit community whose members were always there for one another? Sure it would, but this probably won't happen. You may become close to some people in your group—seeing

them outside of book group and introducing your children to theirs. But this may not happen. Members may not have the time or the inclination to socialize outside of book group, and that is okay too. It's perfectly acceptable just to see these folks once a month and talk about books. Be careful, though, if you do become more socially involved with others in group. You don't have to hide friendship, but don't form a "clique" within the group that might make others uncomfortable, e.g., no private jokes, no significant glances.

8. **If most members like to buy new books, inquire at your local independent bookstore about registering your group.** Most independents will take care of purchasing for book groups, and some may even offer a group discount! Belonging to a book group shouldn't be expensive; most communities have used bookstores where you may be able to find copies. We've had good luck searching online for used books at www.bibliofind.com, where used book dealers can register their wares. Your local library is also an important resource. Most libraries participate in interlibrary loan programs, which let patrons request books from other libraries. If your group plans your reading selections several months in advance, you should be able to locate your reading material at little expense.

9. **Find creative ways to pass your books on when you're finished with them.** Some members will want to keep all the group's reading selections. In fact, it would be great if one person would agree to keep a copy of every book selection. New members could then browse through the group's backlist and even catch up. You can sell your books easily by registering at www.amazon.com. But you may get more pleasure from donating your books to needy libraries or organizations. Find them locally by calling small public libraries, women's shelters, nursing homes, high schools, and charity book drives. Charitable organizations, like the one at www.bookends.org, collect used books for underfunded schools and libraries; check out their website for information on how to donate. Or type "book drive + libraries" into any search engine and explore the many options for donating.

10. **Improve discussions by appointing one member each month to present information on the author and kickstart the conversation.** Effective discussion of the book can begin with a brief biographical summary of the author's life and a reading of important or interesting passages from interviews. Pass around photos, if you find any. Summarize the major trends in reviews and criticism, highlighting any points you'd like your group to consider further. Finally, prepare a few questions or comments to spark discussion. What do you love about the book? What do you hate? What perplexed or surprised you? When one member takes responsibility each month for leading and organizing the discussion, the quality and depth of conversation dramatically improve because each meeting gains focus and purpose.

11. **Learn more about the authors you read by researching their lives and works online.** Start with a search of the author's name at a search engine, like www.google.com, which will turn up links to interviews with the author, home pages, publisher information, and book reviews. If you want more information, investigate book-related websites. www.writerswrite.com and www.readersread.com offer links to online book resources, a wealth of author interviews, and book reviews. www.bookspot.com provides links to authors' homepages and a handy page of links to newspaper, magazine, and Internet book reviews. www.bookpage.com and www.yahoo.com's Books pages also contain interviews, reviews, and general information. Your library's website may also offer online resources for patrons. You can often access from home password-only research sites to which your library subscribes simply by typing in the barcode on your library card. Ask your librarian for information.

12. **Experiment with a theme.** Some book groups read only mysteries, romances, or science fiction. Others concentrate on books by women or anything having to do with Tudor England. Still others will read all the works by and about a particular author. You may be unwilling to change the focus of your group forever, but try it for a few months. Concentrating on a particular type of literature or time period allows you to branch out into related topics. For example, if you focus on African literature, you can listen to and

discuss indigenous music, read up on visual artists, and study some relevant history. Reading all the works of a particular author allows you to chart the changes he or she makes over time: which themes recur? How does the treatment of them change?

13. **Go beyond, "I liked it."** If your group finds it hard to move beyond a discussion of whether or not you liked the book, try some of these strategies: prepare some comments or questions. You don't have to do homework on the book—just make a few notes as you're reading. Ask open-ended questions like, "How did the author create the sense of terror?" rather than, "Did the author create a sense of terror?" Find something that puzzles you or that you don't understand. Our group has had some great discussions about things we don't understand. Move beyond whether or not you liked a particular character by discussing her motivation for behaving as she did, looking at other characters' responses to this character, or thinking about *why* the author might want to create this character. Look beyond character to setting and theme. Ask why the author wrote the story in this particular way. What other ways could the story be told? Finally, broaden the discussion by considering similar books or authors—or even films. If your group has trouble sustaining a discussion about one book, comparing and contrasting with another book or film should open up many avenues for discussion.

14. **A book group is the ideal place to experiment with new genres.** Our group has made a conscious effort to move beyond the novels and memoirs that make up the bulk of our reading to include biographies, short stories, and even children's literature. Changing the type of book you choose for one or two meetings per year is probably the easiest, most painless way to add oomph to your group. Suggest something new for the sake of challenge or change. If your group reads popular fiction, try a volume of poetry or a classic. If you read literary fiction, explore science fiction or a detective novel. Even if you don't think much of the title or genre your group selects, you can still initiate a lively discussion about the merits of generic divisions and the standards for inclusion in a particular genre.

15. **Compare the book to the movie.** Read the book and then watch the video together. What's different about them? Has the director remained faithful to the author's vision? Has the director changed details, but captured the essence of the book? Or has the film totally missed the point? Try to think of movies that are better than the books they are adapted from.

16. **Share a meal.** It can't be a coincidence that our group became closer around the time we started cooking meals for each other. Divide up the responsibilities, keep food choices simple, and everyone will be happy.

17. **Create your own book group rituals.** In the summer months, our group meets frequently to catch films at a local film festival. In December, we take a break from our regular reading schedule to read a children's book and exchange gifts.

18. **Find time to share personal recommendations.** What books or movies have you read or seen recently that members of your group might like? The goal here is to find shared interests to talk about.

19. **Build a greener book group.** Do some of the following: carpool, walk, or bike to meetings if possible. Surely a ten-person group doesn't need to take nine cars to a meeting. Use cloth napkins at meetings. Just throw them in the laundry basket after the meeting. And no, no one will mind if you haven't ironed them. Read a classic of the environmental movement like *Silent Spring* by Rachel Carson. Check your library for book group selections before heading to the bookstore. Make arrangements to share books with other members. When you're finished with books, pass them on to friends, the local library, a nursing home, or homeless shelter.

20. **What if your chosen book deals with a sensitive topic: cancer, suicide, alcoholism, or child abuse?** It's not unusual for someone in the group to have some experience with the issue under discussion, and it is also not unusual for that fact to emerge during discussion. Group members may respond to personal disclosure by feeling uncomfortable and trying to change the subject; however, a

personal disclosure can open up discussion, taking it to a deeper level. How your group responds may depend upon how long you've been meeting, how close you are to one another, and the manner in which the disclosure has been raised. If someone volunteers personal information, listen but do not try to "fix" the problem. If you are the person revealing the information, keep in mind that your book group probably wants the best for you, but may not know how to respond to your disclosure.

21. **Book groups are social events, so build in social time at the beginning or end of your meeting.** Long-lasting book groups endure because members create a supportive, fun group environment. They look forward to seeing each other each month and finding out what the other members think about the book, but they're also eager to find out what's been happening since they last saw each other. They are no longer acquaintances, but friends—even if they only see each other once a month for the book group meeting. How do you create a fun group? Get to know each other better. Find out where people work, who has partners or children, what people do in their spare time. Half an hour spent catching up is time well spent.

22. **Your group can find inspiration by crawling around the web to see what other book groups are up to.** These are some of our favorite places:

    Sisters and Brothers of Hotlanta Book Club at www.sistersbrothers.com. This African-American Literature group is always up to something new. They read great books and take community involvement seriously.

    Mostly We Eat at www.mostlyweeat.org. These people are so organized—they have book reviews, reports on meetings, member profiles.

    The Movie Stars Book Club at www.bookclub.flying-fish.org endeared themselves to us by posting photographs of "the movie stars who would play us if our book group were a movie."

    Redwining at www.redwining.com doesn't follow most of the guidelines we suggest, but they have a great group anyway! See which wines they pair with their reading selections.

    The Roman History Reading Group at www.romanhistory

booksandmore.freeservers.com reads anything and everything about Roman history—this is a group on a mission!

23. **Pursue shared interests outside the setting of a reading group by forming a spin-off group.** Form a film club or learn how to knit or sew together. Learning a language can be a great way to grow intellectually and to broaden your horizons. Call your local recreation department or university's continuing education program to sign up for classes.

24. **Learn these five useful phrases for situations gone haywire**:

    "That is interesting. I'd like to hear what everyone else has to say." You say this to people who habitually go on a bit too much about their own concerns.

    "I am interested in the average annual rainfall in Bolivia, but I would really like to continue talking about the book—I especially want to address question three from A Year of Reading." Okay, you had been discussing expeditions to the Antarctic because that is what your selection is about, but somehow the discussion has meandered into Bolivian climate patterns. Don't complain, just remind everyone to get back to the book.

    "Do you all think we need to start being more formal about scheduling our hosting and food providing? I could be wrong, but it seems like the same people are always volunteering." No need to mention names. Just bring the issue up to the group. The nonvolunteers usually get the message.

    "Would you like to ride with my carpool next month? I think the meetings go better when we all arrive on time." Say this to the habitually late person.

    "Tell us about one of your favorite books. What do you like about it?" This is for the person who hates every book your group reads. Nonstop negativity is easy to deliver, but tough to listen to month after month. Turn the tables. Get them to explain what they like and why. Ask them to recommend a book for the next meeting.

25. **Celebrate each other's personal milestones.** Have everyone sign a card for a birthday. Chip in for a gift and card to celebrate a new baby, a wedding, a new job.

Index of Authors

Index of Titles

About the Authors

Elisabeth Ellington grew up in Georgia and graduated from Vesalius College in Brussels, Belgium, in 1995. She has taught at Brandeis University for several years. Her forthcoming doctoral dissertation focuses on biographies of eighteenth-century women writers. She lives in New Hampshire with her husband, Danny Wouters, a dog, two cats, and ten chickens. Her Seacoast New Hampshire book group has been together for seven years.

Jane Freimiller grew up in Philadelphia and graduated from Haverford College in 1987. After earning a Ph.D. in philosophy from Boston College, she taught at a university for several years. She has also been a sales clerk, office temp, and Web designer. Jane currently lives in London with her husband, Kevin Connolly, and is a member of a neighborhood book group as well as one sponsored by the National Gallery in London